Advance Praise for the Book

Apratim Mukarji's ***Annihilating the Demons of Sri Lanka: An Unfinished Story*** gives a compelling account of current developments in Sri Lanka by a writer deeply committed to secularism, the rule of law and democracy. It begins with the endemic corruption in the dismissed Rajapaksa government, which the new Sirisena–Wickremesinghe government proved unable to overcome. The narrative is woven around cases of massive human rights violations, particularly those surrounding the last war, now before the UN; two signal instances of corruption by the rival parties to government; and the resulting compulsion to silence and corrupt the judiciary and the law enforcement machinery. A particularly chilling aspect of this failure under the Rajapaksa government was the murder of journalist Lasantha Wickrematunge. While seeing some positive signs in the Sirisena–Wickremesinghe government which was elected in 2015, complicity at inter-connected top levels of the State obstructs compliance with international pledges on human rights and reconciliation, particularly with the Tamil minority. The writer sees a possible ray of hope in the left-oriented JVP that was involved in two bloody insurgencies against the failures of the major parties to overcome ethno-religious strife and corruption. But does it not, too, suffer from the phobia for open retrospection that plagues Tamil politics in particular, after the brutal legacy of the LTTE?

The writer also makes shrewd assessments about China's role in the island, its curious inroads into the Tamil media, and the power ambitions of Gotabhaya Rajapaksa. Far from patronising, the writer recognises that the maladies he sees in Sri Lanka are also present in India, where its secular legacy may have so far helped to avoid the worst extremes.

—Rajan Hoole,
Academician, Author and Human Rights Crusader

ANNIHILATING THE DEMONS OF SRI LANKA

An Unfinished Story

Apratim Mukarji

Konark Publishers Pvt Ltd
New Delhi • Seattle

Konark Publishers Pvt Ltd
206, First Floor,
Peacock Lane, Shahpur Jat,
New Delhi - 110 049
Phone: +91-11-41055065
Mob: +91 93552 93900, +91 93552 94900
e-mail: india@konarkpublishers.com
website: www.konarkpublishers.com

Konark Publishers International
8615, 13th Ave SW,
Seattle, WA 98106
Phone: (415) 409-9988
e-mail: us@konarkpublishers.com

Cataloging in Publication Data—DK
Courtesy: D.K. Agencies (P) Ltd. <docinfo@dkagencies.com>

Mukarji, Apratim, 1941- **author.**
Annihilating the demons of Sri Lanka: an unfinished story / Apratim Mukarji.
pages cm
Includes bibliographical references and index.
ISBN 9789322008932

1. Sri Lanka—Politics and government—21st century. 2. Political corruption—Sri Lanka. 3. Social problems—Sri Lanka. I. Title.

LCC DS489.84.M85 2019 | DDC 954.93032 23

Edited by Padma Alva
Cover Jacket by Dushyant Parasher
Typeset by The Laser Printers, New Delhi
Printed and bound in India by Sai Printo Pack Pvt Ltd.

Dedicated to the memory of my friend and
Sri Lankan journalist Rita Sebastian
who suffered enormously for the
wayward journey of her beloved country
and people.

Contents

Preface

SRI LANKA entered my life through a circuitous route and without prior notice. I had become a thorn in the flesh of Marxists who were ruling my home state of West Bengal, in India for ages. Their sheen of love for the people had evaporated; it was no longer a people's government, and the *apparat* and the *apparatchik* had self-promoted themselves into a *vox populi the Pretender*. Professional journalism had been declared people's enemy.

I had long tired of reporting and commenting on the same band of corrupt politicians and the fortuitous opening in distant Sri Lanka enamoured me. My predecessor Mohan K. Tikku needed a respite from the adrenaline-driven, action-packed tenure and I eased into his seat in October 1990 with curiosity to learn about a new country and its people and anticipation of risk and adventure. I am glad to admit that Sri Lanka filled my plate with both the elements.

Sri Lanka has a peculiar charm of its own which all foreign correspondents who live and work there succumb to. Each one of them makes life-long friendships enriching their lives. The memories are invariably sweet and soul-wrenching, particularly for those who were assigned to cover one of the bloodiest and longest insurrections in the world.

But I had never imagined that my connection with Sri Lanka would go beyond reporting. One intolerably hot June morning, I received an urgent phone call from a resourceful publisher in Delhi. He gave me only two weeks' time to write a book on the country. 'Elephant Pass is about to fall to the LTTE,' he began peremptorily. 'The Indian government is very worried, you have little time but you must do it.' My protestations that I had never thought of myself as an author of books were brushed aside; and in less than 24 hours I found myself labouring away at my computer. My first book on the island, *The War in Sri Lanka: Unending Conflict?* was published in 2000.

I returned to Sri Lanka in 2004 to probe the curious case of the longest ceasefire in the history of the conflict till date. My findings were published in my second book on the country, *Sri Lanka: A Dangerous Interlude* (2005).

I visited the country again in November 2017. My curiosity whetted by the unthinkable failure of the government of 'good' governance which was failing to lift a long-suffering people from the morass of dead history and discredited (but not discarded) racism. I returned with a mind over-burdened with memories of the follies piled up by the leadership. My third book on Sri Lanka is, therefore, more critical than what I would have wished it to be.

In mid-2017, I began to conceive this book secure in the knowledge that guidance and help would be readily forthcoming from my sources in the island-nation, knowing as I do the open-mindedness and friendliness of the people. My belief was not misplaced.

My former colleague and friend P.K. Balachandran, who succeeded me as *Hindustan Times* correspondent in Colombo in 1997, extended his helping hand immediately and throughout my journey to Sri Lanka in November 2017 and thereafter. A word from him opened many doors for me and I am glad to acknowledge my gratitude to him.

Academics like Jayadeva Uyangoda and human rights activist Dr Jehan Perera in Colombo, and political economist and social activist Ahilan Kadirgamar and academics Rajan and Kirupaimalar Hoole in Jaffna city were admirably forthright in their assessments of the situation in their country. Politicians too, particularly those who are out of office, were readily available.

Those politicians who ruled over the country and those who were ousted from power in the last presidential and parliamentary elections were, however, reticent (to put it mildly) in granting me interviews even though I had provided enough (as I thought) cushion period. Unlike my previous books, however, I had concentrated this time in probing the common people's mind rather than to go by the often contrived viewpoints of the political class. And I am glad to record that I was not disappointed in my venture.

People, whether in the south and west or in the north and east, were admirably frank, sometimes even brutal, in their assessments of the political, economic and societal issues of Sri Lanka. They helped me comprehend the Sri Lankan situation much better than I otherwise could have.

Lastly, I acknowledge the enormous help in understanding the wounded civilisational framework in which Sri Lanka lives today that I obtained from the publication of the National Peace Council of Sri Lanka, *Write to Reconcile II*. Its young writers—Tamils, Muslims and Sinhalese—have poured out their hearts in their poems and short stories. To read this publication is a privilege for any human being. I thank my friend Jehan Perera for this gift.

Prologue
Sri Lanka: A Suicidal Plunge

ON a gloomy, rainy evening of 26 October 2018, President Maithripala Sirisena and his predecessor and (officially, till that moment) *bete noire* former President Mahinda Rajapaksa carried out a coup of sorts. After peremptorily sacking Prime Minister Ranil Wickremasinghe, Sirisena telephoned Rajapaksa to rush to his official residence, and as Rajapaksa's motorcade was about to start, a second call came informing him that the meeting would be held at the Presidential office at the Old Secretariat on Galle Face Road.

According to unconfirmed reports emanating from the Rajapaksa camp, even when he was being ushered into the President's office, he was completely ignorant of the purpose of the summary summons. Before he had left his official residence, however, the former President had telephoned his brothers, Gotabaya and Basil, to rush along to the President's office. Later reports said that by the time the two brothers arrived, their eldest brother had already become Sri Lanka's latest Prime Minister. However, in his 25 November 2018 statement, Rajapaksa referred to Sirisena's explanatory address to the nation delivered on 28 October 2018, on the circumstances in which the choice for a new premier fell on him and remarked that when the government was entrusted to him 'in such circumstances', he could not in all fairness shun the responsibility.[1] In the process, the incumbent Prime Minister lost his job, and the unlikeliest pair of politicians joined hands to run the country. However, this protestation of innocence was difficult to accept even at that early phase because the secret rendezvous the two were carrying on prior to the dramatic developments of the 26 October 2018 evening was not that secret.

The pulsating power game that unfolded on 26 October 2018 ended short of two months only on 16 December when Rajapaksa counted himself out (having resigned the previous day and issuing a damning statement) and Wickremasinghe retrieved his prime ministership. However, Rajapaksa's open threat to the Tamils for supporting Wickremasinghe and his vow to take revenge by blocking a new constitution sent a chill down the combined spine of the minority communities. In Sri Lankan history, this drama altogether has no parallel by itself till date, and such an upheaval must be rare in the history of any democratic country as well, though similar events may have happened in totalitarian or dictatorial regimes. But Sri Lanka has never been one among them. In other words, by expressing his utter incompatibility with Wickremasinghe through the bizarre act he had indulged in, the President had plainly murdered democracy and played havoc with the country's constitution in the course of a few minutes that October evening. Yet, in a little over a month's time, the edifice that the president had so confidently built to dislodge his Prime Minister out of sheer personal pique was virtually demolished. In a desperate bid to save his face, he surrendered to the Opposition in a last bid to choose anyone else but Wickremasinghe. But this patently, wily move, was rebuffed repeatedly by a united Opposition, and after a futile and thoroughly unconstitutional resistance over two months, Sirisena bowed down to reality.

The series of defeats on the floor of the House for Rajapaksa (two no confidence motions adopted and a confidence vote won by Wickremasinghe) established the majority support for the deposed Prime Minister. The gathering gloom for the purported Prime Minister was reinforced by two substantive defeats in the judiciary, first, the Court of Appeals interim stay on his government in response to a number of petitions by Parliamentarians, lawyers, social activists and others, and, thereafter, the rejection of his challenge to the interim stay by the Supreme Court, Rajapaksa finally resigned from the Prime Minister's post on 15 December 2018. And Wickremasinghe returned to the chair the following day.

As the United National Front (UNF) led by Wickremasinghe in Parliament put up a stiff resistance and refused to accept Sirisena's diktat, the President grudgingly realised, which was publicly admitted only by 1 December 2018, that he had absolutely no other option but to re-invite his current *bete noire*, and swallow the bitter medicine to escape an unavoidable and ignoble impeachment. Following the Court of Appeal interim ruling of 3 December 2018, that restrained Rajapaksa and his ministers from functioning as a government (which had been voted down twice in mid-November in Parliament), the President even admitted that there was no Prime Minister or government in the country at that point of time.

The only way out for him in such a hostile environment would be a favourable judgment by the Supreme Court on the issue of the constitutionality of his act of dissolution of Parliament, which would be available only by 7 December 2018 and was actually delivered six days later. By then, the uncooperative Parliament would have blocked the flow of funds to the government, which indeed had happened by the end of November.

This found Sirisena in a terrible hurry to wriggle out of a situation of his own making, in which Rajapaksa had been his willing partner. In all probability, an unfavourable judgment was the likeliest thing to happen to him and he even expressed his apprehension in this regard.

He, therefore, turned to the Tamils for a rescue act and even at that hour he was being patently dishonest. The best deal for him, considering the tight corner he had pushed himself into, came when the 14-member TNA group in Parliament, which was being wooed by both the contending sides, assured him that if he withdrew his unconstitutional measures of sacking Wickremasinghe (dated 26 October 2018) and dissolving Parliament (9 November 2018), it would not support a UNP bid to impeach him. His fear that the main Opposition party might seek to impeach him was not baseless; several UNP MPs were actually exploring such a step once the President withdrew his disputed gazette notifications. The narrative will make it amply clear, ever since the February 2018 local government elections the National Unity government was tottering on the brink of a collapse at any moment. The 26 October 2018 denouement cannot, therefore, be described as a complete surprise, for despite strict secrecy it was known in Colombo circles that Sirisena and Rajapaksa had been meeting each other. Still, when the swift change of guard came in the Prime Minister's office, the shock proved to be cataclysmic because till then, at least in the public perception, the two highest officials of the state, Sirisena and Rajapaksa, were the worst possible enemies of each other. How then could they embrace each other in such a decisive manner? Could it have been completely spontaneous?

Sirisena's rationale

Apparently realising that his seemingly abrupt action required some explaining in the face of a wide adverse public reaction, the President addressed the nation on 28 October 2018, characterising Wickremasinghe's political conduct as 'uncivilised'.[2] 'Wickremasinghe and his group of closest friends who belonged to a privileged class and did not understand the pulse of the people, conducted themselves as if shaping the future of the country was a fun game they played.' The former Prime Minister's 'political conduct was unbecoming of civilised politics'. Once in the government, he arrogantly and stubbornly avoided collective decisions and tended to take individual decisions. This behaviour led to many conflicts and the President's efforts to correct Wickremasinghe did not produce the desired result. The President maintained that he also tried to persuade Wickremasinghe to be cooperative and consult the senior leaders before taking decisions. 'I suggested to him that we should take our decisions after proper discussions to achieve the goals of good governance. However, he ignored the aspirations of ...the people.' As will be narrated in details in the following chapters, the so-called Central Bank of Sri Lanka (CBSL) Bond scandal that broke out early in the regime of the Unity government was probably the single most potent factor that ruined the relations between the two top leaders of the government, that is the President and the Prime Minister. It was but natural that this scam would occupy an important part of the President's 28 October 2018 statement. Calling the scam nothing less than the 'Central Bank robbery,'

Sirisena said, "The Central Bank robbery was an abortion of the pledge of good governance we had given to the people to eliminate corruption and fraud.' Recalling the days when the scandal was rocking the country, he said that at that time Wickremasinghe behaved very impatiently and restlessly. He even objected to the President's decision to personally visit the CBSL. The visit was followed by the appointment of a Presidential inquiry commission to probe the scam, with the UNP questioning the rationale of the President's action. 'I wish to reiterate here,' he said, 'that Ranil Wickremasinghe must take the responsibility to bring Arjuna Mahendran (the deposed CBSL chairman and since absconding) and a close friend of Wickremasinghe to Sri Lanka,' the President said.

Mentioning the upset outcome of the local government elections in February, 2018—in which the Rajapaksa-led Sri Lanka Podujana Peramuna (SLPP) and allied parties made a dramatic advance towards recapturing power by routing both the main ruling parties—Sirisena said, 'I believe that the result of the local government elections that was held last February was a warning by the people to correct the course of this government. At that moment, I called Wickremasinghe and other leaders of the UNP and explained (that) the "people have taught us a lesson about the way we have governed and we must correct ourselves now." And I told (him), "You have acquired my powers to do what you did, and I silently gave you that power in gratitude as you took (the) leadership to bring me to power." As a result of my gratefulness, which is a noble human quality, the country had to suffer very bad consequences. That was because I allowed him to conduct freely, sometime even acquiring my powers.'

Sirisena also brought forth the sensitive issue of an allegedly India-sponsored assassination plot, and the subsequent appointment of Rajapaksa by replacing Wickremasinghe. 'Recently,' the President said, 'a person called Namal Kumara came before the media and disclosed about a plot to assassinate me and Gotabaya Rajapaksa (former defence secretary). I handed over the task of investigations to (the) Criminal Investigations Department...Within 48 hours of the disclosure made...by the person called Namal Kumara and investigations commenced on the plot, (the) Inspector General of Police (the most senior police officer in Sri Lanka) made a statement stating that there was a doubt about the voices in the tape recording provided by that person.'

'I would like to raise the question,' continued the President, 'with respect, is it suitable for the Police Chief to behave in such a shameless manner and express doubts about the recording, without seeking any technical expert advice on the tape recording, when there was a revelation that a plot was hatched to assassinate the President of the country?' He added that the subsequent investigations carried out by the CID and other agencies including the Intelligence Bureau, showed that this 'is a very serious matter.' In this plot, he added, there was a wide range of information which had not been disclosed to the public.

'There is also an involvement of a Cabinet minister in this plot to assassinate me,' Sirisena alleged. Since then, tremendous pressure had been mounted on the investigations, and there were instances of some responsible intelligence officers refusing to join in the investigations (indicating some personal involvement on their part). Reverting to the topic days later, Sirisena said on November 25, 2018, while talking to foreign correspondents in Colombo, that a forensic examination of the tapes found that the voices in the tapes matched 95 per cent and that some portions had been deleted. The Police Chief also did not explain why two light machine guns were issued to a police unit and why a sniper rifle was missing. 'Despite all this,' he said, 'including the alleged involvement of a cabinet minister (belonging to Wickremasinghe's party) in a plot to kill the Head of State, Wickremasinghe did not get the plot investigated properly. He did not, even once, brief me about progress in the investigation. Meanwhile, his ministerial colleagues were going around saying the assassination plot was but a joke or a drama. Can any leader in the world work with such a person?' As for the bond scam, after the President was informed (the author needs to clarify when since he says 'six months ago' at the end of this sentence) by the concerned departments that it would take at least fifteen years to bring all the guilty persons to justice under the existing Commission Act and that certain amendments must be carried out in order to reduce this time period to just one year, the relevant amendments were submitted by the Presidential Secretariat to Parliament 'six months ago.' Since then, the proposed amendments had been hanging fire. 'Finally, the Amendment Bill to (the) Act on Commission on Bribery or Corruption was presented to Parliament,' but the President was sad to note that Parliament postponed the approval of the Amendments Act 'indefinitely.' Why was it deferred? For whose benefit? Due to pressure from whom? He asked rhetorically.

Sirisena also accused Wickremasinghe of a number of 'fraudulent' deals the government had got into, such as, the EAP Company which owns multi-media arms in television, films radio, many valuable state-owned assets, and awarding of contracts, including 'massive' construction awards like the Kandy Highway Project without a cabinet approval. Referring to the Land Ordinance Special Act, which in effect sought to 'hand over land rights to foreigners', he said that fortunately the bill had been stuck at the Cabinet level. 'This bill, presented under the political and economic vision of Wickremasinghe (and which) would adversely affect the land rights of the country must be totally blocked by us,' he commented. Charging that the committee set up by the former Prime Minister to manage the economy was 'totally fraudulent', he said that the committee's decisions were fraudulent and that as a way out, Sirisena had established the National Economic Council and Wickremasinghe had taken every possible stop to weaken it, he added. He tried to prevent the commission from functioning, and the President said he was clearly stating that the present crisis situation had emerged due to the former Prime Minister's stubborn decisions. Coming to the main allegation against him that his action in sacking Wickremasinghe and appointing Rajapaksa in his place was unconstitutional, he asserted that 'It was entirely constitutional.' 'Wickremasinghe and the UNP complain that the establishment of a new government and appointment of Rajapaksa as Prime Minister was contradictory to the provisions of the Constitution,' he noted. 'But I categorically state that the appointments were made totally in accordance with the Constitution and on (the) advice of legal experts. No constitutional violation was done when (the) appointments were made and (the) removal was enacted. With all respect, I completely reject the charge that what was done was a violation of the Constitution.'

The President, for good measure, invited the UNP members and the Buddhist clergy to support the new government, describing it s an 'open invitation' to break ranks and join the Sirisena-Rajapaksa government.

Apart from directly inviting UNP MPs to defect, he sought to divide the Tamil MPs into two distinct groups, the north-eastern Tamils represented by the TNA and led by R. Sampanthan and the *Malayaha* (plantation or Indian) Tamils represented by the Tamil Progressive Alliance (TPA) led by Mano Ganesan. Meeting them on November 7, 2018, he offered three options before the TPA: join the Rajapaksa government and raise its strength in the House; accept ministerial portfolios and cooperate; else, abstain in the event of a voting in Parliament; and thirdly, instead of Wickremasinghe let any other UNP leader be chosen as Prime Minister. 'As a civilised political entity, we as the TPA team of all six MPs met President Maithripala Sirisena and told him that we cannot accept his invitation to join his government,' Ganesan tweeted.

Undaunted, Sirisena offered the choice of 'staying neutral' to the TNA in the event of a vote in the House. In the next few days, both he and Rajapaksa tried hard to placate the TNA by promising to release the remaining civilian lands still occupied by the army in the Northern Province but to no avail.[3] Rajapaksa offered the lollipop of the release of all the Tamil political prisoners, a long-held demand of the northern Tamils 'very soon', a Tamil language tweet by his MP son Namal said. The tweet claimed, 'President Maithripala Sirisena and Prime Minister Rajapaksa would make a decision (on the issue) very soon.'[4]

Rationale challenged

A leading constitutional lawyer and Member of Parliament, Dr Jayampathy Wickremaratne challenged the (then) anticipated Presidential proclamation for dissolving Parliament by recalling that the original 1978 Constitution, adopted during the J. R. Jayewardene regime, granted the President a 'near-unbridled' power to dissolve Parliament 'at will.' Article 70 gave him the power to do so, subject to just one limitation: if the previous Parliament had been dissolved prior to its completing the (then prevailing) six-year term, the President could only dissolve the succeeding House after its first year was over. At the Presidential election of January 2015 one of the main issues raised was the Executive Presidency. The forces that supported the common candidate of the united Opposition (Sirisena) 'were clearly for limiting presidential powers and strengthening Parliament. One does not have to labour the point,' he pointed out.

The 19th Amendment, which was passed with just one member opposing it, reduced the term of Parliament to five years. The amended 19th Amendment now provides that the President shall not dissolve Parliament until the expiration of a period of not less than four years and six months from the date appointed for its first meeting unless Parliament requests the President to do so by a resolution passed by not less than two-thirds of the whole number of members (including those not present) voting in its favour. 'Thus, Parliament can now be dissolved by the President in the first four and a half years of its term only if 150 Members of Parliament so request by a resolution passed in Parliament,' he said. 'The wording is clear and unambiguous.' 'If the argument that the President can dissolve Parliament at any time at will is correct, then Parliament can be dissolved by the President just one day after the new Parliament meets, even if he had dissolved the previous Parliament before it completed its full term. This shows the absurdity of the argument,' he added.[5]

The enormity of the President's ill-advised actions had alerted the intelligentsia to such an extent that Jayampathy Wickramaratne, in addition to his own input as an MP and a constitutional lawyer, also sought the opinion of a group of constitutional experts on the issue. Their view was put on *Groundviews*, a Sri Lankan website, for wider circulation, prepared by Gehan Gunatilleke, Dinesha Samararatne, Kalana Senaratne and Asanga Welikala. Responding to a question on if the withdrawal of the United People's Freedom Alliance (UPFA) led by the President from the Wickremasinghe government had led to a vacation in the post of Prime Minister, the lawyers clarified that there was no constitutional provision stipulating that the withdrawal of one party from a coalition would automatically lead to a dissolution of the government or the cabinet of ministers or the office of Prime Minister. 'Article 46(4) and (5), which deals with a national government, makes no reference whatsoever to such consequences,' they said.[6] The only legal consequence of the formation of a national (coalition) government was that the ordinary cap on the number of cabinet ministers at 30 and non-cabinet ministers at 40 would stand suspended, with Parliament determining the number of ministers, which could be higher than the ordinary limit. Conversely, if a national government ceased to exist, then the 'only' legal consequence would be that the number of cabinet ministers be reduced to 30 and that of non-cabinet ministers to 40. And 'the President can do this only on the advice of the Prime Minister, as all ministerial appointments and dismissals legally require the President to act on the advice of the Prime Minister (see Articles 45(1) and 46(3),' they pointed out. Was Sirisena legally justified in appointing any MP as prime minister who, in his opinion, was most likely to command the confidence of Parliament? In seeking to answer this question, the lawyers straightaway demolished the constitutionality of Sirisena's action in 'unilaterally' dismissing Wickremasinghe, arguing that he was not authorised by the Constitution to do so 'based on a subjective opinion of the President, as to which Member of Parliament commands the confidence of Parliament.' The provision that the President shall appoint the person, 'who, in (his) opinion, is most likely to command the confidence of Parliament' (Article 42(4) can only be given the right meaning in the context of the specific purpose for which this power is vested in the President. 'The power of the President is a constitutional power to be exercised in the public interest and in the light of relevant facts. It is not something that is personal to him that can be used in any way that he pleases,' they concluded.

They also supported Wickremasinghe's contention that in the light of the 19th Amendment, the Prime Minister ceases to hold office either by death or resignation and thereby ceasing to be an MP or if his government loses the trust of the House following a defeat on the floor of Parliament over the Statement of Government Policy, the Appropriations Bill or a vote of no confidence under Articles 46(2) and 48. None of these conditions prevailed in the instant case.

Was Rajapaksa eligible for his appointment as Prime Minister? The very fact that he had already been elected as President twice in 2005 and 2010 made him ineligible to be President for a third term under Articles 31(2) and 92(c). This automatically would make him inclined to become the next Prime Minister if such an opportunity arose. As it in fact did when Sirisena had his brainwave of getting rid of Wickremasinghe by hook or by crook. However, as Sirisena himself stated later during the crisis, Rajapaksa was only his third choice, the first being Speaker Karu Jayasuriya and the second Sajith Premadasa, the UNP vice-president and former President the late Ranasinghe Premadasa's son. Both had declined the offer and, instead, advised Sirisena to go by the constitutional path of appointing one who commanded the trust of the House. Thus, it was Rajapaksa who was offered the post and which he accepted with alacrity since it offered him a short-cut to power and he would not have to wait till 2020 for an electoral show-down.[7]

A matter of translation?

In the convoluted world of Sri Lankan politics at the time, even the English and Sinhala versions of the Constitution figured prominently in the country-wide debate. The question was if the admitted discrepancy between the English and Sinhala texts of the statute book meant that the Sinhala version granted the President the power to remove a sitting prime minister and reappoint another unilaterally. In response, after acknowledging the existence of the linguistic discrepancy, the lawyers argued that the description of the condition under which the incumbent could be removed as 'by the removal from office or resignation or otherwise' instead of 'by death, resignation or otherwise' (as in the English version) made no material difference to the process through which a Prime Minister might be removed from office. Neither the Sinhala nor the English version of Article 48(1) referred to the President's power to remove a Prime Minister. Thus, treating this apparent discrepancy as a reference to such a power of removal was incongruous in terms of the Constitution (when) 'read as a whole.' Nowhere else in the Sinhala text it was contemplated that a presidential power of dismissal had been retained in the Constitution after the 19th Amendment. The lawyers also rejected the other contention that the president enjoyed the power of dissolving Parliament during the first four and a half years of its five-year term and pointed out that rightfully, the President could have done so only in March 2020.

After two no confidence motions against the new government were carried by the majority of the MPs, it was clear as day that the President's invitation to defect had fallen flat. This development was sought to be countermanded by the rejection of the anti-government motions by both the President and the 'purported' (as the UNP designated Rajapaksa) Prime Minister, further pushing a political solution to further uncertainty and instability. A group of eminent constitutional experts, academics and social activists including political scientists Jayadeva Uyangoda and Paikaisothy Saravanamuttu, and lawyers J. C. Weliamuna, Jayampathy Wickremaratne and Tissa Jayatilaka, countered the President's justification of his actions, arguing that the 1978 Constitution, as amended by the 19th Amendment, was the 'only' constitutional document that should govern the actions of the President with regard to the Prime Minister. According to the Constitution as it stands at present, once a Prime Minister is appointed, his or her office would be vacated only in 'limited' instances, that is, resignation, ceasing to be a Member of Parliament (Article 48), or where he is removed by virtue of the dissolution of the Cabinet which would automatically occur upon the defeat of the Statement of Government Policy or the Appropriation Bill or upon a motion of no-confidence being passed against the government (Article 48). 'As the objective of the 19th Amendment was to move towards a parliamentary democracy, the amendment expressly repealed the power of the President to remove the Prime Minister that existed under (the) provisions of the original 1978 Constitution and its 18th Amendment,' the group noted in the 'Statement on the Constitutional Crisis,' issued in the aftermath of the crisis. The group called upon the

President to forthwith revoke the prorogation of Parliament (which had followed on 9 November 2018) to facilitate (an) immediate resolution of the crisis through Parliament; Speaker Karu Jayasuriya should forthwith convene Parliament to faciliate an immediate resolution of the crisis through Parliament; all government leaders and MPs should abide by and 'not to transgress' the principles and provisions of the Constitution; all political leaders should ensure that violence and unrest were prevented; all MPs should ensure that they would vote in accordance with the people's mandate and 'not in consideration of financial or other benefits offered'; all public servants should ensure that they did not obey any instructions granted by 'unconstitutionally appointed' persons and that they upheld the Constitution and the rule of law; and the Inspector General of Police and the armed forces should ensure that in carrying out their duties, they acted in a non-partisan manner and strictly honoured the Constitution and the rule of law.

However, even though Sirisena's patently unconstitutional offer to the Opposition benches to cross over to his side in order to achieve a 113-seat majority in the 225-seat Parliament, did not materialise yet, to his credit, he fought tenaciously clinging to his belief that nothing was fair or foul in politics. Unfortunately for this lawfully elected but fallen head of state, neither the MPs nor the judiciary helped him achieve his objective. Nevertheless, it was clear that the President had opted for the rather desperate measure of dissolving Parliament and calling for fresh elections (which otherwise would be due only in mid-2020) after it was established that the Sirisena-Rajapaksa combine would not be able to muster a majority support in Parliament.

Supreme Court's spanner

The Supreme Court threw two inevitable spanners into the works of the President. Firstly, the Supreme Court stayed on 13 November 2018 the Presidential dissolution of Parliament and restrained the Election Commission from announcing snap elections. After hearing eleven petitioners and respondents for two days, the court suspended until 7 December 2018 the Presidential proclamation issued by Sirisena which also called for elections to be held on 5 December 2018. Among the petitioners was one of the election commissioners, Ratnajeevan Hoole, who later explained that 'All (the) three commissioners are unhappy with the dissolution of Parliament' but (apart from him) the other two believed that they must comply with a Presidential gazette. But they had also concluded that they would not object to any relief being sought by other petitioners, such as political parties, academics and social activists. In a powerful argument, Hoole's counsel Hezaz Hizbullah said that a franchise was about people getting together and expressing an opinion on who should represent them in Parliament. 'Those privileging Article 33(2)(c) are (saying that) one person's view is more powerful than that of the people and their franchise. There is only one word for it, it is dictatorship'.[8] In the continuing battle between the President and Parliament, speaker Jayasuriya convened the House on 14 November 2018. The Supreme Court stay order also boosted the morale of Wickremasinghe who had chosen a political battle over a legal challenge even though he had solid grounds to fight his dismissal, which was patently unconstitutional and clearly dictated by personal pique. The former Prime Minister said at the time, 'We have the numbers, we are ready to prove that in Parliament on Wednesday (November 14)...The people have won their first victory. Let's go forward and re-establish the sovereignty of the people in our beloved country.' Immediately after his sacking, he had asserted that irrespective of the 26 October 2018 developments, he remained the lawful Prime Minister as he enjoyed the majority support in Parliament. 'As the Prime Minister of Sri Lanka I have come here with the leaders of the United National Front (the alliance led by his party, UNP), clearly showing my majority. We are the largest party in Parliament and it is because of this I was elected as the Prime Minister,' he added.[9]

As the crisis rambled into more than a month and there was no sign of a rapprochement between the two sides, the strategies being followed by them acquired well delineated contours. The game that Srisena initiated and was strengthened by the entry of Rajapaksa was to prevent Wickremasinghe by any means from returning to head the government.

Even though the latter was able to establish his majority twice in Parliament, both the outcomes were summarily rejected by the President. This happened even after the Opposition parties led by the UNP and by Speaker Jayasuriya strictly followed the procedure of voting by the MPs as laid down by the President. The Sirisena-Rajapaksa combine continued to successfully prevent Wickremasinghe from establishing his parliamentary majority. This strategy was adopted after the duo failed in the initial stage to lure members from the Opposition benches to its side even after inducements of ministerial jobs and money were liberally offered. The duo also steadfastly ignored the adverse verdicts by the Supreme Court. On his side, Wickremasinghe chose to strike a tone of moderation, sticking to the constitutional position of the 'illegal' termination of his Prime Ministership, and attempting to maintain cordiality with Sirisena. Even after the President came out with a scathing personal attack on him on 29 October 2018, he kept on saying that he was still willing to work in tandem with the President. On 7 November 2018, he said that he was willing to work with the President 'if given a chance to prove' his majority in Parliament. 'I'll have no problem working with him, that's a question you must ask him. The Constitution doesn't make provision for personal prejudices.' Referring to the Speaker's statement that Rajapaksa would not be recognised as the lawful Prime Minister until he proved his majority in the House, Wickremasinghe said, 'Parliament's power is supreme and that is what the Speaker has upheld. I am confident of having the numbers. The fact that they (Sirisena and Rajapaksa) are delaying the recall (of the House) is because they don't have the numbers. The delay worries me because it makes the country more unstable.'[10]

The vote of no confidence on the Rajapaksa government was held twice, first on 14 November 2018 after nearly three weeks of suspension of Parliament, and then two days later on 16 November, winning on both the occasions by a majority of voice votes. On the first occasion, amid a long-sustained suspense and tremendous chaos, Speaker Jayasuriya said, 'I hereby declare that the appointed (Rajapaksa) government has no majority in this House.'[11] It was 122 votes in support of the motion in a House of 225 members.

However, this verdict was evidently marred by several deficiencies. The no confidence motion was passed without a debate and in utter chaos and without using the electronic voting system to establish the authenticity of the numbers for and against the motion. The manner of conducting the voting was strongly questioned because the Speaker had maintained that the voices and the look on the faces of the members showed that the motion had the approval of the majority of the members present and that he had consequently declared the motion as passed. It was at best a questionable basis for the verdict. 'Politics is now a crass and unabashed pursuit of self-interest and power, irrespective of its impact on institutions so painstakingly built up and so carefully nurtured over the years since 1931 when universal adult franchise was introduced for the first time in the British Empire. The on-going sordid saga relating to the premiership of the country involving the President, two Prime Ministers and the Speaker of Parliament brings out the nature of the disease in all its ugliness. The malaise could become endemic if not checked in time. As of date, Lankans have little or no hope that it will be checked in the absence of a larger than life messianic figure who can take the people on a new path.'[12]

This voting was followed by the Speaker forwarding a letter to the President, signed by 122 MPs, which, however, was not certified by Parliament, explaining what had happened. This letter was rejected by the latter arguing that the correct parliamentary procedures were flouted in getting the no confidence motion passed. The President, in his reply to this letter, which he sent to the Speaker on 14 November 2018, said the Standing Orders and other relevant procedures had not been followed when it came to the moving of the no confidence motion against Prime Minister Rajapaksa and his government. 'The list of signatures attached with the motion has not been certified by Parliament,' the President pointed out, adding that the date of the motion had also been inserted in an 'unacceptable' manner. The parliamentary tradition did not make it necessary for a newly appointed Prime Minister to prove his majority in Parliament (in fact, the usual practice is to allow such a person six months before facing such a motion).

Sirisena also maintained that he was the 'sole appointing authority' with regard to the appointment of a Prime Minister. He referred to the motion's argument that the Gazette Notifications Nos. 2094/43, 2094/43A and 2094/44 dated 26 October 2018 promulgated by the President and the purported acts and appointments referred to therein, were unconstitutional and were 'null and void and of no force or effect in law' and shot back that the gazette notifications in question were issued in accordance to the powers vested in him by the Constitution. It was the Constitution which dictated that he appointed that MP who commanded the most confidence according to his opinion as Prime Minister. He further said there was no need for him to ascertain if the person actually commanded such a majority.

These developments were followed by a new low in parliamentary conduct when on 15 November 2018, utter chaos prevailed in the House with a group of MPs resorting to an assault on the Speaker just as Rajapaksa rose and demanded a snap poll as a means to ending the stalemate. Hurling verbal abuses at Speaker Jayasuriya, MPs belonging to the government side marched towards his chair refusing to participate in the voting that would follow their leader's address. In his address, Rajapaksa disputed Jayasuriya's statement that since the November 14 voting, there was no government or Opposition in Parliament, and called upon 'all parties and MPs to join hands with us to go for fresh elections.' This was apparently a move to neutralise Wickremasinghe's claim that he continued to enjoy parliamentary majority as proved by the carrying of the no confidence motion on the previous day.

Presumably to avoid a repetition of the 14 and 16 November, 2018, Parliamentary proceedings which ended in a zero-sum game and failed to strike a political solution to the stalemate, the President convened on November 18 a meeting of the parliamentary party leaders, including the appointed Prime Minister and the ousted Prime Minister, to decide on the procedure to introduce and debate a fresh no confidence motion.

The guideline set by the President was to adopt a 'tangible, verifiable and legally acceptable' way of conducting the proceedings since, apart from the legality of the first no confidence motion, the Speaker was also in the dock. The voting on the motion should be held by calling out the names of the members and by a show of hands, he said. Alternatively, the electronic voting system should be used. Parliament could not repeat the confused and rough and ready way adopted on 14 and 16 November 2018 when the motion was moved and voted upon. The inability of the Rajapaksa government to defeat the motion was known to all but, for the sake of parliamentary democracy, this had to be established credibly by following the established procedure. This was not done, the Standing Orders were suspended and the voice vote was adopted without giving the MPs time to study the motion and debate it.

A new low

Sri Lanka recorded a new low in parliamentary etiquette when, on 15 November 2018, Rajapaksa's supporters made a blatant attempt to disrupt proceedings and physically threatened Speaker Jayasuriya. This happened when Jayasuriya stated that following the previous day's outcome over the no confidence motion, Parliament at present had neither a government nor an Opposition. The Rajapaksa side refused to accept this ruling and the appointed Prime Minister made a speech inviting the MPs belonging to all parties 'to join hands with us to go for fresh elections.' This demand apparently followed his realisation that as long as the current House stayed, he had no chance of winning the majority vote on any issue. However, this did not go unchallenged and the UNP immediately demanded a floor test to determine which side enjoyed the majority status.

This development acted as a catalyst for an all-out chaos that not just descended on the House but also indicated that the government side was acting according to a pre-determined programme. The government MPs rushed towards the Speaker's chair with one of them injuring himself as he unsuccessfully tried to snatch the Speaker's microphone, and subsequently he had to be hospitalised. The choicest of abuses were showered quite liberally on Jayasuriya, and in a tell-tale sign Rajapaksa remained a mute witness to the mayhem being perpetrated by his MPs. The UNP MPs soon joined the fray and both the sides exchanged blows at each other, leading eventually to an adjournment. Those members who maintained civility later lamented that it turned out to be a 'shameful' day for Parliament.[13]

The following day proved to be still worse. Even before the Speaker had arrived in the House, government MPs occupied his chair. The microphones and telephones on the Speaker's desk had already been ripped out and constant slogan-chanting continued. At 1.30 p.m., the Speaker entered the chamber escorted by thirty policemen and surrounded by the parliamentary staff, and stood in the aisle and with a microphone in his hand and began the proceedings. Government members began to throw chairs, copies of the Constitution and water bottles aimed at the Speaker and MPs sitting across.

As government MPs continued their determined bid to disrupt proceedings, Opposition MPs maintained their calm, and TNA member M.A. Sumanthiran moved a resolution to suspend the day's business, which was passed by a voice vote. This was swiftly followed by a motion of no confidence moved against the Rajapaksa government by the JVP member Anura Kumara Dissanayake and seconded by his colleague Vijitha Herath. The Speaker called for a vote and a loud approving chorus instantly emerged from the Opposition benches, 'The Ayes have it,' declared the Speaker.

Rajapaksa's office later issued the 'official procedure' for presenting and proceeding with no confidence motions in Parliament. It said that it could not accept the two motions passed during the course of the week as they were adopted in violation of the established parliamentary rules. This had occurred despite the Opposition MPs' assurance to the President that they would abide by the set procedure and the Standing Orders of Parliament. The Opposition MPs countered that the violence unleashed by the ruling United Peoples Freedom Front (UPFA) led by the President and the Prime Minister was the reason for the non-observance of the rules and the adoption of the motion by voice vote 'amidst chaos and din.' This defence was also rejected by the Prime Minister's office arguing that commotion and even violence in the House could not be an excuse for flouting the set proceedings. The right course for the Speaker would have been an adjournment of the House and all the contentious issues like the demand for arresting two Opposition MPs for carrying knives inside the chamber could have been civilly discussed and sorted out.[14]

This no-holds-barred fight between the government and the Opposition left no room for any illusion that a rapprochement could be attempted at all at some point of time. As a matter of fact, the situation worsened as the days passed with both the warring sides sharpening their assaults on each other. On 19 November 2018, the UNP declared that it would oppose all financial proposals put up by the secretary to the 'purported' Prime Minister Rajapaksa and warned bureaucrats who were carrying out orders of the Prime Minister and other ministers that they would be held responsible for their actions taken even after being warned and would be liable to punitive action.[15]

Meanwhile, several UNP MPs handed over a resolution to the Secretary-General of Parliament stating that the Secretary to the Prime Minister had no authority to approve any expenditure drawn from the funds of the state. The resolution was signed by six of the MPs. TNA MP M. A. Sumanthiran and the Chief Opposition Whip Anura Kumara Dissanayake (JVP) said that their parties would support the motion. The motion was slated to be moved in the House on 29 November 2018.

Since the matter of moving a no confidence motion against the government eluded a solution, the deputy speaker of Parliament (who was acting on behalf of the Speaker who had stopped attending Parliament fearing further assault on his person) sought the formation of a Select Committee for Parliamentary Affairs to deliberate on the matter and requested the parties to submit their nominations for the purpose. The government demanded that as per the accepted parliamentary practice, the government should enjoy the majority membership in the committee. This, in turn, was opposed by the Opposition which argued that since the subject before the committee would be a no confidence against the Prime Minister and his government, the government's demand could not be accepted.

The Opposition did not rest by wrestling with the government inside Parliament but also sought to corner it further in court. On 23 November

2018, all the 122 MPs who had signed the two no confidence motions filed a Writ of Quo Warranto in the Court of Appeal challenging the Rajapaksa government's continuation in office after the two motions had been passed against it. The MPs requested the court to declare that the Prime Minister, ministers and deputy ministers had no authority to hold government offices following the two 'successful' motions of no confidence passed by Parliament against them. They cited Article 48(2) of the Constitution in their support which said that the government of the day would stand dissolved with the adoption of a no confidence motion. As a precedent, the MPs quoted the case of former MP Geetha Kumarasinghe who lost her seat in 2017 following a Writ of Quo Warranto in the Court of Appeal.[16]

The same day, the ruling group hit back in its own fashion. The Rajapaksa-led UPFA declared that it would not recognise Karu Jayasuriya as the Speaker of Parliament as he had reduced himself to the status of an Opposition spokesman. MP Rohitha Abeygunawardene told reporters that Jayasuriya 'is not a Speaker of Parliament but the Speaker of Srikotha (the headquarters of the UNP)'. Another MP explained that the UPFA MPs would not recognise Jayasuriya in his capacity of the Speaker as he had refused to recognise the UPFA government as the legitimate government of Sri Lanka.

The dispute over the composition of the proposed select committee for Parliamentary Affairs arose because of the inability of the two sides to agree on the relevant procedure to be followed. The ruling party demanded the majority seven members for itself and the Opposition rejected it by arguing that since the committee would be asked to examine the no confidence motion against the government to be moved, the government party could not demand to enjoy the usual privilege. Finally, the UPFA MPs staged a walkout during the voting on 23 November 2018, protesting against the allocation of members to the select committee. In his masterful statement of 25 November 2018, (referred to earlier) Rajapaksa sought to demolish the Opposition case against Sirisena point by point and managed to play the role of an innocent victim of political vendetta. Going through his lengthy narrative, it is pertinent to note that he sticks to his long-held opinions on how, after annihilating the LTTE and Tamil terrorism as such, he had turned Sri Lanka back to progress and development and the economy had been flourishing when he had demitted office in January 2015 and how now the Wickremasinghe-led government had failed to perform its task because of its faulty ideology (neo-capitalist, urban-oriented and elitist, a charge levelled at the beginning of the crisis by Sirisena) and corruption culminating in a dreadful decline which had given rise to country-wide discontent; and how once again back at the helm he would steer the country back to prosperity. 'I have been stressing,' he said, 'ever since I took office as Prime Minister that our foremost aim was to go for an election in order to establish a stable government. However, the objective of the other side (Opposition) is to revive the previous government and to rule the country for as long as possible without holding any election at all. That is the reason for the present political situation.' The repeated postponement of the local government elections was primarily because the government of the day feared a defeat in the face of rising popularity of Rajapaksa. With the rapid decline in the economy and the long-sustained scandal over the Central Bank affair, the Sirisena-Wickremasinghe camp at the time was virtually compelled to surrender to the popular demand for holding the elections.

In the wake of the surprising change of the Prime Minister and subsequent political instability in the country, the Opposition had sought to portray the 'peril' in which the economy had been thrown into as its first direct impact. The deposed finance minister Mangala Samaraweera stated on 4 November 2018, 'The uncertainty created has triggered an immediate negative impact at a time of tremendous fragility in global financial markets. The first impact was felt in the stock market. Between Monday (29 October 2018) and Thursday (1 November 2018) net foreign outflows from the Colombo Stock Exchange were LKR 4 billion in just a 4-day period. For the entire 9-months (270 days) from January to September 2018 the total net outflow from the stock market was LKR 6.1 billion. Foreign investors are selling rapidly due to a sharp drop in confidence in Sri Lanka's economic management. These outflows are putting major pressure on the Sri Lankan Rupee in an already fragile global economy.' He estimated that as a consequence of this development, Sri Lanka's external borrowing costs would almost double.[17]

He expressed his apprehension that if the country failed to meet its external obligations, it might collapse into a situation like Argentina or worse than Venezuela, where similar 'reckless' policies were implemented. 'It is our citizens,' he argued, 'that will suffer as a result of this reckless, opportunistic behaviour. In Argentina, a country with similar challenges…made key policy errors like what we saw last week, interest rates just reached 74 per cent, inflation is 22 per cent, and the peso depreciated 115 per cent this year.'

The accelerated foreign sales of Sri Lankan debt and equity would put significant pressure on the value of the Rupee and would cause domestic interest rates to spike. 'The selling rate of the SL Rupee that had stabilised below 175 (against the US dollar) spiked from 174 to 177.3 in just four days,' he said. 'The old Rajapaksa style of selling off our hard earned reserves to try and defend the Rupee has no doubt already been deployed—this has been proved time and again to be a failed strategy. Lost reserves will make it even more difficult to meet our upcoming external debt repayments. 'The Central Bank might soon be forced to raise domestic interest rates, leading to rising borrowing costs across the board and stifling investment and economic activity.

Samaraweera also claimed that under the Wickremasinghe government, Sri Lanka had just managed to turn around its declining exports and stagnating FDI. In 2017 it saw its best ever exports and FDI and in the first half of 2018 both had continued to grow. 'Unfortunately,' said, 'the blatantly undemocratic, unconstitutional measures by the illegal regime have put at risk our hard won access to the EU market through the GSP+ scheme.' If Sri Lanka eventually lost this market, it would severely undermine its fishing, seafood and apparel sectors, all of which were making 'strong' inroads into the world's largest single market. 'A return to inward-looking, protectionist, regressive policies will put us back on the fast lane to economic crisis,' he warned. He also claimed that these negative developments had already affected Sri Lanka's credit ratings and there was a serious risk of global rating agencies like Moody's and Fitch (which had already commented on this) downgrading their Sri Lanka ratings. Global creditors might be unwilling to lend to the country which would in return affect refinancing the country's $15 billion debt payments in the next three years. Samaraweera pursued his line of attack on Rajapaksa by noting that as the former Finance Minister, he had made allocations to ensure funding until 31 December 2018; however, the country would fall into a crisis from January 2019 onwards. A legitimate government with an adequate majority in Parliament would have had the opportunity to present at least a vote on account which would have covered at a minimum the first three months of the new year enabling payment of pensions, salaries, *samurdhi* payments for poverty alleviation and settlements of debts. 'It is still not too late to re-establish the government that commands the clear majority in Parliament to present a budget/vote on account to authorise expenditure from the consolidated fund from 2019,' he wrote. Sri Lanka has hitherto never defaulted its debt obligations.

'The actions of 26 October 2018 have irreversibly undermined Sri Lanka's credibility in global markets – risking our ability to service future debt as well. We are being pushed towards a state of economic collapse as we stumble on to a road of a Greece-like situation,' he added.[18]

Samaraweera appeared to have crossed the limits when he tried to take credit for 'saving' Rajapaksa from becoming an international pariah. Speaking at a UNP electoral council meeting in Matara district on 2 December 2018, he said, 'The current (Wickremasinghe) government salvaged Sri Lanka from its status of a drop of blood on the world map and prevented Mahinda Rajapaksa from becoming an international criminal. The ex-President now has the opportunity to visit the international community and even to criticise the government, thanks to the present government. We remember how the country was by December 2014. Our country was marked as a bloodstain on the world map. We were accused of violating human rights in the war. An international investigation was to be held even without our involvement. The new government elected in 2015 pointed out to the U.N. in New

York and Geneva that the new government (was) ready to take measures against any human rights violations and punish the culprits. The U.N. halted the international investigations on this government's promise. This government paved the way for the former President to go abroad and boast. If not for this government, he would have been punished by an international court. Mahinda Rajapaksa was able to leave the country because of the trust placed in this government by the international community. (He) should light an oil lamp to Prime Minister Ranil Wickremasinghe's picture. We stopped him from becoming an international criminal.'[19]

However, the former Finance Minister faced a lot of flak on the social media for his injudiciously boastful remark and his act of taking credit for absolving the former President from facing justice for his cruel stint in office. Frances Harrison, a former BBC correspondent and journalist who has done seminal work in exposing Rajapaksa's inglorious record in office, tweeted on 5 December 2018, '…and then claimed to have trickled #tamils on accountability 4 for the war (&UN_HRC member states re-resolution 30/10 to save Mahinda!' Another tweet by Sukumaran said, 'says one who orchestrated a duplication intense campaign of emotional pleas of trial/space for accountability+political solution whilst pledging to demilitarise north-east of #lka by 2018…meanwhile, distorting reconciliation obligations to electorate.'

At around his time, Sirisena, still hell bent on neutralising Wickremasinghe by whatever came handy, announced on 25 November 2018 that a Presidential Commission would be appointed to probe the charges of corruption and fraud against the former Prime Minister. There were 17 reports, he told foreign correspondent in Colombo that day, against Wickremasinghe and his 'cohorts', which had not been investigated because the competent departments were under the Prime Minister's control in the Unity government (January 2015-26 October 2018). The suspected corruption and fraud cases involved 'questionable deals' in respect of land deals and private companies 'from the word go.' If Parliament had passed Wickremasinghe's Special Land Act by voice vote as had happened in the case of the two no confidence motions against Rajapaksa, 'foreigners would have been able to buy up Sri Lanka's lands to the detriment of the country'.[20]

In an interesting exposé of how the Wickremasinghe government was functioning, Sirisena recalled that he had desired the new administration to be run on scientific lines and had appointed a committee for this purpose. The committee submitted its report which was passed on to the Prime Minister. 'But he took no notice of it. He distributed portfolios in the most unscientific manner. For example, the Higher Education Minister was also (the) Minister for Highways. When I went abroad to negotiate agreements, those governments wondered if highway construction was being taught in Sri Lanka's higher education institutions,' said Sirisena. Another anomaly was placing the Central Bank under the Prime Minister and the state banks under the Finance Minister.

Sirisena also accused Wickremasinghe of pursuing neo-liberal policies which were antithetical to the economic interests of Sri Lankans. 'Every leader in every part of the world, including (US President Donald) Trump, puts his country and its people first and pursues policies which will serve their interests, but Wickremasinghe's policies were at variance with this trend. I had to stop many of his proposals with the result, there used to be frequent verbal duels in the cabinet,' he said.

However, in a sign of the eroded prestige and status of the president, the UNP immediately took up the challenge of a probe against Wickremasinghe and demanded the very next day that Sirisena, too, should subject himself to a corruption probe. The party president Kabir Hashim said that while the President, as the Head of State, should also be inquired into. 'The government that operated during this period was in no way a Ranil Wickremasinghe government,' he said. 'President Sirisena, who headed the National Unity government, was not only the Head of State but also the Head of Government. All decisions were made by a cabinet chaired by the President. If there was corruption in the past three and a half years as the President says, the President has equally to share the blame.'[21]

Rajapaksa retaliates

In his statement of 25 November 2018, Rajapaksa sought to turn this argument around by incorporating it in his discourse. 'The former Finance Minister claims that the economy is on a downward trend because of the change of government. The President invited me to take over the government precisely because of the collapse of the economy during the previous government. In such circumstances, what any democratic country would do is to hold a general election and have a new government elected to power.' Rajapaksa also exploited Sirisena's stint as one of his ministers in his government, stating that because he was in our government, he 'knows how we handled difficult situations. We managed to find the money to fight the war. We managed to complete a large number of major development projects that no previous government had been able to get off the ground'.

He also took credit for shielding the people from the effects of the 2007 world food crisis and the worst global economic recession since the 1930s that occurred in 2008, and claimed that Sri Lankans were not even aware of the world-wide crisis. 'Within a period of nine years, my government increased the US dollar per capita income of the country threefold…On the 9 January 2015 we handed an economically stable government to the new UNP government. Four years later, however, the country is now in a perilous state. The most serious aspect of the economic crisis facing this country today is the foreign currency debt burden,' Rajapaksa said.

'Even when the civil war was going on, the economy was not in such a bad state,' he claimed. At that time, too, the debt to GDP ratio was 90 per cent but the proportion of foreign currency debt was not as high as at present. Within a period of about three and a half years, the *Yahapalanaya* (good governance) government had taken a total of more than $20.7 billion in foreign currency loan alone. Due to this debt burden it will take a while to turn things around.

Saying that he was keeping a tab on the Wickremasinghe government's mismanagement of the economy and informing the people from time to time, he remarked, 'It should be plain to everyone that those who are trying to revive the previous government and rule without holding elections, are incapable of turning this country around. It was they who destroyed the stable economy that we had created. That is why they are so reluctant to hold elections.' He appealed to the nationalistic spirit of the people and requested them to extend 'the kind of support they gave us during the war,' in order to get the country out of the economic crisis. 'The President and the people of this country know that only we can extricate this country from the crisis it is in.' He also squarely rejected the Opposition's demand for holding a presidential election, arguing that the problem was in Parliament and that only a general election was necessary.

However, the appointed government's swift action on 29 November 2018 in signing two contracts with two Chinese firms for an infrastructure project drew sharp reactions from around the country as this happened in the midst of the constitutional crisis and with the validity of the government and its actions and decisions wrapped in doubt. Sri Lanka Ports Authority signed the contracts with China Harbour Engineering and Shanghai Zhenhua Heavy Industries, respectively, for enhancing the deep berth capacity of the state-run Jaya Container Terminal in Colombo, worth $32 million, and for purchasing three cranes for the same project worth $25.7 million.[22]

The same day Sri Lanka witnessed a major development in the political crisis. Speaker Jayasuriya met the President to discuss 'available avenues for establishing a legitimate government.' The surprise move was apparently motivated by the continuing failure of Rajapaksa to drum up support for his government among the MPs and the consistent show of the majority strength in Parliament by the Opposition.

If one could go by the available information, the President had reached a conclusion by the end of November that his actions in sacking the former Prime Minister and dissolving Parliament were unconstitutional and that he was ready to make amends. The 'unconstitutional' actions that the TNA sought to be rescinded were: the dissolution of Parliament on 9 November 2018 when Prime Minister

Wickremasinghe enjoyed majority support in it; and the summary dismissal of Wickremasinghe and the arbitrary appointment of Rajapaksa as his replacement on 26 October 2018.[23]

The President's search for such reassurances came in the wake of reports that a campaign had been launched in pro-democracy circles sympathetic to the UNP to get Parliament to impeach Sirisena for the crisis he had landed Sri Lanka in. However, the ground realities did not exactly place the main Opposition party in a situation where it would be feasible for it to go for such a serious move. For one thing, it lacked the numerical strength to bring an impeachment motion against the President on its own. Under the Constitution, moving an impeachment motion against the President successfully would require a backing by at least two-thirds of the total strength of 225 members, which would be 150 members. Even if the UNP enjoyed a simple majority of 113 members, it would have required the support of all the Opposition parties, such as, the TNA, JVP, TPA and others. If the TNA with its 14 members had assured the President of its decision not to support such a motion, there would be no way for the UNP to move ahead with it.

The Constitution allows, under Article 38(2)(I), 'intentional violation of the Constitution' as one of the conditions that merit an impeachment move against the President. The 13 December 2018 verdict of the Supreme Court emboldened the Opposition to think once again in terms of making such a move in order to neutralise the President before he actually embarked upon stymieing a resurrected Wickremasinghe government by his declared intention to not cooperate with the functioning of the cabinet.

The reports also spoke about Sirisena 'mulling' over withdrawing the offending gazette notifications which had unleashed the unprecedented constitutional and political crisis. However, they also indicated that he was still undecided about the timing of such a decision, particularly whether it should be done before or after the Supreme Court verdict on the subject scheduled to be delivered on 7 December 2018. He was apparently trying to explore the little time left to garner enough support to save his face in the meantime. But as things unfolded, his further dishonest attempts were being steadily foiled by the smaller alliances like the TNA and the TPA.

The crisis deepens

During the last three days of November 2018, the united Opposition moved swiftly to mount a pincer attack on the Sirisena-Rajapaksa dispensation. On 29 November 2018, a majority of MPs (123 out of the total 225) voted in favour of a special motion to halt finances to the Prime Minister's office to cripple its functioning. The motion, moved by the UNP, was supported by the TNA and the JVP. It happened on the third consecutive day of the boycott of Parliament by the government loyalists. The boycott followed Speaker Jayasuriya's ruling that he did not recognise the legality of the installation of Rajapaksa as the Prime Minister. However, like in the case of the two no confidence motions passed by Parliament, the special motion was also rejected by the government MPs on the ground that while only a minister could move such a motion, it had been moved by an ordinary MP.[24] This was followed on 30 November 2018, by another development when the same majority of the MPs voted in favour of a parliamentary motion to halt finances to the Rajapaksa cabinet and junior ministers with the government members still continuing their boycott of parliamentary proceedings. The motion to do so was submitted to Parliament by an MP of the Jathika Hela Urumaya or National Heritage Party (an ultra-nationalist Sinhalese party which supported Wickremasinghe. The party, though widely perceived to be a Sinhala-Buddhist party, describes itself as a secular inclusive political entity). Following the one-sided voting, Speaker Jayasuriya announced that the motion to cut down the expenditure of ministers, deputy ministers, and state ministers had been passed and that he would inform the ministry secretaries of the parliamentary decision.[25]

The government MPs declared that they would not accept this vote as well, as they had chosen to ignore the two no trust motions. 'We have mentioned this to the Speaker too. We will not attend such illegal motions,' said SLFP MP Anura Priyadarshana Yapa. The continuing boycott of Parliament by the pro-Rajapaksa members followed the

Speaker's declaration he did not recognise the new government. The latter, on its part, based their response on their determination that the Speaker was no longer a neutral arbitrator and was acting as a spokesman of Wickremasinghe.

The crippling effect

As the two warring camps grappled with each other, the state came to a virtual standstill, perhaps the worst affected being the bureaucrats. While, the two parliamentary resolutions adopted by majority vote on 29 and 30 November 2018, targetted Rajapaksa, in effect it tended to shackle the entire bureaucracy, spread across the island-nation and which was running the day-to-day administration.

While the parliamentary Opposition insisted that the motions must be honoured, what this meant on the ground was unprecedented. The entire cash flow to the ministries and their numerous departments looking after all the aspects of a modern state suddenly dried up. And it was the bureaucrats from the highest to the lowest levels who were called upon to tackle the consequences.[26]

An MP remarked at the time, 'If they (the motions) have been passed with a majority in Parliament, the secretaries (to the ministries) must take note.' But, at the very best, this was a fatuous comment, for putting the motion in practice simply meant crippling the administration and the entire state machinery.

The already grave situation was further complicated by the political executive's haste in taking quick decisions and passing orders for their immediate implementation. 'Ministers' (the inverted comma became a necessary appendage as technically they were no longer validly appointed) were signing orders, expecting their secretaries to carry them out. 'We have never been on a trickier slope, not even during the war years,' a senior bureaucrat in an essential service ministry said. 'As bureaucrats, we work with the government of the day, but when that is a disputed matter, our job gets very hard.' As a powerful mark of protest, a former senior civil servant, Devanesan Nesiah returned his *Deshamanya* (one of the highest civilian honour), explaining in his letter to the

President that since he could no longer take pride in the title conferred on him, he had little option but to return the treasured medal and certificate. Even though the Rajapaksa government pretended to not have been disturbed by the developments and appeared to be working in normal circumstances, it was forced soon to lapse into carrying on with day-to-day routine work.

But the purported Prime Minister refused to concede defeat, and even after the Court of Appeal restrained him and his cabinet of ministers on 3 December 2018 from functioning from their respective offices, Rajapaksa opted to challenge the interim order. The court order followed the adoption of two no trust motions against the Rajapaksa government leading to the situation where there was no government at that juncture.[27] On the day of the order itself, Rajapaksa had stated that he was 'not in agreement' with it and that he would challenge it in the Supreme Court basing his case on the argument that it was the apex court which alone could decide constitutional matters (the President had claimed that his appointment of Rajapaksa as the new Prime Minister was constitutionally appropriate, which was countered by the Opposition and legal experts asserting that it was not) and that the particular point of law was beyond the jurisdiction of the Court of Appeal. The Court of Appeal had issued notices accordingly to Rajapaksa and his ministers, who were respondents in the case, returnable on 12 December 2018.

The petitioners, MPs belonging to the UNP, TNA, JVP, Sri Lanka Muslim Congress and some other parties, argued that on 14 November 2018, Parliament passed a vote of no confidence against the purported government of the 49 respondents, followed by another vote of no confidence adopted on 16 November 2018. They maintained that in terms of Article 48 of the Constitution, the cabinet stood dissolved with effect from 14 November 2018. A leading lawyer J.C. Weliamuna opined that under the circumstances, the President must thereafter appoint a new Prime Minister and a new council of ministers.

As Wickremasinghe continued to enjoy the confidence of the majority of the MPs, the TNA and other Opposition parties, who called on the President the same evening as the Court of Appeal interim order, enjoined him the imperative need to restore the ousted Prime Minister back in his post. But Sirisena, as obdurate as Rajapaksa, once again refused to do so. As a legal recourse to bypass Parliament proved to be of little help, Rajapaksa said in a statement that 'the struggle to establish political stability in this country through the holding of a general election needs the support of the people more than ever at this moment.'[28]

Interestingly, on the very day that the Court of Appeal passed its interim order on Rajapaksa's constitutionality, the President told the TNA members of Parliament that no Prime Minister or government existed in Sri Lanka at the moment, echoing the court verdict which his own Prime Minister was contesting. However, going against all logic, he would not take Wickremasinghe back as his Prime Minister. In fact, he added for good measure that even if Wickremasinghe was backed by all the 225 members of Parliament, he would remain a *persona non grata* for him.

The President's current *bete noire*, however, maintained his reasoned approach and said on 4 December 2018 that the President must not take 'subjective decisions' to the Constitution. 'Don't be like Hitler and other dictators,' he said in a sharp repartee. 'The Prime Minister is decided by parliamentary majority. The President cannot say this is what I want. All we are saying is follow the Constitution.'[29]

Minorities suffer

However, the country did not consist of the Sinhalese politicians alone. There were other communities which had other preoccupations, and the chief among these was the overriding necessity for them to continue to live in a comparatively peaceful environment. Considering the historical proclivity of the country to lapse into communal frenzy in times of great stress and political instability, the growing worry among the Tamils, Muslims and Christians was the obvious inability of the parliamentarians to settle the matter amicably.

An unforeseen fallout of the over-a-month-long tussle between President Sirisena and the ousted Prime Minister Wickremasinghe was the consequences for the minority communities, especially the Sri Lankan

Tamils. Before the latest storm had broken out on the 26 October 2018 evening, the Tamils were living in a situation to which they had been accustomed since the end of the civil war in May 2009. They had learned over the years how to deal with Rajapaksa's presidential term and then the unexpected ushering of a spring of hope with the election of Sirisena and the formation of the national unity government.

The following chapters will narrate how the ethnic Tamils were the least prepared for the sudden and dangerous turn of events in Colombo, especially after they had witnessed a tardy but assured ascent to justice, resettlement, reconciliation and development on their way to a peaceful life after many decades of depredation and calamity. Their hopes for a peaceful era were completely beholden to the adoption of a new constitution by the existing Parliament (the term of which would expire in May 2020) ensuring a future free of communal frenzy and domination of the majority Sinhalese-Buddhist community, and a right to live and prosperity for every citizen irrespective of their ethnicity. Therefore, when the Sirisena-Wickremasinghe government suddenly went into a spin and in a little over one month, both Parliament and the government stopped functioning and a climate of chaos descended over the country, it was the Tamils who could become the worst sufferers. A number of Opposition politicians were already expressing their apprehension that communal riots could erupt at any moment.

The continuing political crisis could embolden anti-social elements to take the law into their hands and 'in such a situation, the country's minorities, especially the Tamils, may become the victims,' warned the Leader of the Opposition in Parliament and Leader of the TNA, R. Sampanthan on 20 November 2018. He had just briefed the Colombo-based foreign diplomats about the fast-paced developments. Describing the events since 26 October 2018, he said, '...such turbulence seriously impairs on-going efforts for a political solution through constitutional reform.' However, any false hope that may still have survived in the minds of the Tamils had to be dispelled when Rajapaksa made his defiant and angry statement after resigning from the Prime Ministership on 15 December 2018. He left no doubt in anybody's mind about the extremely destructive path he was planning to follow in the coming months. After warning that the resurrected UNF government and Sri Lanka would be held hostage to the 'divisive, separatist and anti-national' agenda of TNA, he vowed, 'We will bring the forces opposed to the country to their knees by organising the people.' Pointing out that the Wickremasinghe government was committed to bringing about a new Constitution 'at the behest of the TNA', he said that the draft of a new constitution, already available in public domain, envisaged 'the division of Sri Lanka into none semi-independent federal units.' 'It will abolish the executive presidency', and the new constitution had been drafted by certain individuals 'who turned the country into an ungovernable mess.' However, all was not lost yet, and the UNF-TNA combine would never be able to get the new constitution passed as it lacked the two-thirds majority in Parliament. The SLPP led by him, the SLFP led by Sirisena and other parties in the north-east and the Central Provinces together controlled 54 per cent of the total votes in the country, and thus the road to a new constitution was effectively blocked.

Although 10 long years had passed since the hostilities ended and peace had reigned in the former war zone, almost all the demands of the ethnic Tamils remained unfulfilled. In a few instances, some progress had been made, such as, release of civilian-owned lands in the Northern Province to the original owners but, here too, problems were not fully resolved. For example, the owners who had recovered their lands complained that they could not resume farming as their conditions had deteriorated under military occupation. Sometimes, they were given different portions of land rather than their own which they found difficult to cultivate. About 15 per cent of the occupied lands were still under army control which, as the President had assured, would be returned shortly, but this promise was also stalled due to the political instability.

A similar fate befell the issue of the release of the political prisoners, which both the President and the new Prime Minster had assured would be accomplished soon. Progress in the work in the Office of Missing Persons was of particular concern to the Tamils which had lagged very much and despite the most intense and sustained campaign by the Tamils to expedite. Therefore, the sudden stalemate in Colombo, leading to a collapse of the government, meant that issues which were of far lesser import to the Sinhalese would suffer the most.

Agriculture and fishing were the two main occupations of the people in the north-east, and here too, the Tamils and Muslims had not yet fully got back their rights. On the contrary, a substantial number of Sinhalese fishermen were issued licences to fish in the traditional zones of the minorities.

But, above everything else, it was a new constitution that the Tamils and all other minority communities were looking forward to after many seasons of disappointment. The latest report on constitutional reform was scheduled to be tabled in Parliament on 7 November 2018 but the disruptions in parliamentary proceedings ensured that the fate of the report was left hanging in the balance. Sampanthan was understandably acerbic in his comments, 'It is unacceptable that all these efforts are getting stalled in the absence of a government or a PM. Action should be taken immediately to resolve the crisis.'[30]

Since the Tamils in general believe that the entire Sinhalese political leadership, and not just Mahinda Rajapaksa, is guilty of betraying all the promises made to them by both the previous governments of Rajapaksa and Sirisena-Wickremasinghe, the TNA by lending its unconditional support to the Wickremasinghe camp was committing a major disservice to them. The Tamil Eelam Liberation Organization (TELO), a constituent of the TNA with two MPs, tweeted on 3 December 2018, 'If the TNA supports...UNP, it should be conditional and an agreement needs to be signed. Unless...TNA agrees to this demand...we will take our own decision on it separately.' A senior TNA MP Sritharan also criticised (the) pledge of support to UNP. The TNA's response was not immediately available.

Symptomatic of the feelings of further alienation and discrimination among the minorities generated in the aftermath of the political crisis, the Church of Ceylon issued a statement on 28 October 2018, describing the removal of Wickremasinghe as 'unconstitutional' and warning that 'the arbitrary removal of a sitting Prime Minister in an unconstitutional manner will plunge the nation into a state of instability.' The Church also said that there were no provisions in the present Constitution to remove a sitting Prime Minister as the 19th Amendment had reduced the President's executive powers and transferred such powers to the 'Prime Minister in Parliament.'

Continuing, the Church stated that the democratic framework enshrined in the Sri Lankan Constitution should not be 'abused for political expediency.' Proposing a societal resistance to the President's move, it said, 'We urge the instruments of the State, religious institutions and all peace-loving people of our country to join hands to uphold democratic values and peace with justice for all as well as the rule of law for the greater common good of the people of our country and the preservation of democratic institutions, so that all communities that call Sri Lanka home may live without fear and intimidation.' The Church also called upon the police and the military to 'act with restraint and in an impartial manner while enforcing law and order in the country.'

Presidency devalued

Perhaps a long-lasting deleterious impact the prolonged constitutional and political impasse had on the minority communities was their loss of faith in the presidential system itself. Therefore, when (author to be asked the full name and his party and post held. Does he mean Nimal Siripala?) Siripala insisted that far from losing more powers, he wanted to have more powers granted to the executive president, both the Tamils and Muslims said that they were completely against any such move. 'Sri Lankan Executive Presidents from J. R. Jayewardene to Sirisena have shown that they care for the Tamils only at election time. Once elected, they forget the Tamils,' remarked Suresh Premachandran, leader of the Eelam People's Revolutionary Liberation Front (EPRLF) and a former Tamil National Alliance (TNA) MP. 'So far, every executive president has used the extraordinary powers vested in the post to enhance his or her power instead of using them for the common good. The executive presidency has spurred dictatorial tendencies in Sri Lanka.'[31]

To quote Premachandran again, 'Neither Jayewardene nor Premadasa nor Chandrika Kumaratunga nor Rajapaksa nor Sirisena solved the Tamil problem. For example, none of them acceded to the Tamils' demand for a federal constitution. Maithripala Sirisena, who would not have become President if the Tamils and Muslims had not voted for him overwhelmingly, has not given the Tamils meaningful devolution in the three years and a half he has been in power. Tamil political prisoners are still to be released and a lot of land held by the military in the north is still to be handed back to their Tamil owners.

Urging the Tamils to support the on-going movement for abolition of executive presidency, he said, 'By doing so, the Tamils will be participating in the movement for the restoration of democracy in the country. Not just the Tamils and Muslims but the majority Sinhalese, too, have suffered as a result of the dictatorial tendencies created by the executive presidency system. All communities in Sri Lanka are yearning for the restoration of democracy.

The crisis generated in the last few months of 2018 saw two camps pitted against each other centering around the question of the powers of the Executive President, Sirisena and Rajapaksa. and their followers working for a more powerful presidency and Wickremasinghe and his followers, the minority communities and civil society opposing their design. As expected, the bone of contention was the 19th Amendment to the Constitution.

The Sirisena camp wanted the law to be tweaked to get rid of its 'anomalies'. One such anomaly was the 19A Amendment creating the Independent Police Commission, which was good in itself but in the process the power of sacking the Inspector General of Police had been passed on to the Prime Minister. 'This curbs (the President's) executive power and creates practical problems in the implementation of policies,' was quoted as one such anomaly. Rajapaksa, for his part, wanted the 19th Amendment to be done away with as it made a mockery of the very institution of the Executive President itself by severely clipping its wings.

The minority communities, on the opposite pole, argued that abolition of the office was in the election manifesto of the Opposition led by Sirisena himself and that he was, hence, duty bound to fulfil it. 'The abolition of the executive presidency along with power sharing with the provinces is at the core of the new draft constitution, which had the support of all parties', said M.A. Sumanthiran of the TNA. 'Therefore, the TNA will not support any move to increase the powers of the President by amending the 19A.' Two Muslim parties, All Ceylon Makkal Congress and Sri Lanka Muslim Congress also supported the TNA stand on the issue as they felt that the institution of executive presidency bred dictatorship.

Political sanity restored

Nearly two months had slipped by since the no-holds barred power game erupted, and the country appeared to be groaning under its deleterious impact. All eyes were fixed on the Supreme Court which, after hearing the arguments and counter-arguments for three days from 6 December 2018, in favour and against the President's actions in dissolving Parliament prematurely, preceded by the 26 October 2018 dismissal of the incumbent Prime Minister, finally delivered its judgment on 13 December 2018.

A seven-judge bench presided over by Chief Justice Nalin Perera agreed unanimously that Sirisena violated the Constitution when he dissolved Parliament (on 9 November 2018) and called a snap election nearly two years ahead of the schedule. 'I make order,' Perera said, 'that the November 9 Gazette (decree) sacking Parliament…has no force or effect in law and declare its operation illegal.'[32] Neither President Sirisena nor Prime Minister Rajapaksa responded immediately but the latter's son Namal told reporters outside the Supreme Court premises that they did not agree with the verdict. 'We do not agree with the decision of the court, but we do not have a higher court to appeal to'. The UNP welcomed the verdict as a victory for democracy. 'As a country, we have to be joyful that we have an independent judiciary that acted as a check on an errant executive,' UNP deputy leader Sajith Premadasa, whom Sirisena wanted very much as a substitute for Wickremasinghe said. On 16 December

2018, Wickremasinghe was sworn in as Prime Minister for the second time by Sirisena. Neither Sirisena nor Rajapaksa accepted the verdict with grace, and the people's fond hope of an end to the unseemly bickering and the virtual collapse of administration and the lingering of an air of uncertainty did not materialise. The eagerly anticipated truce between Sirisena and Wickremasinghe, which was thought to be the only possible fallout of the verdict, remained elusive. Conversely, exactly as many feared, far from calming down and engaging himself solely with the task of running the government for the remaining part of the term, the President made no bones about his intention to continue the hounding of Wickremasinghe. Speaking to MPs belonging to the UNP, he said on 17 December 2018, 'Some of your MPs over the phone or when they meet me, say that we must move forward together, but I can't see what the guarantee for such a collective journey is…I don't want to create conflicts. At every turn of this conflict, it is the country that falls back. The prevailing corrupt situation is very strong. There are some extremely corrupt politicians in Parliament. When we consider our Cabinet, there are some corrupted individuals. The promise of good governance, which we gave to our people, has been completely violated. I clearly state that I am not the person who is responsible for this calamity. I made all the sacrifices toward achieving good governance; however, all those sacrifices were destroyed.'[33]

Reiterating his charges of how Wickremasinghe deliberately messed around with the mandated goals of the coalition government, he also referred to the judiciary, saying, 'There is an allegation among the judges in the judiciary service that I do not give appointments in accordance with seniority. I should clearly state I have sent every single name of those who level those charges against me, but the Constitutional Council has rejected those names. In that situation, there has been injustice to those who hold seniority in the field of judiciary. Therefore, the question arises as to how impartial the Constitutional Council has been when appointing judges.'

In an astonishing reference to Rajapaksa's defeat in the Presidential election of 2015, he said, 'As a result of the previous government's misdeeds, President Mahinda Rajapaksa was defeated, which was the first time a President was defeated, and I was elected by 625,000 people voting for me. What was opposed in the previous government was corruption and fraud. But the new people's government that was elected by the people plundered the Central Bank within three months…So, (the) *Yahapalanaya* political concept has been destroyed. The citizen's *Yahapalanaya* expectation has been destroyed.' In the meandering speech, after touching on almost every topic he had dealt with in his 28 October 2018 address to the nation, he came up with another startling observation, 'If Tamil (political) prisoners are to be freed (as demanded by the TNA), then our soldiers (who have been accused of human rights violations during the last phase of the civil war) should also be freed from different court cases that have been filed against them.'

On his part, Rajapaksa contributed handsomely to the re-emerging air of confrontation. 'We will bring the forces opposed to the country to their knees by organising the people…We are now on a direct confrontation with a group of political parties that have continually engaged in various subterfuges to avoid holding elections…The government had to perform demeaning contortions to get the provincial council elections to be postponed…There is no inkling when they will be held…people are now being deprived of a general election.' He reiterated his strong objection to the bringing in of a new constitution, 'at the behest of the TNA', which seeks to divide Sri Lanka into semi-independent federal units. The new constitution would in effect also abolish the executive presidency. Nevertheless, not all was lost yet, and he drew considerable solace from the probability that the UNF-TNA combine would not be able to push the draft constitution through in Parliament as it lacked the essential two-thirds majority. At the end of the constitutional and political crisis, what Sri Lanka probably genuinely gained is the re-assertion of the independence of the Supreme Court. A major asset in a country in a scenario where the governing class is beset with much doubt, suspicions and backstabbing and the governed are left with a feeling of hopelessness for themselves and disdain for their masters. Therefore, the most significant feature of the court's invalidation of three major political decisions made by Sirisena is 'the re-emergence of the judiciary with a clear sense of institutional autonomy and independence.' This is all the more important given the thoroughly negative political consequences a judicial endorsement of the President's actions would have carried. The highest court of the court of the country asserted itself against the arbitrary and capricious exercise of constitutional authority by the head of the executive and refused to be subservient to the executive. It also protected the institutional autonomy of the legislature and ensured the constitutional protection to the Prime Minister and the cabinet. The two judgments of the court will also hopefully define future verdicts. Henceforth, the political class will be doubly cautious in any misadventure with the Constitution and its application. The happy ending with the verdict also highlights the resilience of Sri Lankan democracy and a 'citizens' awakening.' However, the fissures in the state polity have not disappeared, and the resilience of citizens in defending their democracy will once again be put to the test 'within months'.[34]

One question, however, remains to be answered. How will the spectacle of the Sirisena-Rajapaksa duo affect their electoral prospects when the next presidential and parliamentary elections are held? A sample survey of public opinion in Sri Lanka reveals that several eminent Sri Lankans felt that Rajapaksa may not take his outright victory as a given any more, since the joint endeavour by him and Sirisena to manoeuvre Wickremasinghe out of office with the avoidable negative consequences has not gone down well with the people. Even among the hard-core Rajapaksa supporters and among his party members the episode has left a bad taste in the mouth. This opinion is not shared by others who felt that while this may be true of urban voters, Rajapaksa continues to hold tremendous popularity among rural voters, and eventually it is they who will count. Both the views were on account of the Sinhala-Buddhist constituency. As far as the minority voters are concerned, there is no divergence of views. The Tamils, Muslims and Christians have sensed the coming of bad times and they are definitely free of any illusion. Sri Lankan history contains too many tell-tale lessons for them to make any further mistake.

Prologue – Sri Lanka: A Suicidal Plunge

NOTES

1. NewsIn Asia, 'On October 26 an interim government was formed to hold elections, says Rajapaksa,' 25 November 2018, https://newsin.asia/on-october-26-an-interim-government-was-formed-to-hold-elections-says-rajapaksa/
2. President Maithripala Sirisena's Address to the Nation on 28 October 2018, Presidential Media Division, Colombo, Sri Lanka, http://www.president.gov.lk/
3. Meera Srinivasan, 'Sirisena reaches out to Tamil leadership,' *The Hindu*, 8 November, 2018
4. Press Trust of India, 'Tamil prisoners may be freed to tilt scales in favour of Lanka's Rajapaksa,' *The Hindu*, 4 November 2018.
5. Jayampathy Wickremaratne, 'On Dissolution of Parliament,' *LankaeNews*, 9 November 2018.
6. NewsIn Asia, 'Lawyers opposed to Lankan President Sirisena's actions state their case point by point,' 2 December 2018, https://newsin.asia.lawyers-opposed-tolankan-president-sirisenas-actions-state-their case-point-by-point/
7. Meera Srinivasan, 'Rajapaksa was only third choice: Sirisena,' *The Hindu*, 25 November 2018.
8. Article 33 (2)(c) of the Constitution of 1978 reads, while defining the Executive President's powers, 'to receive and recognise, and to appoint and accredit, Ambassadors, High Commissioners, Plenipotentiaries and other diplomatic agents.'
9. NewsIn Asia, "Sri Lanka's sacked PM says he will not step down as he enjoys majority in House," 27 October 2018, https://newsin.asia/sri-lankas-sackedpm-says-he-will-not-step-down-as-he-enjoys-majority-in-house/
10. Meera Srinivasan, 'Willing to work with Sirisena No room for prejudices, says Ranil,' *The Hindu*, 8 November 2018.
11. Meera Srinivasan, 'Sri Lanka Parliament votes against Rajapaksa govt, Speaker Karu Jayasuriya declares it doesn't have majority,' *The Hindu*, 15 November 2018.
12. NewsIn Asia, 'Breaking constitutional and parliamentary norms appear to be the new norm in Lanka,' 14 November 2018, https://newsin.asia/breakingconstitutional-and-parliamentary-norms-appears-to-be-new norm-in-lanka/
13. Meera Srinivasan, 'Chaos in House as Rajapaksa refuses to endorse vote,' *The Hindu*, 16 November 2018.
14. NewsIn Asia, 'Lankan Prime Minister's Office releases official procedure in regard to No Confidence Motions,' 17 November 2018, https://newsin.asia/lankan-prime-ministers-office-releases-official-procedure-in-regard-to-noconfidence-motions/

15. NewsIn Asia, 'Lankan Opposition threatens to block financial proposals made by Prime Minister Rajapaksa's Office,' 19 November 2018, https://newsin.asia/lankan-opposition-threatens-to block-financial-proposals-made-by-primeminister-rajapaksas-office/
16. NewsIn Asia, '122 Lankan MPs file Writ of Quo Warranto in Court of Appeal against Rajapaksa's government,' 23 November 2018, https://newsin.asia/122-lankan-mps-file-writ-of-quo-warranto-in-court-of-appeal-against-rajapaksas-premiership/
17. NewsIn Asia, 'Sirisena-Rajapaksa "coup" has put the Lankan economy in peril, says ousted Finance Minister,'4 November 2018, https://newsin,asia/sirisenarajapaksa-coup-has-put-the-lankan-economy-in-peril-says-ousted-financeminister/
18. Mangala Samaraweera, 'Sri Lanka: Plunging into an Economic Abyss,' *Sri Lanka Guardian Columns*, 21 November 2018, http://www.slguardian.org/2018/11/sri-lanka-plunging-into-economic-abyss.html
19. Financial Times, Mangala claims Ranil saved Mahinda from becoming an international criminal, 1 October 2018, http://www.ft.lk/news/Mangala-claims-Ranil-saved-Mahinda-from-becoming-an-international-criminal/56-663825
20. NewsIn Asia, 'Presidential Commission to probe alleged misdeeds of ousted Lankan PM Wickremasinghe,' 25 November 2018, https://newsin.asia/
21. NewsIn Asia, 'Sri Lanka's UNP says President should be included in corruption probe on former govt,' 26 November 2018, https://newsin.asia/sri-lankas-unp-says-president-should-be-included-in-corruption-probe-on-former-govt/
22. Reuters, 'Lanka signs port deals with China,' 29 November 2018.
23. NewsIn Asia, 'TNA says it won't support any impeachment move if President withdraws unconstitutional actions,' 1 December 2018, http://southasiajournal.net/tna-says-it-wont-support-any-impeachment-move-if-president-withdraws-unconstitutional-actions/
24. NewsIn Asia, 'Sri Lanka Parliament votes to cut finances to PM's office,' 29 November 2018, https://newsin.asia/sri-lankan-parliament-votes-to-cut-finances-to-pms-office/
25. NewsIn Asia, 'Sri Lanka Parliament votes to cut finances to ministries and junior ministries,' 30 November 2018, https://newsin.asia/sri-lanka-parliament-votes-to-cut-finances-to-ministries-and-junior-ministries/
26. Meera Srinivasan, 'A test for Sri Lanka's bureaucracy,' *The Hindu*, 1 December 2018.
27. Meera Srinivasan, 'Court restrains Rajapaksa from functioning as PM,' *The Hindu*, 4 December 2018; and Meera Srinivasan, 'Don't act like Hitler, Ranil tells President Sirisena,' *The Hindu*, 5 December 2018.
28. NewsIn Asia, 'Sirisena refuses to re-appoint Wickremasinghe even as Appeal Court stays Rajapaksa Premiership,' 3 December 2018, https://newsin.asia/

rajapaksa-to-challenge-stay-on-premiership-in-supreme-court-as-prez-sirisena-vows-not-to-re-appoint-wickremesinghe/

29. Meera Srinivasan, 'Don't act like Hitler, Ranil tells President Sirisena,' *The Hindu*, 5 December 2018.

30. Meera Srinivasan, 'Minorities could become victims of Sri Lanka's crisis: Sampanthan,' *The Hindu*, 21 November 2018.

31. NewsIn Asia, 'Lankan minorities oppose increasing President's powers, want abolition of Executive Presidency,' 9 December 2018, https://newsin.asia/lankan-minorities-oppose-increasing-presidents-powers-want-abolition-of-executive-presidency/

32. AFP, 'Court rules against Sri Lanka President, impeachment edges closer,' 13 December 2018.

33. NewsIn Asia, 'Sirisena says it'll be very hard to go on a "collective journey with a corrupt UNP",' 17 December 2018, https://newsin.asia/sirisena-says-itll-be-very-hard-to-go-on-a-collective-journey-with-a-corrupt-unp/

34. Jayadeva Uyangoda, 'Restoration of political sanity,' *The Hindu*, 17 December 2018.

Introduction

IT was like a tropical storm breaking out in a clear blue sky. From 8 January 2015 (when the last presidential election was held), it had been smooth sailing for a popular government. The unprecedented and unexpected victory of the combined Opposition had to make its way through a very dark period indeed. In particular, the election campaign during late November 2014 and early January 2015 proved to be a violent one, with the ruling party mounting a series of attacks on the Opposition. The entrenched mafia in power had no intention of quitting office peacefully. However, the perilous campaign gave way to a smooth sailing for the subsequently formed *Yahapalanaya* government, run by a unique combination of two hitherto sworn political enemies—the right-of-centre pro-capitalist United National Party (UNP) and the left-of-centre socialist Sri Lanka Freedom Party (SLFP) along with several parties of sundry ideologies—but united in opposition to President Mahinda Rajapaksa.

Even before the first month of government was over, a scam of mammoth proportions broke out, engulfing the political space and the media, and the *rainbow coalition*—banded together by a common urgency to defeat an intolerably authoritarian President and welcomed in turn by the harassed population of all the racial and religious communities with relief—began to face a rising tide of popular disenchantment. By the time the third year was out, the coalition was tottering on the brink of an immediate split. The crisis was exacerbated by the results of the 8 February 2018 local government elections, which showed that popular support for the ruling coalition had evaporated. Rajapaksa, who supported a new party, Sri Lanka Podujana Peramuna (SLPP), built up by his brother, Basil, and loyalists, emerged as the largest party in the local government elections. He immediately demanded a snap poll. In the late-March, his party moved a no-confidence motion against the government. Obviously, something had gone horribly wrong, but what was it?

Over-confidence backfires

Going back three years, when Rajapaksa announced the mid-term presidential election on 20 November 2014, he was under no compulsion to do so. In fact, his announcement surprised both his country and the world at large. He had another clear two years left in his second term as President and faced no challenge to his rule. The Rajapaksa 'clan', consisted of his brothers, his two elder sons, some 31 other relatives, along with a coterie of politicians, 'newborn' tycoons promoted by him, and a band of faithful bureaucrats, officers of the armed forces and intelligence agency. All of whom made up an intimidating group of people who held the country in thraldom. It was widely believed at the time, but officially denied by the government, that between 2005 when Rajapaksa first became President and 2013 he and his brothers, including the eldest Chamal, who was the speaker in Parliament, controlled over 70 per cent of the national Budget. In the 2014 budget, the various ministries under the brothers directly accounted for 47 per cent of allocated funds. Such was their enormous clout. It was in fact an all-embracing autocracy.[1]

Democracy subverted

The story of how Rajapaksa spread his wings over every aspect of life after his electoral victory in 2005 is fascinating and a lesson on how to subvert the democratic system of governance into a family fiefdom.

His first step was to appoint brother Gotabaya[2] to the most pivotal post of Defence Secretary with complete control over the armed services plus the civilian police (which is usually under the interior or home ministry in a democracy), and, most importantly the intelligence services, again a domain of the interior or home ministry in a democratic set-up. While another brother Basil was appointed senior presidential adviser and minister of economic development. Chamal became the speaker of Parliament. The eldest son Namal won a seat in Parliament and consequently grew into one of the most influential parliamentarians, as well as his heir apparent. Numerous other members of the extended Rajapaksa family were put in control of various state-owned institutions.

After covering the central administration and legislature (luckily the judiciary was yet to be encroached upon which the President would eventually do at the fag end of his two-term rule), Rajapaksa turned his attention to the provinces.

Since the government had been formed with an overwhelming support of the majority Sinhalese community, it ingeniously framed a policy to usurp the jurisdiction of the popularly elected provincial councils, to gain a grip over the lives of the provincial population.[3]

This astute political move was accomplished through the introduction of the *Divi Neguma* (life upliftment) Act. In the garb of introducing a poverty alleviation scheme through community-level organisations, this piece of legislation facilitated the effective transfer of the control of the provincial councils over the implementation of the various pro-people benefit schemes for social uplift to the central government in Colombo. By taking over the management of these schemes, the Rajapaksa government (which in turn was being controlled by the first family) could directly influence the lives of about a million individuals. In reality, however, just one individual, Basil Rajapaksa as the Minister of Economic Development, became the sole controller, with wide discretionary powers and funds to the tune of $614 million, as well as overriding powers that had constitutionally devolved to the provinces. This unconstitutional act had in fact been rejected by Chief Justice Shirani Bandaranaike of the Supreme Court[4], stating that the court was not in favour of the enabling bill. This display of judicial independence invited the presidential wrath, leading to a patently contrived impeachment of the Chief Justice, a process in which the speaker of Parliament obediently played his choreographed role.[5] As we will see in subsequent pages, this demeaning of the judiciary and the constitution would later constitute one of the major charges against the President and lead eventually to his ouster from power.

The first South Asian country to have a food stamp facility to help the poorest people obtain bare minimum nutrition, Sri Lanka has always enjoyed higher socio-economic parameters than its neighbours. But no previous government had ever sought to exploit the pro-poor and developmental schemes for political ends. This situation changed with the introduction of the Life Upliftment programme. The political exploitation of this omnibus development scheme was frequently exposed when pro-government political rallies and processions were held in the provinces in which beneficiaries were willy-nilly persuaded to participate. The political domination of the Rajapaksa clan was thus perpetuated in the most crucial electoral constituency of the country—the Sinhala-speaking population concentrated in the south, central, west and eastern parts of the island, accounting for 72 per cent of the total population. The politically astute President Rajapaksa had thus ensured continued support of the majority of the Sinhalese for his present and future career. Even when he lost the election in 2015, he had garnered 55 per cent of the Sinhalese vote and was raring to come back to power once again after winning overwhelmingly in the local government elections in 2018. He had already emerged as a real threat to the stability of the NDF government in the remaining months of its tenure.

An interesting feature of Sri Lankan democracy—the oldest in South Asia—had always been its frequent and prolonged cohabitation with autocracy. Its authoritarianism (or semi-authoritarianism, as per political scientist Jayadeva Uyangoda) may be described as an in-house or internalised ideology since it was established and perpetuated by the very constitutional institution of the popularly elected President. For all practical purposes, the executive President came to be above the constitution, thanks to the immunity clause. This clause put the executive President beyond judicial review; nothing that he did could be challenged in court. This was possible because there was no post-enactment judicial review, enabling pre-constitution laws to continue to be operational. This apparently anti-democratic situation was rectified to a large extent by the 19th Amendment brought in by the present government.[6]

What the people were witnessing and experiencing in the Rajapaksa presidency had already been internalised during the first two presidencies that of J.R. Jayewardene, the mastermind of the system who brought it about in the 1978 Constitution, followed by Ranasinghe Premadasa who succeeded in creating a virtual reign of terror. The Sri Lankan model is said to be a combination of the American and French presidential systems sans their safeguards.[7] It was but a single step to take to corrupt the democratic system to authoritarianism, which culminated in sheer brutality and inhumanity under Rajapaksa.

Always determined to acquire supreme political power, Jayewardene made his first move when still a junior minister in the UNP government of Prime Minister Dudley Senanayake (1965-70). Delivering a keynote address to the Association for the Advancement of Science on 14 December 1966, he outlined his vision for executive presidency based on the US and French models. He openly argued for a strong executive President elected by the people and not subject to the whims and fancies of a Parliament. Senanayake, with whom Jayewardene's relations had deteriorated, was strongly opposed to the idea.

He revived the idea when the Parliament was converted into a constituent assembly to draft a republican constitution during the United Front Government under the premiership of Sirimavo Bandaranaike (1970-77). He was the Leader of the Opposition in Parliament at the time and his advocacy of executive presidency was strongly supported by his party's MP and Chief Opposition Whip Premadasa, another over-ambitious and marginally less democratic-minded leader. As Senanayake, the party leader, was strongly against the proposal, Jayewardene's proposal did not receive the support of the majority of the UNP MPs either. As expected, the United Front Government opposed the motion fiercely and it was rejected in the Constituent Assembly.

The United Front government brought in the new Republican Constitution on 22 May 1972, and the Governor-General, under the Soulbury Constitution, gave way to a President, who had a more or less a ceremonial role. Power was vested in Parliament, and while President William Gopallawa was the titular Head of the State, the real power was retained by Prime Minister Bandaranaike.

After the death of Senanayake in April 1973, Jayewardene became the leader of the UNP. An astute and shrewd politician, he established his leadership soon and brought the party under his full control. He was in a position now to pursue his dream of an executive presidency, without a whimper of objection from within the party.

The change to an executive presidency system was a key aspect of the UNP electoral campaign in the general election held in July 1977. It was described as an important promise in the manifesto. The UNP swept the polls and obtained 141 of the 168 seats in Parliament. Once sworn in as Prime Minister, Jayewardene started to move fast towards his long-cherished vision of an executive presidency.

Steps towards achieving his goal were taken with the help of the leading lawyer Mark Fernando. An amendment to the republican constitution was drafted in August 1977, and following the cabinet approval, a draft amendment was sent to the Constitutional Court, which prevailed at the time, as an urgent bill. It was approved within the stipulated 24 hours. The bill was debated and adopted by Parliament on 22 September 1977 and introduced as the Second Constitutional Amendment. Executive powers were transferred to the President and Jayewardene became the first Executive President of Sri Lanka on 4 February 1978, coinciding with the 30th anniversary of independence.

Jayewardene realised his long-time political dream and became an 'absolute ruler' with unlimited power. Barely a year into his rule, Jayewardene replaced the 1972 Constitution with a new Constitution. Popularly referred to as the 'JR Constitution', it was formally promulgated on 7 September 1978 after a process which started with the setting up of a Parliamentary Select Committee on 3 November 1977.[8]

A balloon goes up

However, a balloon went up in early 2018 following the stunning victory at local government polls by the Rajapaksa-backed party and the Joint Opposition that if they won the 2020 presidential election, Gotabaya, the former Defence Secretary, would be President. A carefully crafted campaign began with a few party MPs 'claiming' that Gotabaya would be the 2020 presidential candidate. He himself said that if the political parties associated with the Rajapaksas decided to nominate him as their presidential candidate, 'I definitely will have to accept it.' Interestingly, his definition of the ideal candidate fitted him perfectly. He said, 'Definitely, an individual who loves this country and who could protect the sovereignty, territorial integrity, unitary status of this country, should be the candidate. He should be able to ensure that (the) life of war heroes is safe.[9] The prospective candidate should be a 'character' that could work hard, develop the economy and should be somebody who doesn't engage in revengeful, venomous politics (sic). Such a character should come to limelight from the masses.'[10]

Since Mahinda Rajapaksa cannot become President again under the 19th Amendment to the Constitution but nevertheless wants to wield power, in case his candidate wins, the next best option for him would be to nominate one of his brothers for the job and Gotabaya is clearly the best choice available. In their various interviews and other interactions, both the brothers have given enough indications of this eventuality. Both have emphasised the supreme necessity of protecting Sri Lanka's sovereignty and territorial integrity and vow to do everything necessary to achieve this. The meaning of these pronouncements is obvious enough. Protecting the sovereignty could imply continued defiance of the international demand for war crimes tribunals manned by hybrid benches; and maintaining the territorial integrity would signify nullification of the constitutional reform process.[11]

Expectations belied

Meanwhile, a look back to the end of the civil war in May 2009. There were great expectations all over the country and especially in the north-east, as well as in the world at large, that with the dawn of peace Sri Lanka was now poised to step into a new world of reconciliation and reconstruction, racial harmony, economic development and a settled democratic discourse.

Swift action by the government was anticipated, with the international community ready to pitch in with guidance and assistance. The priorities were well-marked. They were:

1) The resettlement of Internally Displaced Persons (IDPs) and refugees to their original habitats and inclusive of the restoration of their means of livelihood. These people were overwhelmingly Tamil but with substantial numbers of Muslims (ethnically cleansed by the LTTE from the Eastern Province in the early 1990s), and a smaller number of Sinhalese who had fled the Jaffna peninsula in the wake of the 1983 anti-Tamil riots in the south.
2) Restoration and augmentation of the basic commercial, educational, health, industrial, professional and societal infrastructure.
3) Fulfilment of the political aspirations of the Tamils, namely a meaningful political autonomy for the Northern and Eastern Provinces through the adoption of constitutional provisions for an adequate devolution of power between the central and provincial assemblies and government. In essence, through the long-withheld implementation of the 13th Amendment to the constitution, as spelt out in the 1987 India-Sri Lanka Accord.

The post-war reality proved to be diametrically opposite to the anticipations. State repression intensified; political dissension was literally smothered and suppressed, as was the media with independent journalists, physically done away with, jailed or hounded out of the country. The Tamil question was seemingly buried for no apparent intention to address the vexing issue of devolution of powers to the Northern Province, though (as we will soon see) at every opportunity the President reiterated his intention to do justice to the Tamils. In addition, the Rajapaksa government's attention was increasingly dedicated to denying and defying the call of the international community to account for the unresolved deaths of thousands of civilians during the final phase of the civil war (June 2008-May 2009).

More tragically, Rajapaksa employed various tactics to slither out of the rising crescendo of demands for action. His goal was clearly to keep misleading his people and the world.

Even before the war ended, he started talking about his firm intention to implement the 13th Amendment devolving more powers to the provinces. In October 2008, he said in an attempt to shift the blame to the minorities, 'There is no political will on either side (the government and the rebels) to implement the amendment. In the south (the Sinhalese region), because it is a political issue and as a political leader, I have said that after twenty years we have the intention of implementing this for the first time. We have given that assurance to the Tamil people of my country and to the international community. We are going to do it. This is not to satisfy anybody. It is my duty by the people of this country and let me repeat, I myself will take charge of the political process and see it through politically.'[12]

He further said that the political process had already been set in the Eastern Province (liberated earlier in 2008), election to the provincial council had been held and a government had been installed. 'I will be doing the same thing as soon as possible in (the Northern) Province after we clear it of terrorists. The people must be able to express their true feelings and elect their true representatives. At present such a situation does not exist.'

He also detailed his priorities in this respect and talked about a 'just and enduring' political solution to the ethnic question 'based on the four Ds—demilitarisation, democratisation, development and devolution to be implemented in that precise order because without demilitarisation, it was not possible to achieve anything—no democratisation, no development, no devolution. It is pointless to give the Tamils devolution when they are not ready to accept it or one cannot implement it,' he argued. Characterised of a personalised approach to a national and historical issue, his subsequent pronouncement on the subject made during another interview did not help the prevailing situation and in fact introduced an element of bemusement. He said, 'Now my theory is—there are no minorities in Sri Lanka, there are only those who love the country and those who don't.'[13]

It is not clear if he ever realised that through the series of interviews he was increasingly exposing his innate dislike and distrust of the Tamils.

Continuing his unique discourse, he said a year later that the 'pro-LTTE' Tamil National Alliance (TNA), consisting of former militant organisations and some south-based political parties and the Muslim parties had not responded to his earlier call for talks because they were 'not interested' as long as LTTE chief Velupillai Prabhakaran was alive. He said, 'Now they must understand that there is no option for them but to talk.' As he was the President and the leader of the country, they had to come and negotiate and have a dialogue with him. However, if they felt that they could not 'cope' with him, new leaders would come up and he would deal with them.[14&15]

His sense of guilt was clearly visible; at the same time, he could not stop himself from sniping at the Tamils and interestingly he also threatened the leadership simultaneously.[16]

When this book talks about the 'festering wounds', it seeks to focus on certain disabilities of the Sri Lankan leadership to break out of communal constraints and be able to perceive their country and people as one indivisible entity. His ego bloated by his epochal victory in the 26-year-old Civil War and hurling the world's most dangerous guerrilla force to oblivion, Rajapaksa was in his true elements in this series of interviews to *The Hindu* newspaper.

Later in the year, he returned to his theme. He said, 'Development is important. Without development and peace, we cannot have democracy. Democracy is very important because we are a democratic country—and then devolution. We have said we must get to know the minds of the people. Politicians have their own theories, but people—the new generation—have different views. What we want is reconfirmation of what they want.' He was apparently seeking to replace the experienced senior leadership by an inexperienced younger leadership which would facilitate bargaining and in turn, make the younger leaders beholden to him for his patronage. This was certainly a very unstatesmanlike approach.

Rajapaksa's protestations of genuine desire to do good to the Tamils barely managed to hide his actual intention of not acceding to any substantive demand of the community. When asked, in the last quoted interview, if he could spell out a 'clear political solution' even if he would not reveal the specifics, he remained deliberately vague, 'Yes, but first I will find out their views. We want to appoint a committee from both (the) sides (presumably the Tamils and Muslims on the one side and the government on the other) and discuss all this.' The 'present' TNA leadership must realise, he warned, that they could not get what Prabhakaran wanted by using guns, weapons or terrorism. They (the TNA) could not 'terrorise' the country 'that way'. They also had to understand that what the government had refused to give Prabhakaran, it would not give to others. They had to be 'realistic and fair' in this process and know the feelings of others as well. While saying all this in a curious mix of toughness and sweet reasonableness, he kept on emphasising the overarching role of the Sinhalese community in national affairs. Throughout his bout of sermonising, the President, in effect took no notice of the TNA's contemporary statement that it would accept a devolution package 'within the united Sri Lanka'.

But what was really happening in Sri Lanka at the time? In a representative kaleidoscope of the disturbing developments in those days, here are some samples. One newspaper headline said, Tamil journalist was killed, says Channel 4 documentary (*The Hindu*, 22 November 2013), reporting that '...the footage showing a young woman being captured by men in army fatigue, and later lying unconscious or dead with a gash across her face is the Tamil propagandist Isipriya, who the Sri Lanka government maintained, had died in combat (more than four years after the war had ended).' When contacted, the Sri Lankan army spokesman Brigadier Ruwan Wanigasooriya termed the video clip a 'completely false creation by Channel 4.' He also alleged that the clip had been released with the motive of influencing the UK and India to boycott the forthcoming Commonwealth Heads of Government Meeting (CHOGM) to be held in Sri Lanka.

As there were indications that India might choose to abandon its steadfast opposition to Rajapaksa and actually decide to attend the CHOGM, Callum Macrae, the director of the celebrated documentaries

The Killing Fields of Sri Lanka and *No fire Zone,* appealed to New Delhi to heed his call, *Don't Shelve Human Rights* (*The Times of India,* Kolkata edition, 6 November 2013). He wrote, '...while the UK and Australia hide their reluctance to confront Sri Lanka's crimes behind a fake commitment to the 'greater good' of the Commonwealth, Rajapaksa hides his guilt behind a phoney veneer of 'anti-imperialism'. The rest of the Commonwealth, led by India, needs to confront both of these false postures.'

Macrae's fear was not baseless. While, Indian Prime Minister Manmohan Singh, skipped the CHOGM summit, it was by no means a boycott. India was, in fact, represented at a lower level, the bare minimum downgrade that Singh could effect to demonstrate his government's concerns over Rajapaksa's ill-treatment of the Tamils. He was to have attended the summit and then visit Jaffna, as the British Prime Minister David Cameron did. *The Hindu* wrote, 'Once again foreign policy objectives have been sacrificed at the altar of political expediency. After Pakistan and Bangladesh, the surrender by...Singh and the Congress to political opposition and a narrow regional view on Sri Lanka is not surprising, but it is disappointing all the same.' (Surrender on CHOGM, *The Hindu,* 11 November 2013). The reference was to the resolution adopted unanimously by the Tamil Nadu Assembly and jointly sponsored by the two main Tamil parties—the Dravida Munnetra Kazhagam (DMK) and the All India Anna DMK (AIADMK)—calling upon the Indian government to boycott the summit. While the ruling and Opposition parties passed the resolution to register their protest at the treatment of the Tamils in the north-east by the Sri Lankan government, the editorial noted the hollowness of their gesture by pointing out that the same politicians did not care about the Northern Provincial Council elections, held by a reluctant Colombo because of the constant pressure exerted by New Delhi, which at long last gifted the community its first elected government. This view was shared by a noted Si Lankan diplomat and writer as well. A former permanent representative of his country at the UN in Geneva, Dayan Jayatilleka advanced the same logic—'The presence or absence of the Indian Prime Minister at CHOGM and India's vote on an international inquiry mechanism at the UNHRC in March 2014, are cards that must not be thrown away. As Ronald Reagan cautioned, once you've played your last card, you no longer have it. India must not gain the Tamil minority of the island only to lose Sri Lanka. India's Sri Lanka policy must not seem as if it has been formulated at the Madras Cafe.'[17]

London played it better

The inglorious Indian retreat was in sharp contrast to the British Prime Minister's visit on the same occasion not just to Colombo but also to Jaffna and his forthright comment, 'I am the first PM or President to go to the north of Sri Lanka since 1948 (when the island won its independence from the UK). I want to shine a light on chilling events there first hand.' He was greeted by a fairly large number of people, mostly relatives of the disappeared, who demanded justice from the Sri Lankan government.

However, undaunted by the sustained UN and Western campaign to put his government to task, Rajapaksa lectured his guests not to turn the CHOGM into a punitive or judgmental body and instead concentrate on a collective developmental drive. He also chose to gloss over Prime Minister Singh's absence at the summit, pointing out that the latter did not attend the previous summit at Perth either.[18]

The Poll Surprise

Coming back to the developments in November 2014, it was obvious that Rajapaksa had calculated a third stint in power in order to further secure his family's grip over Sri Lanka, backed by the unholy alliance built over the first two terms. However, it was the timing, and not the decision, that surprised the people. The manner in which the constitution was amended—by having it passed by a subservient Parliament and then by impeaching the inconvenient Chief Justice of the Supreme Court Shirani Bandaranaike in an untenable manner and thereafter had it approved by her successor (a former attorney-general and at the time Chief Presidential Adviser) Mohan Peiris—created the impression that Rajapaksa was in no hurry to vie for an unprecedented third term since he was in an unassailable position. The Constitution empowered him to call for a snap poll after he completed three years in office. Moreover, when Rajapaksa sought the Supreme Court's clearance in November 2014, seeking a third term, it was assumed that he would do so at a time of his choosing. Thus, there was no compelling reason for him to act as he, nevertheless, did rather sooner than expected.

The clinching issue for Rajapaksa appeared to be his confidence of winning the mid-term poll. This was evident when, right in the beginning of his election campaign, he rhetorically asked, 'I am in the ring. Where is my opponent?' He was sure of securing the support of his main vote bank, the rural Sinhalese electorate, carefully nurtured over the years with a host of welfare schemes, notably *Divi Neguma*. And indeed the largest chunk of the national electorate did not fail him. But still he lost because of a dramatically changed public mindset, a revenge-seeking combination of the minority communities and the liberal urban Sinhalese. Over 80 per cent of the Tamil votes and a sizeable majority of the Muslim votes—who had historically sided with the Sinhalese—went against him. He seemed to have been well-aware of chances of the Tamils ditching him, for he appealed in a sort of tongue-in-cheek fashion while campaigning in Jaffna to vote for 'the known devil rather than the unknown one'.

At the same time Rajapaksa, unbeknown to him, was also being called upon to fight an unseen foe, his image of a fearsome autocrat and the groundswell for removing him from power. The latter element was in the shadows till the very end, and that was by itself a gripping story and a lesson in how democracy always reasserts itself in the face of dictatorship, camouflaged or not.

It all began with the blatantly unconstitutional removal of Chief Justice Bandaranaike in January 2013, two years before Rajapaksa's defeat came about. The secret campaign to ensure the President's defeat in the next election began when constitutional lawyer J.C. Weliamuna and constitutional law expert Jayampathy Wickremaratne, emerged in due course, as key civil society voices that sought to give form to the simmering anger in the country, targeting a regime change that they perceived as the only way out of the deep morass Sri Lankans found themselves in.[19]

Tracing the roots of the anti-Rajapaksa sentiment, which would later grow strong enough to unseat him, Weliamuna said, 'University teachers also put together a huge struggle at that time. It was clear that different sections of society were deeply concerned with the regime's authoritarian ways.'

Gradually, the activist-lawyers succeeded in mobilising dissenting sections against the government, ignoring threats and intimidation by the state. Weliamuna himself faced a grenade attack on his home in 2009. As international pressure over Sri Lanka's abysmal human rights record sharpened, the government, increasingly feeling cornered, chose the convenient vehicle of branding critical voices as 'traitors'. As also usual in such cases, media support for the anti-Rajapaksa movement was missing, with the state media accounting for the bulk space and the independent section preferring to be wise before the act. It was only independent journalists who were still braving the odds in a virtual police state; but they were eliminated or put in jail or managed to escape. This virtual clamp-down on the media was definitely dampening for the burgeoning pro-democracy movement but it did not deter it in any way.

A point was reached when the civil society could not advance its agenda any further and decided to canvass for support with the Opposition parties. 'They also began to collaborate with the liberal Buddhist monk Sobitha Thero's National Movement for Social Justice. All the different segments of the movement came to an understanding that they would henceforth campaign for abolition of the executive presidency since this lay at the root of distortion of democracy and negation of the constitution witnessed so far.'

During the campaign, Sirisena had also promised that he would bring about a sea change in the governance of the country, including a host of welfare measures to bring relief to the embattled population. He promised to achieve all this within the first hundred days of his presidency. This decision helped to induct more politically conscious people from diverse backgrounds, broadening the reach of the still-undercover campaign.

The Trojan Horse Act

The clinching issue in setting up a united effective electoral opposition to the President was two-fold: a unanimous choice of a common candidate acceptable to a group with widely diverse ideologies and whoever was chosen should be capable of contesting and defeating the formidable President who was still basking in the glory of crushing the Liberation Tigers of Tamil Eelam (LTTE).

The group, as Weliamuna recalled, was only too conscious of the hard task in hand. The chosen candidate had to be as acceptable as Rajapaksa was to a sizeable majority of the Sinhalese electorate and also a charismatic and invincible leader. To resolve this dilemma, it was now necessary for the political actors involved to step in. And this the actors did with aplomb. The return to the political field of former President Chandrika Bandaranaike Kumaratunga, who had retreated into self-exile from politics in 2005 after having been out-smarted by her Prime Minister Rajapaksa, and the reasoned role played by former Prime Minister Ranil Wickremasinghe proved crucial.

The activist-politician group was still toying with the idea of a candidate from the Sri Lanka Freedom Party (founded by Kumaratunga's father, long led by her mother Sirimavo and later by Chandrika herself) when Rajapaksa called a snap poll, causing surprise and disarray in the Opposition camp. The President had already started thumping his chest and inviting an opponent to fight him, convinced there was none.

Several closed-door meetings later, facilitated by the use of 'technology conducive to greater privacy', the group's thinking cleared. However, there was no clarity in the narrative of how the group zeroed in on Maithripala Sirisena,[20] a low-profile health minister in the Rajapaksa government and general secretary of his faction of the SLFP with a strong rural support base, but he was obviously ripe for the picking.

Till then, the President's camp had no inkling that its own 'Quisling' was biding time to stab them in the back. It was still planning its campaign on the presumption that Wickremasinghe, who was the natural choice, would be the Opposition candidate. 'Once Sirisena crossed over,'

Weliamuna recalled, 'they had to redesign the entire campaign and the time was limited.'

The political leadership provided by Kumaratunga and Wickremasinghe was 'just fantastic'; equally successful was the joint Opposition team's efforts to consolidate its election campaign points around issues, such as, abuse of power, family rule, and corruption, issues which obviously resonated well with the people.

The Opposition campaign quickly roped in non-political persons like former diplomats, academics and social activists. The campaign became a collective effort and the credit could not be claimed by any one person. Many of such volunteers themselves had been victims of authoritarianism, risked their lives or were forced into self-exile. Weliamuna summed up the supreme lesson learned from the exercise in the following words, 'To change the world, you don't need millions. You just need a few determined people.'

A tectonic shift

All the protracted and secret preparations involving various political personalities from different persuasions, intellectuals, social and political activists, on the one hand and an electorate ready to take a plunge for change on the other, merged into a neatly orchestrated exhibition of popular will and the result is now part of Sri Lankan history. The massive popular mandate given on 8 January 2015 went decisively in favour of the virtually unknown political entity, Maithripala Sirisena, and in the process threw out the fearsome strongman Mahinda Rajapaksa from his entrenched seat of power. Sirisena bagged 51.26 per cent of the popular vote and Rajapaksa 47.58 per cent. A quiet revolution by democratic means turned the island-nation away from the abyss it had descended into. Sirisena appointed Ranil Wickremasinghe his Prime Minister and the new government took shape in quick time and its agenda of good governance was set in motion.

The most significant feature of this tectonic change was the 'peaceful' transfer of power, though the government ordered a probe into an alleged coup plot by the outgoing President immediately after assumption of office by the new government. The electoral outcome was a testimony to the resilience of Sri Lanka's democracy after having gone through so much violence, bloodshed and war in the previous decades. It was ironic in a sense that Rajapaksa, given his nature, did not resist much, but this could be attributed to the fact that his conspiracy to stage a coup was already known to the new government, and so he just became careful.[21]

What the people apparently appreciated was the *rainbow coalition*'s slogan of 'regime change for good governance'. It was amazing that a concept which was a part of the neo-liberal political discourse had been appropriated in the vernacular and political imagination for the revival of democratic politics. Sirisena's election campaign stressed democratic and corruption-free governance, an end to family rule and cronyism, and reviving the autonomy of key institutions of governance, specifically the legislature and the judiciary. This was a kind of home-grown democratic reform agenda evolved primarily against the years of Rajapaksa's 'semi-authoritarianism and family-centric style of governance'.

State reform and governance reform were the two types of political reforms advocated by the National Democratic Front (NDF), the official name of the coalition. Constitutional reform was the base of the state reform agenda. The cry for the abolition of executive presidency[22], which lay at the root of reforming the existing system by abolishing the 18th Amendment—which had rendered the incumbent a new Caesar—was another element that caught the people's imagination.

The Sirisena-Wickremasinghe duo and the coalition under their leadership did not let the hot iron to cool off and struck fast by going for parliamentary elections on 19 August in the same year. The outcome was as expected. The Prime Minister-led United Front for Good Governance (UFGG) and UNP won 106 seats in the 225-seat Parliament and the Rajapaksa-led United People's Freedom Alliance (UPFA) scored in 95 seats. The remaining 24 seats were shared by the Tamil National Alliance (TNA, an alliance of 18 Tamil parties based in the north-east) winning 16 seats; the leftist-Buddhist-chauvinist Janatha Vimukthi

Peramuna (JVP), Sri Lanka Muslim Congress (SLMC), and Eelam People's Democratic Party (EPDP) claiming the remaining eight seats.

What truly surprised observers was that despite the complete lack of any promise on greater devolution of powers to the provinces and restoring the minorities' rights—which had traditionally been the catchwords to influence minority voting in the previous elections—it did not deter the Tamils and Muslims from voting enthusiastically for the Opposition candidate. On the top of this, these two communities continued to repose their faith in the new government despite the many disappointments over its subsequent performance. Devolution is still a far cry, as the Northern Provincial government has found out to its dismay. The office of the Executive President remains as powerful as before though there have been driblets of reform. It is the continuing cronyism and resultant corruption that ultimately brought about the near-downfall of the government and the internal crisis between February and April 2018. But a notice was served and while the Prime Minister survived by winning the 4 April 2018 no-confidence motion in Parliament convincingly, the inevitable outcome in the next presidential election, due on in January 2020, could already be glimpsed in a silhouette. Unless Sirisena and Wikremsinghe resolved their sharp differences, worked unitedly and were seen publicly to be doing so, while carrying their respective parties together without bad-mouthing and back-stabbing each other, Rajapaksa would no longer remain a distant threat but a real-time wolf at the door.

When the former President gleefully announced on 16 March 2018, that 'we are close to toppling the government' by moving a no-confidence motion against the Prime Minister in Parliament, he sounded reasonably confident. 'The UNP's own members are doing that. I don't have to do much,' he said, implying that a section of the Prime Minister's party would defect to the Opposition. As narrated in the coming pages, this fond hope did not materialise on the evening of 4 April 2018 when Parliament voted on the motion with the UNP members voting solidly against the motion, but the continuing in-fighting in the government—mainly due to the President's desperate and ill-advised manoeuvres to weaken the Prime Minister—helped the former President to keep his plans afloat.

NOTES

1 Apratim Mukarji, 'Sri Lanka: Correcting the Wayward State,' *World Affairs*, April-June Summer 2015, Vol. 19, No. 2, and 'The Sri Lankan Polity: A Case of Constitutional Autocracy,' *World Affairs*, New Delhi, Summer 2014, April-June, Vol. 18, No. 2.

2 It is fascinating to see how Mahinda Rajapaksa defends his blatantly undemocratic act of putting his brothers in pivotal positions in his government. In an interview to Arun Janardhanan of *The Indian Express*, Kolkata ed. 24 March 2018, he says, "Ours has always been a very united family. Gotabaya and Basil came from overseas to help me in my presidential campaign in 2005, and on my request, they both stayed back to help me administer the country. I did not get them involved in my government simply because they were my brothers, but because they had abilities that the country could use. I think they both proved themselves in the tasks they undertook. But both have left their mark. After I lost power in January 2015, both have faced persecution by this government. We have never had any falling out among ourselves."

3 Based on interviews with Bradman Veerakoon, former principal advisor to the former President, Ranasinghe Premadasa, and Dr Paikiasothy Saravanamuttu, Director, Centre for Policy Alternatives, Colombo, 18 December 2012.

4 R.K. Radhakrishnan, 'Sri Lankan parliament impeaches Chief Justice,' *The Hindu*, 10 January 2013. The Chief Justice was impeached by Parliament "effectively throwing the judiciary into disarray and signaling a breakdown of the Constitution. A host of procedural issues delayed the debate on the day before and the vote on 10 January 2013. But Speaker Chamal Rajapaksa allowed the vote to go ahead late that day. He later announced that the President would be informed that the impeachment motion was passed with 155 votes for the motion and 49 against. The report on which the impeachment motion was debated, prepared by a Parliamentary Select Committee that probed allegations of misconduct by the Chief Justice, was earlier quashed by a court. The Parliament, nevertheless, went ahead with the debate on a report that had been struck down as void. "Is this Parliament to say, 'We can read the Constitution. Art. 125 says it is the sole and exclusive jurisdiction of the Supreme Court to interpret the Constitution, but we don't agree with that. Because we don't agree with that, we don't accept that," asked M.A. Sumanthiran, an MP, who belongs to the hopelessly outnumbered Opposition in Parliament. The stand of his party, the Tamil National Alliance, was that the entire report on which the entire debate was based, did not exist. Meanwhile, a group of senior lawyers wrote to the Supreme Court judges, asking them not to accept a new Chief Justice to protect the independence of the judiciary. The attempt to remove the Chief Justice from office is without

any legal basis and contrary to the Constitution and the law of the land," Lawyers Collective said in the letter to the Supreme Court judges. "As you are well aware you are obliged (as are we) to honour and follow the decisions of our courts whether we agree with (them) or not. Thus, disagreements in other quarters (are) irrelevant." The Centre for Policy Alternatives (CPA), a think tank, said that "the unnecessary and regrettable move by the legislature today has deeply debilitating consequences for constitutional governance." The United States, the first country to react, said that it was deeply concerned by the impeachment proceedings against the Chief Justice which were conducted in defiance of a Supreme Court order. "The impeachment calls into question issues about the separation of powers in Sri Lanka and the impact of its absence on democratic institution." "With this, the rule of law system in Sri Lanka comes to an end," the Hong Kong-based Asian Human Rights Commission said. "This is the culmination of the scheme of the 1978 Constitution which is a constitution, not of a democracy, but of a dictatorship." Chief Justice Bandaranaike was removed from office on 13 January 2013, and was reinstated in her office by President Maithripala Sirisena on 29 January 2015.

5 Puneeth Nagaraj, 'Not Uplifting,' *The Hindu,* 7 December 2012.

6 T. Ramakrishnan, 'Need safeguards against majoritarianism,' *The Hindu,* 27 January 2016.

7 Veeragathy Thanabalasingham, 'J.R. Jayewardene chained Sri Lanka to the demonic Executive Presidency,' *Daily Express,* reproduced in NewsIn. Asia, 10 February 2018, https://newsin.asia/j-r-jayewardene-chained-sri-lanka-to-the-demonic-executivepresidency/

8 Ibid.

9 The reference is to the term 'war heroes' given by the Rajapaksa regime to defence force officers who won the war against the Tamil Tigers and later were accused of perpetrating the genocide. Even the successor government balked at the risk of going ahead with their trials, as demanded by the U.N. and the international community. It is a safe bet that if the Rajapaksas come back to power, Sri Lanka would stick to their earlier stand. The present government is clearly not likely to accede to the international pressure, and the present tussle is over the UN's demand that foreign and presumably independent judges must be included in the benches to be set up for the purpose.

10 Interview to *Ceylon Today,* 3 March 2018.

11 Interview to *The Indian Express,* Kolkata ed.

12 Interview to *The Hindu,* New Delhi, 29 October 2008.

13 Interview to *The Hindu,* 6 July 2009.

14 Interview to *The Hindu,* 20 February 2010

15 Interview to *The Hindu,* 22 November 2010

16 Astonishingly, his views have hardly changed since he was thrown out of power three years ago. See his interview to *The Indian Express*, ibid. He was quoted saying, 'My message to the Tamil people of Sri Lanka is that they should not be influenced by the propaganda of overseas-based organisations and various other interested parties. The Tamil people of Sri Lanka should realise that there are Tamil communities living in India, Malaysia, Singapore, South Africa and many other countries and they all lead normal lives. However, in Sri Lanka, we see the Tamil people are being deliberately denied a normal life by forces that want to use them to carve out an independent Tamil state. Even after the war ended, this attempt has not ceased because foreign parties are keeping alive the hope of incremental progression towards a separate state.'

17 Dayan Jayatilleka, 'Learn to keep your friends close,' *The Hindu*, 21 October 2013.

18 Meera Srinivasan, 'Rajapaksa satisfied with India's representation at Commonwealth meeting,' *The Hindu*, 15 November 2013.

19 Meera Srinivasan, 'Working behind the scenes for change in Sri Lanka,' *The Hindu*, 18 January 2015.

20 It can be conjectured that once it was decided that the candidate should be from the President's own party, the group may have sounded likely dissidents, and that was how it zeroed in on Sirisena. The latter may have been looking around for just such a chance, and as the requirements of both the sides clicked, he was chosen. My experience says that nothing is ultimately secret in Sri Lanka where people know or claim to know the details of one's private life. Scratch a politician and he or she starts telling you intimate stories of his or her rivals. But all this is really guesswork, and one wishes that Weliamuna was more forthcoming on this interesting aspect of the whole adventure. The then station chief of India's spy agency Research and Analysis Wing (RAW) in Colombo, Ilango (described by sources in Colombo as a "pompous" fellow who was openly boastful about his activities played a major role in persuading Wickremasinghe from contesting against Rajapaksa and was in close touch with Chandrika Bandaranaike Kumaratunga, who was said to have persuaded Sirisena to defect to the Opposition camp. *Reuters* reported from Colombo and New Delhi on 18 January 2015 that the Indian agent was accused of playing a role in convincing Wickremasinghe not to contest against the incumbent President and stand aside for someone who could be sure of winning. All the three personalities involved, Wickremasinghe, Kumaratunga and Rajapaksa, either denied or refused to respond to Reuters' queries in this regard. But unnamed Indian officials and a Sri Lankan MP confirmed that Ilango was in touch with both Wickremasinghe and Kumaratunga. What was on record was the withdrawal of the agent from Colombo after the then Defence Secretary and the President's brother, Gotabaya Rajapaksa,

complained to India's National Security Adviser Ajit Doval, who at that time was visiting Colombo to attend a defence seminar. Sources in Colombo told this author that while the story of how Sirisena was roped in in place of Wickremasinghe was widely known at the time and the role that Ilango played in the drama but nobody talked about it openly. True to the atmosphere at the time, it was kept under wraps even by the media.

21 Jayadeva Uyangoda, 'For a fresh beginning in Sri Lanka,' *The Hindu*, 10 January 2015, written just a day after the results were out. Prof. Uyangoda appears to be unaware of the coup bid which had not yet come out in the open.

22 Elaborately dealt with above.

1

Counting Wounds— A Country in Search of a Statesman

If you are thinking about yourself only,
close your eyes and think twice.
This is our small country.

—Binguni Liyanage, *Sacrifices* (Write to Reconcile II)

ONE of the most enduring epithets that Time has bequeathed to Sri Lanka is euphemistically attributed to a certain Bishop Hebbar who presumably remarked that Serendip (Sri Lanka in old Persian), was a land 'where every prospect pleases, only Man is vile'.

Sri Lanka's history tells us that the good Bishop hit the bull's eye; he could not have been more prescient. Nature has been bountiful to the island, showering it with resources of many kinds, leaving little room for man to grumble about.

Before proceeding further, one cannot do better than listen to a Sri Lankan voice, 'If Sri Lanka's political and legal history since independence demonstrates one fact, it is the fundamental dishonesty of those whom we elect to serve us. Even the rare exceptions to this rule have failed to emulate an Ambedkar, a Gandhi or a Nehru whose visions and dreams lifted Indian society from its depths and fashioned an inimitable national spirit which carried that country through decades of communal turmoil. This has been our singular loss.'[1]

Less than three years later, as the political flip-flop had pushed further the prospects of a national reconciliation in the wake of a government defeat in the 10 February 2018 local government elections, the tallest Tamil leader and Leader of the Opposition in Parliament, R. Sampanthan addressed President Sirisena (who was present on the occasion in Jaffna) thus: 'We want a statesman to rise in this country who can say, "I resolved the country's national question," and we think you can do it, and it is our expectation that it will be done.'[2]

As we look at today's Sri Lanka, we see in essence the ashes of 'missed opportunities' dotting its post-independence landscape. While the process of racial discrimination was initiated by the British administration as part of its imperial doctrine of divide and rule, it is impossible to miss the Sinhalese political leadership's seemingly pathological inability to treat the minority communities as equal citizens. One may perhaps say that the festering wounds and the wounded psyche that pockmark the country's journey since independence owe their origins to this pathological and ideological malady. A narrowness of mind afflicts the Sinhalese polity, holding the country back to its continued denial of natural justice to weaker communities.

There is reason to believe that the Tamil cry for a federal state, which lies at the root of political and societal upheavals that shook the country for decades and reverberates even today, could have had a nuanced history if Tamil leaders in colonial Ceylon (now known as Sri Lanka) had the foresight to bring it to the fore right then. In fact, Tamil scholars trace the series of missed opportunities right from 1929 when S.W.R.D. Bandaranaike, who eventually became Prime Minister, mooted the concept of a Ceylonese Federation. The first Prime Minister D.S. Senanayake even talked about an India-Ceylon Federation[3], an impossible and incomprehensible concept to most Sinhalese at any time. But, even as early as that time, the portents of future communal problems had raised their ugly heads. Strangely enough, the concept escaped the attention of Tamil leaders at the time. No Tamil leader of eminence fought for a federal constitution at the time of independence in 1948, when the future of the country was being determined. Tamil leaders could have initiated a debate on federalism then, demanding a federal constitution. The Tamil Congress under the leadership of G.G. Ponnambalam, which represented Tamil communal interests, fought instead for a 50:50 representation formula in Parliament, that is asking for half the seats while in truth the minority communities accounted for a little over 30 per cent, with the Tamils alone constituting about a quarter of the total population. So this demand was patently absurd.[4]

The scholars feel that this was probably a mistake and Ponnambalam may have chosen to go for an equal parliamentary representation with the fond hope that the Tamils, enamoured of him, would help in his becoming the Prime Minister. What it did was to antagonise the Sinhalese who felt that the demand for equal representation in Parliament was unwarranted.

The Sinhalese leadership was equally compromised by narrow considerations. D.S. Senanayake had secured the cooperation of the Tamil leadership through personal guarantees of good intent and the offer of ministries. The first Parliament had over 40 per cent of the seats represented by candidates from the minorities or left-inclined candidates influenced by the minorities such as, the Ceylon or ethnic Tamils, Tamils of Indian origin, Muslims and Burghers.

A strike by stealth

This cosy minority numerical strength was jettisoned by the Ceylon Citizenship Act of December, 1948, and the Indian and Pakistani Residents (Citizenship) Act of 1949 which paved the way for denying citizenship to thousands of Indians who had voting rights, had participated in the elections and sent their own representatives to Parliament. All this happened because citizenship was denied to those who may have lived for decades and generations in the country but did not possess birth certificates either for themselves or for their forefathers. The irony of this legislative charade, to be strengthened later by a judicial charade (recounted below), was that many Sinhalese politicians at the time did not possess those documents either.

These two Acts were followed by a third law, the Parliamentary Elections Amendment Act of 1949, which further reduced the political clout that the combined legislative strength of all the minority communities plus the Left parties enjoyed in Parliament. As a result of this legislation, the minority representation in Parliament was reduced to less than 20 per cent of the total strength from the previously held over-40 per cent strength. Viewed against the subsequent history, this could also be called a devilish trick by the Sinhalese leadership as it sought to nip in the bud the rising aspirations of the minorities in the face of majority domination in an independent country.

This was accomplished by making the plantation or Indian Tamils non-citizens overnight who at the time accounted for about 10 per cent of the total population or about a third of the minority population. At that time, the plantation Tamils directly held seven parliamentary seats and could influence the voting pattern in twenty other constituencies, all of which used to vote against the ruling UNP led by Senanayake. The propaganda unleashed in the Sinhalese areas was that the Indians would eventually run over the country in continuous waves of migration reducing the majority community to the beggarly status of a minority in their own country.[5] A sinister bogey that has been revived and is thriving in today's post-war Sri Lanka.

This marked the second occasion when the ethnic Tamil leadership failed to rise and oppose the Sinhalese move. Leaders belonging to both the UNP and the Tamil Congress either voted in favour of the bills or failed to seriously put a resistance to it. The Tamil Congress leader Ponnambalam, who had by then been inducted into the UNP Cabinet, opposed the first bill and supported the second. The Sinhalese elite discovered early in independent Sri Lanka that they could call the bluff of their Tamil counterparts, especially the 'Colombo Tamils', who lived and prospered along with them in the salubrious capital city.

Leftist Sinhalese parliamentarians, however, did not commit the sin of racial parochialism. As scholar Kumari Jayewardena pointed out[6], the vote in Parliament that disenfranchised the plantation Tamils was not a communal vote. Strenuous opposition to these bills was mobilised by the major Left parties—the Trotskyite Lanka Sama Samaj Party led by Dr N.M. Perera, the Bolshevik Leninist Party led by Dr Colvin De Silva and the Communist Party led by Pieter Keuneman. Most MPs from these parties were Sinhalese. A prominent Buddhist and doctor H. Sri Nissanka opposed these pieces of legislation on the grounds that they ignored the first principle of law. Other prominent Sinhalese independents who voted against the bills were Wilmot Perera, R.S. Pelpola, M.R.A. Iriyagolla and Lakhsman Rajapakse.

The authors of *The Broken Palmyra* felt it was perhaps nearer the truth to say that the voting on the bills that changed the history of the island for ever was more on class, rather than, on communal lines. It might even be wrong to say that Senanayake was involved in a 'deep anti-Tamil conspiracy' to bring about Sinhalese domination. Nor is it possible to make a case that Senanayake was hatching a diabolical master plan to colonise Tamil areas with Sinhalese settlers. When work for the Gal Oya settlement scheme in the Eastern Province had been completed, the first preference was given to people from the province. It was only after about six months, when faced with the paucity of local applicants, that the doors were opened to applicants from other provinces.

As regards the Citizenship Act 1948 and its sequel, what almost certainly motivated Senanayake was his alarm over the strength in Parliament of the working class-based Left parties, comprising 20 of the 95 seats in the House. This number definitely looked formidable against the ruling UNP's strength of 41 seats in the 1947 elections, seven short of a simple majority. At the time, even the possibility of a coalition government with the left parties was conceivable. It must be remembered that all these were happening in the years following the end of the Second World War, when the spectre of an eventual and inevitable world domination by communism seemed a real threat to the liberal democratic world, and every democracy shaped its policies accordingly.

In this scenario, the ruling party would naturally think of perpetuating its political and class domination by knocking out the weakest section of the working class, the plantation Tamils. The dividends of the act were available when in the 1952 elections the UNP's strength went up to 54.

The authors mentioned above describe the passage of the three bills in 1948 and 1949 as 'the first and most grievous blow against democracy: with Tamil connivance'. Dr Perera said at the time, 'I thought racialism of this type died with Houston Chamberlain and Adolph Hitler. I do not believe that anyone claiming to be a statesman would ask us to accede to a bill of this nature... We cannot proceed as if we were God's chosen race quite apart from the rest of the world; that we and we alone have the right to be citizens of this country.'

Tamil Congress leader S.J.V. Chelvanayagam strongly dissented from these bills and, in protest, left the party to form a new party, the Federal Party, which twenty-five years later absorbed other Tamil parties and emerged as the Tamil United Liberation Front (TULF). His two other eminent associates in forming the new party were Dr E.M.V. Naganathan and C. Vanniasingham who also assisted Chelvanayagam during negotiations that led to the 1957 Bandaranaike-Chelvanayagam Pact. The agreement was the first attempt to find a political solution to the Sinhalese-Tamil divide, which of course fell through in the face of a strong resistance by the die-hard Sinhalese Buddhist opinion. Of historical interest was also the leading role played by J.R. Jayewardene, who took advantage of the situation to improve the downward prospects of his party, the UNP, by further instigating the already hardened majority sentiments.

Subsequent history shows that apart from the majority community's disdain for and discrimination against the minority plantation Tamils as reflected in the government's policies and Parliament's acts, the Sinhalese-dominated judiciary, too, threw in its lot in legitimising injustice and even more shockingly, the Privy Council finally took part in the sordid drama. In sum total, the majesty of justice, which seeks to be fair to every person irrespective of his or her identity, was sullied in the very initial stage of independent Sri Lanka.

The history of plantation Tamils is a long chronicle of exploitation and inhumanity. They were brought to Sri Lanka from southern India by British planters (quite a few used to die on ships, suffocated as they were in extremely hot and crowded holds) to clear jungles in the Kandy district; plant tea bushes and once the plantations were set up they continued to work as bonded labour condemned to live in line rooms isolated from the outside world in extremely unhygienic conditions. Special permissions were required for outsiders to enter the plantations.

Added to this life of misery was the Kandyan population's anger against the newcomers whose lands were taken over by the planters. They could not afford to be angry with those who were responsible for taking over their lands; therefore, they chose to be virulently antagonistic towards the hapless Indian Tamils. In course of time, the Kandyan elite also joined in the bandwagon of berating the Tamils of Indian origin for no fault of theirs.

However, it was the judiciary's failure to be fair when judging the challenges to the Citizenship Act of 1948 and Parliamentary Elections Amendment Act of 1949 that quickened the pace of the dark history. In quashing the petitions, the Kegalle District Court threw to the winds the first principle of the Soulbury Constitution guaranteeing equal justice to all.

The authors of *The Broken Palmyra* write, 'Everyone—both sides to the dispute—knew that the series of legislation represented a legal conjuring trick. Everyone knew that the intended victims were the Indians. Racist sentiments expressed during the course of the (parliamentary) debate were proof of that. The sting of the legislation was obscured by being distributed in three separate acts. Each act, taken by itself, may seem fairly respectable. A judge may thus hold them each to be valid without appearing to be too partial. However, by every accepted universal norm the legislation was unjust and discriminatory and many in this country agreed with that. Thus, Great Britain helped to strike the first blow against democracy in independent Ceylon. Many felt at that time as also later that the quality of British justice meted out by the Privy

Council (was) not unaffected by Britain's other interests. The tea plantations were largely British-owned and Britain had a naval base in Trincomalee.' (pp. 4-7)

The treatment meted out to the plantation Tamils, as correctly foreseen by a few ethnic Tamil leaders like Chelvanayagam, would, in the years to come, engulf the ethnic Tamils and Muslims as well, completing the dehumanising process. In a corollary, the moderate Tamil leadership would eventually yield place to militancy, culminating in the 26-year-old Civil War. History would come a full circle with the defeat of the LTTE in May 2009 leaving the stage open for the new age majoritarian chauvinism to step in.

Some of the milestones in this journey were the Official Language Act of 1956, a product of the prolonged *swabasa* (mother tongue) movement which had started on a demand for replacement of the English language by the Sinhala and Tamil languages and ended up by excluding Tamil and making Sinhala the sole official language to conduct official business. It was only logical for the Tamils to conclude that they had been reduced to the status of second-class citizens in their own country. It was after fifty long years that with the coming to power of the NDF government in 2015 that Tamil was once again elevated to the status of an official language.

The government's capitulation over the language issue was accompanied by the abrogation of the Bandaranaike-Chelvanayagam Pact, which had never got off the ground in the first place. Yet, a perusal of the agreement proves beyond doubt that had these two acts of betrayal not happened, the Tamil discontent would not have led to the cry for separation.[7]

A glance through the island's history shows time and again how opportunities were missed by the two conflicting communities for rapprochement, more milestones to mark human perfidy were set up on the road ahead. But what perhaps eclipsed others was the majority community's campaign to change the national narrative with full official patronage. However, it is argued that obsessed with its theory of Sinhalese 'perfidy', the Tamil leadership of the day, the Federal Party and the TULF, at least twice missed the right track and, in consequence, further isolated itself from national politics. The first of the two occasions was available when the government handled the general strike of 1980 (newspapers of the time frequently used the word 'smashed' to convey the severity of the police repression let loose on the strikers) with an iron hand and the second when the hugely fraudulent referendum was stage-managed by the government two years later, all under Jayawardene's stewardship. At both times, the Tamil leadership chose to label the popular protests as 'southern issues' and decided to remain aloof. The decisions only succeeded in isolating the Tamil leadership further from the concerns of the Sinhalese community rendering it irrelevant in national issues. On the other hand, there was the shining example of two Leftist Sinhalese leaders who made it a mission in their abruptly curtailed lives to bring solace to the Tamils, Sarath Muttetuwegama and Vijaya Kumaratunga.

Nevertheless, the treatment of the Tamils by the Sinhalese is by far the worst festering wound inflicted on the country and people continue to reap the bitter harvest. Considerable solace has been administered with the change of government in 2015 but the healing process appears to have been halted mid-way, and in sheer desperation the Tamil leadership is crying out for a 'statesman' to appear and save them. As the Rajapaksa clan had started flexing its muscles in the aftermath of the massive defeat inflicted on the ruling parties, the Tamils' wait for a statesman to appear and do justice to the long-suffering community may well prove to be a never-ending one.

The turning point

By 2013, the politically conscious people had begun to realise that authoritarianism had reached dangerous levels, and that it was time a resistance movement was built up. The country had been scandalised by the manner of removal of the Supreme Court Chief Justice[8], and this had served to heighten the urgency for resistance. However, the strike would have to be a stealthy one followed by steps initiated to remove the root cause of repeated bouts of authoritarianism.

This was why the joint Opposition group decided to work for the abolition of executive presidency and destruction of the roots of what happened during those significant two years, 2013-2015. Despite having experienced universal franchise first in South Asia and having carried out political leadership changes through successive general elections since independence, a *shadow state* had been allowed to exist since 1971 as part of the violent state response to the first rebellion of the Marxist organisation JVP.

It was the chilling effect of the 1971 state repression by the Sirimavo Bandaranaike government with a large-scale use of forced disappearances of arrested suspects or accused that seemed to have defined the nature of political violence in Sri Lanka. Apprehending that the state reaction on any form of political resistance would be the kind of ruthless killings witnessed at that time, the rebels took to adopting equally cruel strategies. This in its turn was seen to have created justification for the state's retaliation which took the form of widespread use of forced disappearances.

The result of this cycle of violence involving the state and its challengers in the two southern rebellions, coupled with the growing civil war in the north-east, facilitated the growth of a *shadow state* within Sri Lanka. The Ministry of Defence, which till now controls the police force as well, apart from the three armed services of army, navy and air force—quite contrary to the usual practice in democracies where police and intelligence services are controlled by interior or home ministries—resorted to extreme forms of violence considered justifiable and legitimate so as to control every form of political activism. Thus, there was absolutely no room left for political activism against the government by way of political discourse.

In this scenario, the real control of Sri Lankan politics was vested in the Defence Ministry which was empowered to mobilise intelligence services and the paramilitary forces. Peaceful political competition, which should be the norm in a democracy, was replaced so early in the life of independent Sri Lanka, by a 'strategy of annihilation' of all political opposition.[9] The country still officially remained a democratic republic but its democracy was disabled and only a pretence of the real thing. With the coming into power of the Sirisena-Wickremasinghe government, most of the edifice has been dismantled, but the job is not yet fully done. Abuses still occur, and even if numerically negligible, citizens continue to face a diminished form of state reprisals like abductions, beatings, detentions and even murders.[10]

But the most sensitive issue that clinched the 2015 elections in favour of the *rainbow coalition* was, corruption, and the exposure of the Central Bank of Sri Lanka bond scam within the first month of its tenure that acted like a fuse which ultimately burnt its way to almost bringing down the government by the end of 2017.

History of a scam

Within a few days of the formation of the government by President Maithripala Sirisena, Prime Minister Ranil Wickremasinghe made his most important appointment[11], placing his long-time economic adviser Arjuna Mahendran to the governorship of the Central Bank of Sri Lanka. In less than a month thereafter, a massive financial scandal broke out involving the Governor. The repercussions of that scam have continued to rock the government since then, and quickened its pace after the 10 February 2018, local government elections when the two ruling parties fared very badly, and the discarded despot Mahinda Rajapaksa surged ahead with a massive popular support fortuitously regained.

This roller-coaster journey in popular support can only be appreciated if the state of affairs in February 2018 were put in perspective. The reign of corruption that characterised the Rajapaksa regime had disgusted the people so much that they opted for the slogan 'good governance' with alacrity and relief. Thus, the shock of realising that the new regime had already been corrupted, angered them very much, and they struck a blow at the first opportunity, that is the local government elections. The government had anticipated such an outcome and hence, was taking its own time to schedule and reschedule the polls till they could not be postponed any further. The last elections to the 340-odd local bodies (comprising 23 municipal councils, 41 urban councils and 271 provincial councils) were held way back in 2011. As these elections traditionally were shorn of any political importance and were seen as more of a routine low-key affair, neither the government nor the political parties were bothered about the prolonged gap in electing new bodies. However, as the Central Bank bond scandal broke out and national politics suddenly warmed up, enabling the ousted President to smell an opportunity to challenge the coalition government through elections, demands for local polls became a clamour in 2017.

Complications arose for the government to respond suitably to this challenge, because it was the President's party which balked at the prospects of facing the electorate. Only too conscious of the resounding failure to honour the commitments to the people to ensure a corruption-free administration, bringing swift justice to the perpetrators of state terrorism, creating jobs and ushering in substantial economic development, the President prevaricated, stalling for time. As popular disenchantment surfaced, the Rajapaksa camp got emboldened. Pro-Rajapaksa elements within the Sirisena faction of the SLFP did not want to wait anymore to bring the wobbly government down. The President was thus forced by circumstances to delay the elections further. From the dominant partner UNP's perspective, the time was already propitious, and it was, therefore, raring to go for the polls, as it felt that the President's party was now in a very weak state of health.

Even after a gazette notification was issued on 27 October 2017 setting 28 January 2018 as the election day, a clear three months' time in hand, the polls were further postponed to 10 February 2018. But the Sirisena-led SLFP still could not elude its fate. The results showed that even if the party was still a ruling party, it had emphatically lost the popular mandate to rule. The aftermath, with the Rajapaksa-led SLFP faction baying for blood, and the stronger UNP (though it, too, had considerable ground) itching for more dominance in the government, ran true to the script.

It was in this backdrop that the bond scam proved to be handy for all the three parties to advance their respective and mutually exclusive agendas. Going by one account of how the scam was instituted, a blogger 'Business Basil' had predicted a mere three days after the 8 January 2015 presidential election when the new Cabinet was yet to be formed that 'Perpetual Treasuries Ltd (PTL) owned by Free Lanka Capital Holdings will mostly get a large amount of business volumes of Treasury Bills and Treasury Bonds business in (the) new *Yahapalanaya* government of Maithripala-Ranil regime since (the) new governor of (the) Central Bank is tipped to be (the) Free Lanka Capital's driving force Arjun Aloysius' father-in-law Arjuna Mahendran who is also the top economic adviser of Wickremasinghe.' Under the mutual agreement between the two parties, the Prime Minister is in charge of all the economic ministries and the foreign ministry.

Pointing out that the Cabinet was yet to be formed, that the prognosis for the new President and his government was excellent, that 'they' had campaigned on a platform of good governance, meritocracy, transparency and freedom from corruption, a commentator remarked that against such a background, the suggestion of the sorts 'Business Basil' made seemed 'unwarranted, premature and wholly speculative'.[12]

But in any event, the blogger proved to be right. The government was not even two months old when the storm broke. The allegation was that the PTL benefitted at the auction from a combination of insider information and a late decision to issue an unprecedented volume of bonds. For those who knew how Perpetual did business, it didn't come as a total shock. The company was connected with pumping up stocks and dumping them at high prices on the Employees' Provident Fund, which appeared to be a willing participant in the scheme. What, however, shook the market and subsequently the nation was that the new government was complicit in allowing the fraud that had happened at the bond auction.

Digging up facts of the story, however, proved tough as most informed people refused to talk and those who opened their mouths did so on the condition of anonymity. It was obvious that the culture of fear would not go away so early in the country.

By all accounts, Aloysius was a well-connected man, at ease with both the Rajapaksa regime and its successor. The then finance minister Ravi Karunanayake who lost his job subsequently, was frequently mentioned by sources while recounting Aloysius' exploits, though he himself later denied any 'special' relationship with the man in the eye of the storm. *The Sunday Times*, Colombo, reported that all attempts to interview Aloysius were stymied by both the father-in-law and the son-in-law. The latter was described as a 'deal-maker' who got things done by using contacts, forging alliances or by other means. This was a man who was smart enough to install the sister of a former Central Bank Governor in one of his companies.

However, he was not a director of the PTL when the Central Bank bond auction took place. In fact, his resignation took place a week before his father-in-law was appointed the Central Bank governor. But he had remained in other companies of the group and his influence in high places remained intact. His father-in-law, Arjuna Mahendran, was earlier appointed Chairman of the Board of Investment and his father was appointed to various senior foreign ministry postings by Ranil Wickremasinghe in his earlier *avatar* as Prime Minister. Clearly, the connections ran deep and long. Aloysius himself belongs to a rich and powerful family, his grandfather having been a close associate of Ranasinghe Premadasa. It was the grandfather, himself an honourable man, who facilitated Arjun's entry into the stock market by either giving him some shares or access to the sale proceeds of those shares. The journey started out well but Perpetual soon slipped into murky territory, targetting a 'complicit' Employees Provident Fund (EPF) as a dumping ground for inflated shares.

Perpetual Capital and Perpetual Asset Management quietly joined a tiny posse that kept on helping pump up the value of certain shares and unload them on to the EPF. Two of these were Ceylon Grain Elevators and Lanka Orix Leaving Co. 'There was a sort of an insider ring being created with certain people within the EPF and the Central Bank,' to quote an anonymous source.

It was Opposition MP Harsha de Silva who was one of the first to point out that the EPF was investing in non-blue chip companies in a questionable manner, such as, buying shares of such companies at around LKR 50-80 each at end-2015 and selling them to EPF three months later at LKR 250 each. The price of the little-valued but now artificially priced very high stocks, would then fall dramatically back to the earlier level and would 'slay' everyone who had rushed to buy the share after its inflated price became known. Ironically, some of Arjun's own friends lost millions of rupees overnight in this market piracy.

After having cornered several windfall profits by under-pricing while buying and over-pricing while selling good and bad shares, the Central Bank bond issue gave Aloysius another windfall bonanza. In August 2016, his Perpetual Capital group started buying National Development Bank (NDB) shares using two margin trading accounts. It first collected some small quantities, then expanded volumes gradually. By the end of 2016, around 3.9 million NDB shares were privately transferred to Aloysius' group, then the equities were transferred within the group. The motive for this complicated process was not clear but the transactions were not illegal.

As the scandal over the Central Bank bond issue hit the country towards the end of 2017, when this author was visiting Sri Lanka, the enormity of it stunned the people and everybody at the time was talking and writing about it, of the principal players including both businessmen and politicians and about how their hopes for an honest administration had been belied. The popular anger and scepticism were palpable. 'So much for their clean administration,' sneered Basil Fernando, a strapping app cab driver who had transported me from the Katunayake airport early one November morning to the hotel in Colombo. He also predicted with surprising confidence that Mahinda Rajapaksa would definitely come back to power in January 2020 when the next presidential election was due. His enthusiasm for Rajapaksa was understandable as he was a member of his party. But his prediction, which sounded almost unbelievable, was echoed and re-echoed every time I probed the minds of the Sri Lankans or asked them questions, including members of the minority communities. The possible contours of the local government polls were well-etched almost two months before they were held.

In his 3 January 2018 television address to the nation, President Sirisena, however, disclosed that according to the findings of the Presidential Commission of Inquiry to investigate and inquire into Serious Acts of Fraud, Corruption and Abuse of Power, States Resources and Privileges, the criminal acts involving the EPF and the NDB, among other state resources, had actually begun way back in 2008 when Rajapaksa was in his first term of presidency. '(The) Commission states that funds of the Employees Provident Fund (EPF) were lost mostly during that period,' he said.

The report also stated that the Perpetual Treasuries Ltd. (PTL) had made profits through 'illegal' means with the involvement of Arjuna Mahendran, Central Bank officials and some outside individuals. During the auction held on 27 February 2015 alone, the PTL made a 'minimum' windfall profit of LKR 688 million. Further investigations might reveal an even more shocking extent of illegal profit. 'As revealed during the investigations,' the President said, 'PTL has made undue profit of LKR 11,145 million in the secondary market (made in just five months). In this the EPF and other government institutions had lost more than LKR 8,524 million or LKR 8.5 billion.'

The report exposed the helplessness of Central Bank officials before Mahendran, and it was felt that because they kept mum without ever questioning the Governor's unilateral decisions, 'such incorrect decisions were made'. Mahendran interfered in bond auctions 'through a system of incorrect and unconventional methods'. He was also responsible for passing on internal information to outsiders. Without identifying anybody or any entity, it said: 'One party has used such information to obtain undue monetary profits.'

Commenting on the most sensitive question thrown up by Prime Minister Wikremasinghe's role in the scam, the report said that his responsibility in Mahendran's appointment as the Central Bank Governor was 'proper'. The Prime Minister made his statement in Parliament regarding the appointment 'believing in the facts presented by Mahendran and Samarasiri[13], especially the promises made by (the former). (But) the Prime Minister should not have done that.'

Besides, these facts were available with the COPE committee but the Prime Minister did not mention it. Therefore, he did not take the 'proper' action against the Governor. Referring to the sacked finance minister Ravi Karunanayake, the Commission referred to the payment of the rent for the penthouse apartment owned by the Aloysius family and the family's Walt and Rowe Co. and held Karunanayake responsible for these lapses, recommending the government to take necessary action against him under the section of bribery and corruption and further legal action under the penal codes for giving false evidence at the Commission's hearing.

Sirisena concluded his address by making a few political remarks. He said that the people had been very visibly interested in learning the truth about the scam. Secondly, some people inside and outside Parliament made snide remarks that similar to previous Inquiry Commissions, this Commission would also end up by producing a report which would never be acted upon. Thirdly, he denied that his purpose for appointing the two Inquiry Commissions was to target 'any' political party. 'We must be happy over our independent and impartial judiciary,' he said. 'I must state all of us will provide our maximum support for this process.'

Disillusioned people

As I began to probe the minds of people at large as regards their government, oft repeating the question 'Are you satisfied with the performance of this government?', I was taken by surprise by the uniformity of their response. My interlocutors represented a wide spectrum of Sri Lankans, ranging from hardened and cynical politicians to sharp-minded political scientists, journalists, students, housewives, the urban proletariat, small shopkeepers, auto rickshaw drivers and municipal workers. The sum-total of their response was that they had been unfairly short-changed by a government they had put their faith in.

This overall disillusionment had a lot to do with the promises the 'rainbow coalition' had made in its election campaign and the new NDF government's subsequent failure to keep most of those promises. Above all, the seemingly well-intentioned government was perceived to have been exasperatingly slow in honouring its commitments.

The resounding defeat in the local government polls and the subsequent crisis in the coalition had two dimensions. The first was the pressure from the Rajapaksa camp for the Wickremasinghe government to resign, interpreting the election results as a referendum on the government as well as loss of its popular mandate won three years ago. The government could easily have brushed off the pressure by arguing that while Rajapaksa's new party could only poll 44 per cent of the popular vote, the ruling parties had garnered nearly 52 per cent of the votes between themselves.[14]

It was also important to note that despite the adverse election results, the Rajapaksa camp only had 50 MPs in its fold. Thus, the balance of power within Parliament had not changed, until the Opposition succeeded in instigating some of the government MPs to defect. That was exactly what the former President was doing prior to the 4 April 2018 debate on the no confidence motion. 'Some of the ministers and MPs from the ruling coalition have approached us,' he claimed, 'some crossovers may take place in future.'[15] Rajapaksa's confidence stemmed specifically from the substantial number of SLFP ministers and MPs who continued to be with Sirisena only because he was the President. In fact, some of them even openly campaigned for the Rajapaksa nominees in the local poll elections. Rajapaksa was actually being modest when he said that some of the SLFP MPs might cross over. What he and his brothers were already targetting was to get the SLFP members away from the leadership. They sought to pull the rug from under his feet by engineering defections and leaving Sirisena to be of little political value—a President without followers.

In the aftermath of the 10 February 2018 debacle, Rajapaksa seemed to have succeeded in indirectly igniting the hostility and disunity within the ruling coalition further and shaking the very foundations of the government. The Prime Minister's party, the UNP, got 32 per cent of the total vote share in the local body elections while the United People's Freedom Alliance (UPFA) and SLFP led by the President could garner a much lower 12 per cent, more or less reflecting the difference in popular support for them in the last parliamentary elections. Yet, Sirisena seemed to be determined to get rid of Wickremasinghe through the Central Bank bond scam probe and by constantly poaching into the latter's exclusive domain of economic decisions. His frequent refrain during the period was the alleged mishandling of the economy—a topic that Rajapaksa too emphasised at every opportunity—and stressing on the urgency of correcting the situation. He also felt that the Prime Minister had been ignoring him on policy issues. Thus, it became impossible for the coalition to contest the local body elections unitedly; on the contrary, their style of campaigning conveyed the impression that they were actually battling each other rather than unitedly fighting their challenger.[16]

While the two parties remained partners in the government, they quickly transformed themselves into rivals and adversaries in the polls. In particular, the phantom of the bond scam, allowing private runaway windfall profits at the cost of public funds, impacted severely on the credibility and transparency of the government. Besides, the slowness in pursuing the various corruption cases pending against the former President and his brothers had antagonised the people further, a point that the President kept on highlighting during this period.

It was symptomatic of the breakdown in the relationship that during the local government election campaign, Sirisena used the Central Bank bond scam as much as Rajapaksa did, if not more, to directly attack his Prime Minister. In hindsight, it seems that it was Wickremasinghe's unique forbearance by ignoring such a sustained attack that saved the coalition from falling apart during and after the elections. Besides, for months onward, Sirisena's party members, including ministers, kept on broadcasting their determination to edge Wickremasinghe out of power.

Sirisena himself showed an unethical alacrity to replace Wickremasinghe, though he did not have the constitutional authority to do so. As a matter of fact, he could not even sack a minister. In turn, the over-enthusiasm of the SLFP camp galvanised the UNP ministers and MPs, and even though quite a few of them had publicly declared their intention to replace Wickremasinghe with another party MP, they now closed ranks and stood solidly behind the beleaguered Prime Minister.

The extent of bitterness generated between the government and the Opposition led to an unprecedented eruption of violence in Parliament on 10 January 2018 when the Prime Minister was making a statement on the bond scam. Opposition MPs launched a protest in the middle of the House as the statement was being read out, demanding that the Speaker divulge the details of the scam revealed by the report of the Presidential Commission of Inquiry. A missile was eventually hurled at the Prime Minister, forcing the Speaker to adjourn the sitting for 10 minutes. A minister tweeted, 'I am told that never in history had there been a brawl in the Chamber like the one just now.' Another minister tweeted, 'Utter pandemonium in Parliament. Apparently someone threw an object at the Prime Minister while he was speaking in the Chamber... Disgraceful.'

In his statement, Wickremasinghe sought to convert the post-scam scenario into an advantage for the government, arguing that in sharp contrast to the previous experience, his government had taken prompt action to punish the guilty, proving that the rule of law was once again prevailing in the country. 'People still find this to be strange. It is a victory for the people,' he claimed.

However, the in-fighting in the government continued, with the President complaining that a 'small' group within the government was criticising him for taking up the probe into the scam and finding out the guilty with all seriousness. He alleged that apart from criticising his action, these individuals had also financed social media trolls that spread hate and insults against him. 'I can handle the criticisms from the Opposition, but the ones that are criticising me within the government are in a way acting against the principles of Ven. Sobitha Thero.' The reference was to a universally respected liberal Buddhist monk who led a social movement against injustice. He said that his action was necessary as there was a huge outcry from the public as well as civil society organisations to probe the fraud. 'We were not appointed to fill our own pockets or to rob the money,' he added. 'I did what I promised to the people...When I contested for the 2015 presidential election as the common candidate, there were instances where stones were thrown, stages were set on fire and the state media (were) used to the maximum to criticise us. But we overcame all those barriers and finally won the hearts of the people.'

It was during this phase of continuous see-saw battle between the two sides that the President one day stormed out of a Cabinet meeting, infuriated by public criticism of him by UNP MPs. This was regarded as the very first instance of an executive President walking out of a Cabinet meeting he was presiding over. Later on, he identified the MPs by name and concluded by saying that a country could not be ruled under such circumstances. His angry walkout was soon followed by the Prime Minister and some senior ministers from both the parties visiting him and persuading him to return to the Cabinet meeting. This incident also happened in the wake of the Supreme Court rejecting the President's plea to allow him to continue in office for an additional year after his 5-year term ended on 9 January 2020. The issue raised was that he would be reduced to a lame-duck President. His plea for an extension in office also flew in the face of his solemn promise to abolish executive presidency if elected to power.

In his letter dated 8 January 2018, Sirisena had sought the Supreme Court's opinion on whether his five-year term in office could be extended to a six-year one, as 'certain ambiguities' had arisen following the Attorney-General's view that the 19th Amendment to the Constitution (which his government had brought in to limit the President's term of office to two terms). His logic was that when he was elected President and took office on 9 January 2015, his term in office was for six years under the then existing constitutional provision and that he was, therefore, entitled to stay in office for six years. However, when his government passed the 19th Amendment, apart from restricting the presidency to two stints, the tenure was also reduced from six to five years. Besides, as the Centre for Policy Alternative (CPA), which had challenged Sirisena's bid to stay an additional year in office, argued, the amendment was specific in emphasising that the reduced tenure would be applicable in the case of the incumbent President (Sirisena) as well.

Sirisena's real purpose was to continue in office till August 2020 so that he could preside over the choosing of SLFP candidates for the parliamentary elections due that month. Besides, he appeared to have calculated that with another year in office, he could pursue the corruption cases instituted by his government against the Rajapaksa brothers; settle his running feud with his Prime Minister and the UNP and in the process, regain his primacy over his partners. He may also have based his calculation on the assumption that the Supreme Court might opt for a political, rather than a strictly legal point of view while examining his plea. His carefully nurtured plan was thwarted as the apex court chose instead, to give a strictly legal interpretation to the law.[17]

In the month following the President's constitutional setback, the feuding parties grew more abusive, aggressive and desperate to outdo each other. As a result, popular disgust for the ruling parties and the government soared so much that one could openly hear critical comments which were unthinkable three years earlier: 'If the Rajapaksas come back, irrespective of their record, the people would heave a sigh of relief as they can rid of these good-for-nothing people, who do not even know if they are coming or going.'

As the President found himself increasingly cornered by the twin assaults mounted on him by the Wickremasinghe and Rajapaksa camps, he gave up and aborted his move to topple the Prime Minister. However, at the same time he vowed to overhaul the Cabinet. On 19 February 2018, his spokesperson and minister S.B. Dissanayake announced that the SLFP and umbrella organisation UPFA had decided to remain in the unity government.

On the night of 18 February 2018, Sirisena met Wickremasinghe and Speaker Karu Jayasurya, who had brokered peace between the two quarrelling sides. However, within minutes of the peace deal and a settlement struck, Sirisena relapsed into his quest for redemption from Wickremasinghe when a UNP minister conveyed to him the 'readiness' of as many as 113 MPs, from both the parties, to challenge the government on the floor of the House. When the House reconvened next morning, the boast of mythical 113 votes, which would have been the magic majority number in the 225-seat Parliament, had shrunk to a beggarly 20; and Sirisena's hopes were dashed once again.

The Prime Minister's victory on 4 April 2018 when the no confidence motion was defeated (in which the TNA played a major role irrespective of its numerical strength in Parliament, a story which will be narrated shortly), only served to heighten the infighting in the government and the coalition. For one thing, as many as 16 of the SLFP MPs staged a defection and began to sit on the Opposition benches, stating that since they had voted in favour of the no confidence motion against the Prime Minister, they could no longer associate themselves with the government. 'If only the UNP had removed Wickremasinghe and put up somebody else, the coalition government would have sailed smoothly and it would have enjoyed two-thirds majority in Parliament. But certain forces scuttled that prospect by insisting that Wickremasinghe must remain (PM),' one of the defectors said. At the same time, they clarified that they would continue to support the President and that they would not join the Joint Opposition backed by Rajapaksa.

The President went a step further to complicate an already complex political crisis by proroguing Parliament on 12 April till 8 May 2018. This came as a big surprise to all the parties as he had just appointed four new ministers. At this juncture, he was left with just 25 SLFP MPs with him. At the end of the day, the President stood further weakened, and the Prime Minister and the UNP had emerged more powerful. It was clear to all that governance—not to speak of good governance—had been bid goodbye at least for the present.[18]

Now, the TNA story. Even though it was widely anticipated that the Tamil National Alliance would vote against the no-confidence motion simply because the Tamils could under no circumstances help the Rajapaksas in their design, the decision was taken only on the eve of the voting. All the 16 MPs (including the member of the Eelam People's Revolutionary Liberation Force which had left the TNA) voted against the motion. The impact of the TNA support went much beyond its numerical strength. The UNP was united behind the Prime Minister, and having realised that his game had failed, the President asked his party MPs to abstain from voting, thus helping Wickremasinghe to defeat the motion.

However, in a twist which could only be dictated by the Rajapaksas' antipathy towards the Tamils, the ire and wrath of the supporters of the motion turned against the TNA which was somehow perceived (quite correctly, as it turned out) to have saved the Prime Minister on the day. Crude attempts were made to communalise the issue by racist elements supportive of a Rajapaksa return to power. Some hawkish elements tried to spread canards that the LTTE and pro-LTTE elements in the diaspora got the TNA to support Wickremasinghe because he was going to give the Tamil Tigers a separate state through a federal constitution.[19]

The absurdity of this assertion is self-evident. The relationship between the LTTE and its supporters and the TNA is one of intense hatred. As Jeyaraj points out, anyone with a modicum of genuine understanding about contemporary Tamil politics would laugh off these tragi-comic allegations. If the LTTE had ever thought of federalism or development as being equal to a separate state the Tamil Tigers would have accepted devolution long ago. They did not. On the contrary, they perceived devolution and federalism as a betrayal of the Tamil struggle for separation. They treated all Tamil politicians who strove for political settlement with maximum devolution as traitors and killed them as in the case of constitutional expert Dr Neelan Thiruchelvam. While the LTTE did not exist in Sri Lanka any more, overseas LTTE members remained strongly opposed to the current constitution making exercise. That was why they displayed venomous hatred towards the TNA leaders R. Sampanthan and M.A. Sumanthiran who were fully supportive of and immersed in the constitutional exercise. The 'Tigerish' elements also hated Ranil Wickremasinghe and Chandrika Kumaratunga because both the leaders had tried to achieve a negotiated political settlement of the ethnic issue. The LTTE also knew that it was Ranil Wickremasinghe who was cooperating fully in the constitutional exercise. Besides, instead of strengthening, the LTTE would like to destabilise the state, and the best way for that was to ensure the collapse of the Sirisena-Wickremasinghe government. It would have liked the no confidence motion to succeed, unseating the Prime Minister resulting in utter confusion and chaos in the country.

However, the Rajapaksa camp appeared to have decided to capitalise on the allegation of a link between the Tamil Tigers and the TNA ignoring the absurdity of it to profit politically. As the country moves towards the next elections, rumours are thrown up regularly warning of the possibility of a revival of rebellion in the north and that unidentified 'foreign elements' and western funds were busy working towards this end. Therefore, so the retrograde logic ran, the Rajapaksas must return to power to save the country once again from 'subversive' elements and international 'conspirators'.

Meanwhile, following the impressive performance of the Mahinda Rajapaksa-backed new party Sri Lanka Podujana Peramuna (Sri Lanka People's Front) in the local government elections, the Opposition leaders got going with remarkable alacrity. His brother Basil, now a leader of the SLPP, announced on 19 February 2018, that the party would start a 'mega development drive' in local villages to help them gain economic stability. Recalling that the Rajapaksa government had launched measures to develop infrastructure and roads in local villages across the country, he said that the new party would resume the drive to maintain and improve upon the rural infrastructure for the benefit of the local villagers. 'If villages are developed, the government will benefit and we can reach out for further investments from international investors. We will have talks with the central government.' Some of the key projects which the party hoped to implement at the local level were to setting up a renewable energy plant and water facilities for the local farmers and villagers. Basil Rajapaksa was quoted saying, 'Currently there are many people in the villages who do not have (access to) clean water and due to this, they suffer from chronic diseases.'

NOTES

1 Kishali Pinto-Jayewardene, 'Measuring the Maturity of the Sri Lankan Electorate,' *Sunday Times*, Colombo, 25 July 2015.

2 Meera Srinivasan, 'Sirisena urged to "rise as a statesman",' *The Hindu*, 20 March 2018.

3 As claimed by the then *Times of India* political correspondent Darem that Senanayake told him in 1942 when the World War II was raging and Ceylon survived on aid from Britain and India—the latter supplying essential commodities—that he would prefer an India-Ceylon federation. Senanayake also believed that Ceylon's long-term security needs would be better looked after by India. However, with the end of the war in 1945 and a change in the economic fortunes of his country, Senanayake, the first Prime Minister, was quick to change his tune as he was increasingly called upon to address urgent political issues. The UNP, the party he led, zeroed in on the issue of the citizenship of Indian-origin Tamils and initiated a long and painful process designed to deprive citizenship to the majority of those Tamils, described in detail in these pages.

4 Rajan Hoole, Daya Somasundaram, K.Sritharan and Rajani Thirangama, University of Jaffna, Jaffna, *The Broken Palmyra The Tamil Crisis in Sri Lanka: An Inside Account*, The Sri Lanka Studies Institute, Claremont, CA, USA, March 1990, reprinted 1992.

5 One increasingly encounters a similar discourse in India where Hindutva groups led by the ruling Bharatiya Janata Party propagate that Muslims from the neighbouring countries are gradually changing the demographic pattern of the country. A national citizenship register has also been launched, initially in the north-eastern state of Assam where Bengali-speaking Muslims constitute the majority in several districts. The idea of the register is to check every resident's origin and date of entry into Assam and then deport those who would fail to satisfy the qualifications of being genuine Indian citizens. Those already enumerated and declared non-citizens include a large number of long-time voters, including a prominent MP and leader of a major Muslim political party in the state, raising a stink about the controversial exercise. More on the subject can be found below.

6 Articles published in *Lanka Guardian*, June/July, 1984, not archived.

7 The Bandaranaike-Chelvanayagam Pact contained the following provisions: 1) Tamil would be made the language of administration and of record in the Northern and Eastern Provinces; 2) Court proceedings in these provinces would be conducted and recorded in Tamil; 3) Administration throughout the country would be decentralised through district councils; and 4) There would be a reasonable restriction of the Tamil provinces by the Sinhalas. This was the first, though soon aborted, promise of setting up provincial councils on devolved powers.

8 Dealt in details above and below.

9 Basil Fernando, 'Sri Lanka: Contrasting the Political Climate in Burma and Sri Lanka,' *Asian Human Rights Commission*, 29 November 2012.

10 Steven Butler, 'Lots of talk but little progress in Sri Lanka over journalist murders,' Committee to Protect Journalists, 9 January 2018. The incidents of attacks on journalists recorded after the NDF government assumed power are related in *Chapter Five: Human Rights Withering Away and Restoration.*

11 NewsIn Asia website, 'Wickremasinghe tightens grip over Sri Lankan economic and foreign policies,' 31 May 2017. Through a Cabinet-level and junior minister level reshuffle of his Cabinet, Ranil Wickremasinghe tightened his grip over a major part of the coalition government. Among the new junior minister-level appointees were Eran Wickremaratne, a close associate of the Prime Minister; Harsha de Silva, a second loyalist; and Wasanrtha Senanayake; and the only SLFP MP to make the grade at that time was Lakshman Yapa Abeywardena in the post of a state minister of enterprise development.

12 Namini Wijedasa, 'All about Arjun Aloysius the Perpetual Treasuries "James Bond" implicated in the Central Bank bond scam,' *DBSJeyaraj.com.* on Facebook, 3 December 2016, courtesy *The Sunday Times.*

13 P. Samarasiri, who was the Deputy Governor of the Central Bank under Mahendran. He retired in August 2017. On 27 September 2017, the successor and current Central Bank governor Dr Indrajit Coomaraswamy stoutly defended the career of Samarasiri, arguing that the Presidential Commission of Inquiry, did not interrogate him on any alleged misdemeanour. He said that he was taking full responsibility for allowing Samarasiri to remove certain documents and files from his office and scoffed at the allegation that the latter did remove documents and files relating to the Central Bank bond scam. He also defended his officers and said that if any of them was later found guilty in the case, proper disciplinary action would be taken against him.

14 Jayadeva Uyangoda, 'Back to the chessboard?,' *The Hindu*, 16 March 2018.

15 Interview to *The Indian Express*, Kolkata ed., 24 March 2018, *ibid.*

16 In a series of tweets released at the time, the Prime Minister unleashed a publicity blitz recording the achievements of the UNP while ruling the country, giving the impression to the uninitiated, that the government was a one-party affair rather than a coalition. This was reciprocated in kind by Sirisena who similarly highlighted the achievements of the ministries controlled by his party.

17 NewsIn Asia, 'Impact of Lankan Supreme Court's denial of extra year to President Sirisena,' 15 January 2018.

18 NewsIn Asia, 'Political crisis drives Lankan President to prorogue parliament till May 8,' 12 April 2018.

19 D.B.S. Jeyaraj, 'How and Why the TNA Helped Defeat the No Confidence Motion Against Premier Wickremasinghe,' *DBSJeyaraj.com*, 14 April 2018.

2

Why do the Wounds Fester?

In your post war glee, are you listening?
In your post war dance, are you watching?
—Piumi Wijesundara, *Doll House* (Write to Reconcile II)

IT is noteworthy that Buddhist *vikkhus* (monks), who are of course exclusively Sinhalese, have historically played a leading role in the socio-political life of Sri Lanka. Their role in toughening the state's posture towards the minority communities is well-documented. They rest their case on the simplistic dictum that anyone can live in Sri Lanka as long as Sinhala Buddhists can enjoy 'cultural, religious, economic, political and linguistic hegemony'. It is thereby implied that the minorities must accept this as a fact of life and learn to live with it. However, the diversity in the religious composition of society prompted that the state remains neutral in religious affairs.[1]

As we have seen, the state's endeavour to preserve its neutrality, inherited from the colonial rule and enshrined in the Soulbury Constitution, began to face intensifying pressure from the Buddhist clergy since independence, but as long as D.S. Senanayake was at the helm of national affairs, it stood its ground.

He was succeeded by J.R. Jayewardene who had already utilised the Buddhist clergy's agitation against the Indian-origin Tamils in the Kandy district on the issue of their citizenship rights. His game at the time was to enhance his own clout in the ruling UNP and challenge the Prime Minister's leadership. As long as Senanayake lived, Jayewardene did not succeed in his design, but upon his death it did not take long for Jayewardene to emerge as the successor and also to work steadfastly to achieving his goal in life, that of replacing the Soulbury Constitution with an executive presidency form of government and becoming the first person to hold the office. In all these endeavours, his proximity to the clergy was a major help.

Since then, the process of politicisation of the main religion and its resultant metamorphosis into unabashed fundamentalism went ahead, giving rise at times to what would now be called terrorism, like the assassination of Prime Minister S.W.R.D. Bandaranaike at the hands of a monk. By the time this happened, Bandaranaike who had started in his political career as a liberal, had turned the full circle and sacrificed his ideology at the altar of majoritarian chauvinism by fully supporting the demand for declaring the 'only Sinhala' policy. Yet, he was at one time a votary of giving an equal status to the Sinhala and Tamil languages. As the Sinhala-Buddhist clergy continued to score point after point with the willing collaboration of the Sinhalese leadership, they were able to capture the main space in Sri Lankan polity, including determining state policies.

There was a subtle evidence of this mastery of the clergy over the political leadership made available in 2018. May Day is always a big day for Sri Lankans; apart from it being a national holiday, the working classes and all the political parties take out huge processions all over the country celebrating the day. President Premadasa in fact was assassinated on this day in 1993 when he was leading his party's May Day parade in Colombo.

In an unprecedented move in 2018, however, the government decided to postpone the International Workers' Day from May 1 to May 7 to avoid a clash with the biggest Buddhist festival, the Vesak Day which marks the birth, enlightenment and death of Lord Buddha. The government order in this respect specifically mentioned that the postponement had been decided upon 'giving priority for religious activities in (the) Vesak week'. It was explained that the decision was taken after considering a request made by the *Maha Sangha,* a venerated and influential body of the Buddhist clergy.

However, the Buddhist move was threatened when the trade unionists, traditionally a powerful lobby in the island, protested against this unprecedented disruption of an annual international event. Media reports quoted Linus Jayatilleke, president of the United Federation of Labour, arguing that May Days had never been postponed in the country excepting on two extraordinary circumstances.

He said that the May Day events were banned in 1987 when the UNP was in power because of the prevailing political situation. The second occasion was when Chandrika Kumaratunga was the President with a ban on May Day processions due to security alerts; however, related public meetings were allowed. The people, nevertheless, disobeyed the ban order and took out processions. 'May 1 is significant internationally and commemorates the crucial gains by working class struggles. The government may have ulterior motives to do this, fearing that it might not be possible to mobilise large numbers (of processionists) from its own trade unions... It's not just about Vesak, whether it is (the) Christmas or any other religious festival, May Day events will not interfere with those and must be held on May 1,' Jayatilleke said.[2]

Sinhala-Buddhist fundamentalism defined

What is Sinhala-Buddhist fundamentalism? While scholars of various world religions have at times differed, it is well accepted in academic circles that the definition of fundamentalism that is provided by the Fundamentalism Project (1987-1995), funded by the American Academy of Arts and Sciences and directed by Professors Martin E. Marty and R. Scott Appleby, meets all the requirements since it fits into the pattern of fundamentalism evident in all the world religions. We, therefore, need to take a quick glance at the definition.

The study concluded that regardless of religion, fundamentalism has several *commonalities* (italics added), such as:

* Men are to lead and women and children to follow. Wives are to be subservient to their husbands. Often, this subservience applies to sisters toward their brothers. A woman's role in life is to be a homemaker.
* The rules of their religion are complex and rigid and must be followed. Therefore, to avoid any confusion, children of fundamentalists must be sequestrated in an environment of like-minded adherents to the correspondent fundamentalist religion. Especially so in their schooling.
* There is *no* pluralism. Their rules apply to everyone everywhere.
* There is a distinct group of insiders and all others are outsiders. Insiders are nurtured and cared for. Outsiders are cast off and fought.
* They pine for an older age and a past when their religion was pure, as largely they no longer see it as such. Often, this time never fully existed, but they have nostalgic view of a Utopian past and they long to acquire it.[3]

The above study conveys the impression that when an undefinable fear grips a majority community, fundamentalism creeps in and gradually acquires the capacity to pervade the communal mindset. More or less, all the members of such a community begin to think on issues concerning themselves and about minority communities on similar lines. It is fear again which appears to require a strict disciplinary approach to keep the flock free of religio-political contamination. The overall endeavour is to erase the narrative of a diverse society by replacing it with new interpretations of history and, in the process, blurring the distinction between mythology and history.

This particular process has been in vogue in India where the majority Hindu community, led by the currently ruling Bharatiya Janata Party (BJP) and its ideological mentor Rashtriya Swayamsevak Sangh (RSS), along with the latter's affiliates, known by the omnibus nomenclature of Sangh Parivar, plus a host of recently-spewed regional outfits, have succeeded in persuading BJP-run state governments to revise school history textbooks to insert myths in place of facts. Their attacks on dissenters like intellectuals, apart from propaganda, have reached the level of assassinations with justice seldom catching up with perpetrators. The Hindu fundamentalism has even invaded the food and dress habits of minorities, forcing the closure of meat shops and non-availability of cooked meat in restaurants and hotels, forcing cancellation of shooting and exhibition of films considered derogatory to Hindu gods and goddesses, and even forcing book launches to cancel scheduled panel discussions on topics which are anathema to the so-called Hindutva zealots.[4]

A vicious grip

Admittedly, the situation in Sri Lanka is relatively less alarming than what is happening in its northern neighbour, but one important difference between the two countries is the long-established grip of the Buddhist clergy over the state; independent India has till now never experienced any religious hegemony despite having millions of faithful adherents of the two main religions practised, Hinduism and Islam. This is clearly the triumph of pluralism and diversity in the Indian society. India is yet to witness any demolition of this virtue, though as we have seen above, concerted and determined attempts are being made towards that end at this very hour.

As we have seen and will continue to record, the Sri Lankan state had surrendered to the diktat of the mighty *mahanayakes* with their unshakable base in Kandy all the way back in the late 1950s. India had for long been administered by secularist political parties, and more significantly, secularism is enshrined in its constitution[5]. It is only since 2014 with the installation of the BJP-led National Democratic Alliance (NDA) in New Delhi that a serious assault has been mounted on the constitutional validity of the concept and practise of secularism. In a two-way campaign to remove the constitutional tag, and at the same time, benefitting electorally from its continuation in the Indian state, for 'psuedo-secularism' as the rightist Hindu establishment prefers to describe the practise of secularism is looked upon as a potent weapon to constantly beat the rival political parties.

On the other hand, the 'democratic, socialist republic' of Sri Lanka, as the 1978 Constitution reads, 'shall give to Buddhism the foremost place and accordingly it shall be the duty of the State to protect and foster the Buddha *Sasana*, while assuring to all religions the rights granted by Articles 19 and 14(1)(e).' The Constitution designated Sinhala as the official language of the country (this was amended by the NDA government in 2015 which has designated both Sinhala and Tamil as the national languages).

It is argued that Sinhala-Buddhist fundamentalism differs from other forms of fundamentalisms as there is no rigidity or strictness regarding behavioural standards and believers do not form a coherent, readily identifiable group. Although there is no sacred text or scripture that serves as a blueprint for society, some scholars aver that the mytho-historical tract, the *Mahavamsa*, carries canonical authority. One of them points out that this text 'has become the warrant for the interlocked beliefs that the island and its government have traditionally been Sinhala and Buddhist.'[6] This flies in the face of the ethnic Tamils' position that the north-east of the country was historically a Hindu Tamil kingdom.

It is also argued that the Sinhala-Buddhist fundamentalism is determined not only by historical tradition and ideology, but by politics as well. It is used as a platform for politicians and patriots since the late-nineteenth century, is concerned directly with power and dominance, especially dominance by the ethnic majority, the Sinhalese. This has been examined in detail in the introduction and the previous chapter.

However, it is important to note that Sinhala-Buddhist fundamentalism is not an omnibus entity but contains within itself various inter-conflicting strands of thought and approach to different issues. For instance, the differences between Sarvodaya Shramadana Movement (SSM) and the Premadasa government cropped up over two interpretative variations of Sinhala Buddhist fundamentalism. The SSM's formulation could be described as 'socially engaging' and the government's as 'political'. The political stand emphasises identity without requiring that the government follow or enact Buddhist values and the SSM stresses the primacy of values over identity.[7]

Even the much-vaunted Buddha *Sasana*, according to Chandra R. de Silva, is a divided house presenting a variety of views relating to the ideal, social and political order among Buddhist monks in Sri Lanka. This subterranean division is sought to be masked by the great concern for an appearance of a 'unified' front, and the continuing tensions and contradictions between the Buddhist doctrinal tradition and the twentieth century nationalist ideology among Sinhala-Buddhist monks. This fact provides clues on strategies that might be adopted to foster greater tolerance. However, tolerance, not to speak of greater tolerance, appears to be a non-existent virtue of the Sinhala-Buddhist fundamentalism. Otherwise, the label of fundamentalism would not have been relevant in the first place.

As a matter of fact, it is a tragedy of Shakespearean proportions for Sri Lanka that Buddhism, perceived to be a religion of peace, has proved to be the most provocative and violent element in its contemporary history. A history that is replete with stories of violence between the two principal communities, the Sinhalese and the ethnic Tamils. Violence originating from the Sinhalese-Buddhists' desire to tailor the socio-economic-political scenario to ensure the continued supremacy of their religion, and the minority community's strong sense of Tamil nationalism and a separate identity which eventually led to a thirty-year-long civil war, devastating the north-eastern region and leaving behind a host of festering wounds on the body-politic and a wounded national psyche. Beneath this bleak and dehumanising history lies the constant refrain of violence, either state-sponsored or terrorism-related.

Underbelly of modernity

Since Sri Lanka is a modern nation-state, it is expected to control violence legally and rationally. Yet, its history tells a different story, Sri Lanka ranking at one time as one of the most violent countries in the world. However, 'anticipation of violence' may be as damaging and harmful as violence itself, and the disclaimer that it brings to the claim of modernity, namely, that it controls violence through legal and rational means, when in truth, it does not.

There is a hypothesis that the end-product of progress and development, that is the texture of modernity available to everyday life, may not be what it seems to be: 'terror might lurk in the intestines of the modern.' The argument is not that the texture of modernity itself is violent. This claim, while true, does not interrupt the logic of modernity. It is the claim of modernity that it controls violence legally and rationally that invites further examination. 'In this framing, the perpetration of violence is *authored* (italics added) by the state, or is replied to 'justly' by the state.' The argument seeks to alter the term that constitutes these claims, and to establish that the anticipation of violence—rather than its perpetration—occupies an incomprehensible place in the logic of the modern. It is a place that cannot easily be marked, quantified and responded to.[8]

Further, the majority-minority divide in the perspective of Sinhala-Buddhist fundamentalism can be examined in a different context altogether, that of the impact of land reforms and nationalist ideology on Indian-origin or plantation Tamils. Faced with the dominant Sinhalese narrative which refuses to recognise the plurality of Sri Lankan society thus isolating the minorities from being part of its cultural policy and its definition of nationhood, ethnic minorities have generally been conditioned to live through the mechanism of negotiation and accommodation.

It is a commentary on societal complexities that even within the 'negotiating and accommodating' minorities, one community may come to feel and behave like a superior to the other. In an examination of how identities can be differently interpreted, it is noted that in both the Sinhalese and Tamil contexts, the Muslim is defined as 'being subordinate and in an accommodating role' in relation to the dominant one, forcing the former to be identified with 'a larger pan-Islamic world'. In other words, Sri Lankan Muslims, who were originally influenced by sufism and Iranian religious traditions, could no longer cope with the rising levels of discrimination practised by the majority Sinhalese and the minority Tamils, gradually developed a form of Islamic fundamentalism more as a shield against the 'other' forms fundamentalisms and increasingly identified themselves with a 'heroic Arab past'. This form of Islamic fundamentalism is defined as 'the construction of an Islamic/ Muslim identity based on the memory of a heroic Arab past and an avowed ideological commitment to Islamic doctrinal practices and beliefs'.[9]

Is religious fundamentalism gaining over all other forms of fundamentalism in Sri Lanka? As a matter of fact, this question may well be put in a larger context altogether, such as, is this the trend all over the world? After all, as political Islam—often degenerating into terrorism and thus popularly confused as Islamic terrorism—faces increasing resistance from other religions, the overall trend tends to heighten the religious identity further and in certain narratives this becomes the 'only' identity.

But there is an opposite trend as well. For example, in Sri Lanka the majority of the Sinhalese Anglican Christians at one point saw themselves as a separate religious community from the Sinhalese Buddhists. But, later on, after the British left and the Buddhists came to dominate, Sinhalese Anglican Christians 'have been forced to show their loyalty to the nation through the revival of a shared 'history' and language rather than through religious affiliation...the history of this convert group is best discussed in relation to the organisation of state power in Sri Lanka.' In short, in the present context, indigenisation means Sinhalisation, a movement toward empowerment.[10]

This author was always taken by surprise when he discovered that a Sinhalese bearing a Christian name was in reality a practising Buddhist. From his experience with the Indian Christian community, it was rather difficult for him to appreciate this subterranean conversion from one religion to another. He had seen Hindus converting to Islam and adopting Islamic names or Hindus converted to Christianity changing into Christian names; therefore, the Sri Lankan experience was always baffling for him.

This apparently contradictory behaviour is explained by a hopelessly outnumbered minority group, accounting for a mere 7.6 per cent of the total population (Census 2012), trying to create a niche for itself by seeking to curry favour with the dominant majority Sinhalese-Buddhists.

However, there is a reverse trend in conversions as well. While the Sinhalese Buddhists are resentful about an alleged papal 'conspiracy' to convert Buddhists, barring stray cases of conversion, there is scarce evidence of any concerted campaign. However, the markedly higher growth of the Christian population in the hill country than that of the other religious groups can only be explained by conversion.

Papal 'conspiracy': A non-existent ghost?

The alleged papal conspiracy to carry on large-scale conversions in Sri Lanka is believed to be based on the Ecumenical Council of Vatican II (1962-1965) directing the Catholic Church on a revised path towards conversion. The Synod for the Bishops of Asia, held in Rome in 1998, held forth the view that Christianity had become a part of Asian culture through centuries of existence in the continent, facilitated by a process of indigenisation of specifics like hymns rendered in Asian languages, church services Asianised, etc. The relevant policy, drawn by the Asian Synod held in New Delhi and proclaimed by the Pope on 6 November 1999, called upon Catholics to convert Asians to Christianity, pointing out that Europe was converted in the first millennium, America and Africa in the second millennium, and now it was the turn of Asia to go Christian, talking of reaping 'a great harvest of faith' in the continent. The Church also noted the rising economic power of Asian countries like China, India, Indonesia and others and how they were attractive for foreign direct investment.[11]

Elaborating on Jesus's 'saving plan on Asian plains', the proclamation noted it was in fact in Asia that 'God revealed and fulfilled His saving purpose from the beginning'. In the fullness of time, He sent His only-begotten son, Jesus Christ the Saviour, who took flesh 'as an Asian'. Because Jesus was born, lived, died and rose from the dead in the Holy Land, that a small portion of Western Asia became a land of promise and hope for 'all' mankind. Jesus knew and lived in this land. God, in fact, had long before 'chosen' this people and revealed Himself to them in preparation for the Saviour's coming. So the proclamation goes on and on. Incidentally, the reader would be advised to mark the word 'chosen' for its return below in the context of the Sinhala-Buddhist fundamentalism in Sri Lanka.

However, an examination of the Sinhalese Buddhists' great concern for a large-scale conversion drive is found to be largely misplaced. The common complaint or grievance of both the Buddhist fundamentalist Bodu Bala Sena (BBS) and the Hindu fundamentalist Siva Senai (SS), (which denies having any connection to the Indian, Maharashtra-based Shiv Sena but, apart from the similarity in its identity, also behaves in a similar fashion to the Indian organisation) is that Buddhists and Hindus are being converted to Christianity through material and spiritual inducements. It has been alleged that the mushrooming of Western-funded non-governmental organisations (NGOs) in Sri Lanka during the course of the civil war had intensified such religious conversions both in the conflict-affected Eastern and Northern Provinces as well as elsewhere. The BBS also carries out a hate campaign against the Muslims due to the latter's relatively higher birth rate, apart from other reasons.[12]

However, it is statistically established that while the birth rates of Buddhist, Hindu and Christian Sri Lankans have declined to the levels of developed countries during the last 30 years, that of Muslims remains significantly higher. Faith-wise population statistics during 1981-2012 show that while the Buddhist population rose by 38.72 per cent, the Hindus by just 11.47 per cent, the Christians by 37.29 per cent and the Muslims grew by a whopping 75.41 per cent. This is further corroborated by the data relating to the proportion of each religious community in the total population. While the Buddhists' share rose only marginally from 69.30 per cent in 1981 to 70.10 per cent in 2012, that of the Hindus actually declined from 15.48 per cent (1981) to 12.58 per cent in (2012) and that of the Christians increased marginally from 7.61 per cent (1981) to 7.62 per cent (2012), the Muslims' share rose significantly from 7.56 per cent (1981) to 9.66 per cent (2012).

Conversions from the Buddhist and Hindu faiths to Christianity in Sri Lanka began with the Portuguese rule (beginning in 1505) either by inducement or by choice, such as, marriage, a trend which has continued till date. The question raised by strident Buddhists is the allegation of a regular and powerful conversion drive by the Christian Church—instigated and aided by western NGOs out of a much wider design to weaken the Buddhist role in the island—deserves further investigation. The Buddhist clergy also levels serious charges of continuing conversion of Buddhists to Islam in order to raise the Muslim population.

In the post-1977 period, statistics show that lesser numbers of Buddhists and Hindus have been embracing Islam than before, again either by choice like marriage, or to obtain Middle Eastern job visas.

Interestingly, intra-faith conversions are also taking place within the Christian community with the Anglican Church gaining at the cost of the Catholic Church, which is said to be a world-wide phenomenon.

These interfaith migrations have also affected the break-ups of district-wise population of their practitioners. There were 24 districts in the country in 1981, of which seventeen were Buddhist-majority (including Trincomalee in the Eastern Province), five were Hindu-majority and one each was of Muslim and Christian-majority. It is noted that 'majority' here denotes a simple majority and not a 50 per cent plus strength.

Census of 2012 showed several changes from the 1981 enumeration. There were now 16, one less, Buddhist-majority districts as Trincomalee had been merged with the Eastern Province. Similarly, the Hindu-majority districts had gained by one, the Killinochhi district; the Muslim-majority districts were now two (with the Trincomalee district recording a Muslim majority), while the Christian-majority district had remained unchanged (Mannar district).

The above statistics show that at the national level, there is no evidence of substantive religious conversions taking place in Sri Lanka contrary to the shrill Buddhist propaganda. If there were any considerable extents of religious conversions at the national level, the number of Christians would have risen which has not happened. As we have already seen, intra-faith conversions have certainly taken place, placing the Anglicans above the Roman Christians in numbers.

As for the admittedly higher Muslim population, it is obvious and, also statistically supported, that Muslims are greater in number today not because of conversions from the other two religions but by the process of a birth rate which is significantly higher than the national average. In that sense, the Hindus (who are all Tamil-speaking) should be the most aggrieved people in Sri Lanka as they have registered the sharpest fall in their population, from 15.48 per cent (1981) to 12.58 per cent (2012).

An analysis of the Census figures for the Nuwara Eliya district, however, reveals that conversions to the Anglican form of Christianity and a higher birth rate of Christians have both contributed to the highest Christian population growth rate recorded, 45.38 per cent, beating the Muslim population growth rate of 41.70 per cent. Similarly, a higher Christian population growth rate between 1987 and 2012, compared to the other religious groups in the Batticaloa and Trincomalee districts, indicates that they, too, may have witnessed conversions to Christianity. Of course, during this period there was a sharp decline in the Buddhist population as Sinhalese residents fled the Eastern Province in the wake of the civil war. Conversely, there was a major increase in the Buddhist population in the Mullaitivu district by over 672 per cent after the war ended and the army resettled thousands of them in Weli Oya Divisional Secretariat area adjoining the Trincomalee district. The Christian population increased in the Vavuniya district between 1981 and 2012 caused principally by inter-religious and intra-religious conversions. The inter-district migrations of the Hindu population within the Northern district were apparently influenced by the fluctuating fortunes of the civil war. As the Muslims increasingly left the Mannar district in the Eastern Province in the wake of the LTTE's anti-Muslim drive, their population declined there dramatically and, in equal measures, rose in the adjoining Puttalam of the North-Western Province where they mostly resettled. The Hindu population in Puttalam also rose at the time they fled for safety.

While population diversity is prevalent in the Northern, Eastern and Western Provinces with interruptions and variations caused by the civil war, it is the Southern Province which historically and continuously holds on to a solid Buddhist majority. According to the 2012 Census, the Hambantota district had the highest Buddhist population at 96.74 per cent, followed by Matara (94.14) and Galle (93.94). Moneragala, adjoining Hambantota, had the second largest concentration of Buddhists with 94.61 per cent. Conversely, the southern districts had less than one per cent Christians. Going by the rate of growth, however, the Christian population far outstripped the Buddhist population between the two censuses. It grew by 295.39 per cent in Hambantota, by 98.31 per cent in Matara and by 93.13 per cent in Galle. Moreover, it was the Anglicans who outnumbered the Roman Catholics, implying a very high incidence of intra-faith conversions, again conforming to the world trend. Christianity at the same time gained at the cost of Hinduism in the Badulla and Moneragala districts of the Uva Province, and also due to internal migration. The Hindus in the Gampaha district in the Western Province almost doubled between 1981 and 2012, again because of large-scale internal migrations from the war zone.

An analysis of the above data leads to the conclusion that by the time the next census is due, the Muslims will emerge as the second largest population group in Sri Lanka, to be followed by the Hindus and Christians in that order.[13] To that extent, the Sinhala-Buddhist fundamentalists' cry of a so-called papal conspiracy working in Sri Lanka is a false alarm.

The majority's fear psychosis

Most objective analyses of the problems that afflict Sri Lanka lead to the conclusion that Buddhists fear other faiths will overrun theirs and this lies at the root of their fundamentalist approach to the racial and religious question. Intolerance is invariably born in such an environment, leading invariably to violence and societal division.

But why should the majority community be fearful of the far lesser numbers of the minority communities? One analysis is that it is the question of land and not so much that of religion that lies at the root of this fear psychosis. It points out that the Sinhalese Buddhists have for ages identified themselves with the land in which they live, christening Sri Lanka as *Sinhadipa* (the island of the Sinhalese) and *Dhammadipa* (the island containing the Buddha's teachings). From this follows the Buddhists' concept of natural domination and minority subordination.

The subsequent ethno-religious majoritarianism, which seeks to absorb or disregard the minority communities, saw the 1972 constitution providing Buddhism a special status which was later reiterated by the 1978 constitution. A corollary to this was the Sinhalese insistence that Sri Lanka cannot but be a unitary state, leading to denying devolution of power to the other minority communities living in concentration in various parts of the country, such as the Tamils in the north-east, and the next stage that followed, the 30-year-long civil war and the continued denial of devolution in the post-war period.

If we pause a bit and take a look at India, where the majority Hindu community has been waging a kind of war against the minority communities, especially the Muslims in the last four years or so, we see another example of a fear psychosis that seems to have gripped the majority community in a country. A major difference is, of course, the absence of a secessionist movement on the scale of the Tamil militancy in Sri Lanka. Though the Kashmir situation offers a very serious challenge to the Indian state, the Indian case is very different as, apart from local disaffection, an extra-territorial dispute with Pakistan has distorted it right from the beginning. Today, Pakistan has become an integral player in the Kashmir situation, forcing India to engage with it though, in essence, the dispute in the Indian state is between the state and the Muslim population in the Kashmir valley. This external factor is absent in the Sri Lankan case.

Coming back to the issue of majoritarianism and Sinhala-Buddhist fundamentalism in Sri Lanka, it is an established fact that the LTTE's absolute defeat in May 2009 has further emboldened Sinhalese Buddhist nationalists, and some of them, supported by certain extremist Buddhist clergy and politicians, have targetted the island's Muslims and some Christians. It is a fact that the anti-Muslim campaign gained a strong foothold during the Rajapaksa regime (2005-15) through the majoritarian ethno-religious policies which were dictated by the Sinhalese Buddhist nationalist ideology, on constant display during the period, on television channels, movies and newspapers. During the ten years of his rule, Rajapaksa tried his best to encroach upon Tamil and Muslim-majority regions by erecting Buddha statues and temples with hardly any Buddhists in the vicinity, changing Tamil village names to Sinhalese names and instructing the Department of Archaeology to take over certain areas by claiming that they were historically connected to Buddhism. With his defeat and the coming into power of the national unity government in January 2015, religious bigotry has largely given way to a tolerant society but the threat of Rajapaksa returning to the centre-stage is never far away. His continuing politicking along nationalist lines, coupled with dormant anti-Muslim sentiment, make religious violence a very real threat in the years ahead.[14] This assessment came painfully true in March 2018, when prolonged anti-Muslim riots took place in the Kandy district, forcing President Sirisena to declare an island-wide emergency which was lifted only several days later. The episode left behind financial and emotional scars which would take a long time to heal. Though Rajapaksa adopted a very different role at the time, sounding quite convincingly like a liberal leader and playing a personal role in the mitigation of the disturbed environment, the active role in nurturing the Bodu Bala Sena, the perpetrators of the riots, was not hidden from the country.

Why should a majority community in a country be fearful of minority communities? One rather simplified but correct answer would be: this happens when the majority community is burdened with a minority complex. This in any case helps explain the Sinhalese Buddhists' suspicion and apprehensions about 'designs' of the Hindus, Muslims and Christians to outnumber them in order to snatch Sri Lanka from them. Hence, various measures were adopted over several decades to ensure that Sri Lanka remains theirs forever, particularly by insisting that the constitution enshrines the unshakable supremacy of Buddhism by making a suitable declaration. During his tenure in Sri Lanka, this author was often confronted with remarks which betrayed this peculiar mind-set, such as, 'Tamils, Muslims and Christians have other countries to fall back upon, but Sri Lanka is all that we have. We cannot afford to lose it. We must be on an eternal vigil.'

Integral to the Sinhalese Buddhists' view of the Sri Lankan Muslims is their formulation that the latter are in essence 'aliens'. Obviously this formulation is derived from the sense that Muslims are 'different' from the majority community. No less than Anagarika Dharmapala, a leading nationalist Sinhalese Buddhist monk, wrote in 1915 that a 'Mohammedan' is 'an alien to the Sinhalese by religion, face and language'.[15] This was a clear symptom of a closed mind to the concept of diversity within a country.

Inflammatory statements from 'responsible' quarters continue to keep the majoritarian flag afloat in Sri Lanka. Scholar monk, Walpola Rahula was reported as saying in 1996, 'Sri Lanka is a Buddhist Sinhala country. Seventy per cent of the country consists of Buddhists and Sinhala people. Also, Sri Lanka is the only Buddhist Sinhala country in the world. If we don't live here, are the LTTE and some of the Tamil parties asking us to jump in to the sea?'[16] A former Sri Lanka army chief, who also led the army in defeating the LTTE in May 2009 and later joined politics and became an MP and minister, said a year before the war ended, that the country belonged to the Sinhalese but there were minority communities and we (the Sinhalese) treated them like our (their) own. However, they must not try to, under the pretext of being a minority, demand undue things.[17] A leader of the fundamentalist Bodu Bala Sena was quite emphatic about the geographical difference between his country and Saudi Arabia and advised an unnamed 'you' to accept the culture and not to behave in a manner that could harm it.[18]

A healing touch, at last

In keeping with its image of a liberal, progressive administration, the Sirisena-Wickremasinghe regime took a welcome and sorely needed step by appointing an Inter-Religious Advisory Committee to advise it on cultural and religious issues confronting the country from time to time. President Sirisena, while announcing the decision to set up such a body on 25 February 2017, said that the government's objective was to build peace and reconciliation among all communities by enhancing the religious reconciliation among the Buddhists, Catholics (Christians), Muslims and Hindu devotees. 'Issues are arisen on some occasions due to the activities of extremists,' he said, addressing several religious leaders from all the religions practised in Sri Lanka. But it is the responsibility of everybody to find solutions for them with understanding.[19]

A few months after the government set up the Inter-religious Advisory Committee, the executive director of the National Peace Council Dr Jehan Perera, a well-known peace activist, quoted in this book earlier, said at a National Inter-religious symposium that the nation was now free. 'We feared bombs during the war,' he said. 'We feared 'white vans' (a euphemism for unmarked vans used in abductions of political dissidents and independent activists by intelligence and security agencies during the Rajapaksa regime) during the last government. Today we are governed by the two main political parties. There is a certain agreement and consensus. We need a new consensus through a new constitution agreed to by all the people. There should be agreement regarding the solution to the National Question and we need economic development.'

While internet searches for reports on further activities on behalf of the government-appointed Inter-religious Advisory Committee yielded no result apart from the President's initial announcement, the activist-run National Peace Council, a 10-year-old initiative, has been working steadily on reconciliation programmes throughout the country.

A far more stable environment than before admittedly exists in Sri Lanka today, but as the March 2018 religious flare-up in the Kandy district, showed, the peace achieved is in reality a fragile one; and until a nimble state mechanism is set up to nip in the bud any attempt to disturb the calm, sustained peace will remain more illusory rather than a tangible achievement.

Cow-vigilantism in Sri Lanka?

Those who know their Sri Lanka would find it difficult to believe that the current Hindu vigilantism against cow-slaughter and beef-eating in India has transported itself to the neighbour where all the religious communities traditionally eat beef, including Hindus. Beef and beef dishes are highly popular for their relative cheapness and nutritional values. Tamil restaurants do not serve beef but Hindu Tamils eat beef in Sinhalese and Muslim restaurants. This has been the norm so far.

But a surprising change has occurred, though still restricted to small areas in the north and the south. About two years ago, a new Hindu organisation called *Shiva Senai* (Soldiers of Lord Shiva) was set up in the Jaffna peninsula and gained some notoriety in the mid-2018 when it launched a protest against cow slaughter. The movement was quickly rewarded, and cow slaughter was banned in parts of the Chavakachcheri town. The slogan raised by the agitators was significant, 'This is the land of Hindus and Buddhists. We worship the cow. Our tradition must be respected.'[20]

Two things invite immediate attention: the complete absence of any reference to the Muslims who also live in Sri Lanka, including in its northern and eastern parts. Secondly, a Tamil organisation was speaking on behalf of the Buddhists who are all Sinhala-speaking. Only 10 years earlier, Chavakachcheri and the rest of the north had seen the end of the Tamils *vs.* The State war. As this book amply shows, there is little love lost between the Buddhist-Sinhalese and the Tamils, most of whom are Hindus.

This unexpected anti-Muslim agitation surfaced at a time when Sri Lanka had been witnessing far more serious assaults on the Muslim community in the central and southern parts of the country. A fair number of anti-Muslim riots have occurred in the last four or five years inviting rising concern from national and international quarters.

This also came in the wake of an official relationship established between the Bodu Bala Sena, the RSS, the VHP and several other Hindutva organisations of India. Reports suggest that there is an Indian connection to the Shiva Senai outfit, too.

Analyses of communal riots in India point to the conclusion that in almost all such incidents, Muslim business establishments were the prime targets while attacks on Muslim homes and individuals definitely were also included. The same conclusion was reached while analysing the anti-Muslim riots which had taken place in the Rajapaksa regime and thereafter. And as we will see presently in this book, one major purpose of the anti-Tamil riots that had occurred in Sri Lanka in the 1950s through the 1980s until the advent of the LTTE on the scene, were primarily targetted at Tamil business establishments. At the time of the 1983 riots, Colombo economy was dominated to a significant extent by big Tamil-owned-and-run companies, and at the end of the riots none had escaped unscathed. In India too, the anti-Muslim riots played havoc with Muslim businesses, wiping out entire business districts which were later taken over by Hindus as their own business establishments.[21]

The so-called Shiva Senai's decision to bring the Buddhists into its range of concept and programme is apparently intriguing, apart from the obvious contradiction in logic and history. Does this signify that a new and otherwise unthinkable alliance is being built upon the common plank of hatred for Muslims? Even though Buddhists, including monks, are beef-eaters as indeed are Hindus, a shared anti-minority feeling is probably unfolding some undisclosed agenda of the two communities. Otherwise, it is not possible to explain why the Tamil leadership maintained silence while concentrating its entire energy on fighting for a political solution to the national question. The Tamils' tallest leader R. Sampanthan eventually issued a statement in which he actually advised the Muslims to heed the concern of the Hindus and skirted showing any sympathy to the Muslims. And the sudden Tamil ire against the Muslims did not remain confined to that religious minority group, but spread to affect the Christians as well. At the time of the 10 February 2018 local government elections, some Tamil political groups and media ran a regular campaign against re-nomination of the Jaffna mayor Emmanuel Arnold, as a protest against the 'Christian domination' of Tamil parties. Does this not portend a new danger for Sri Lanka? While Muslims rarely became part of the Tamil militancy, Christians played a considerable role in it, especially in the LTTE. While the LTTE drove the Muslims and Buddhists out of the northern and eastern regions, there was never any anti-Christian move by it.

That the incidents in Jaffna were not isolated was soon proved when Buddhist-Sinhalese took up the cause of cow-slaughter in the south. Just as the Tamils had chosen the Chavakachcheri town, where a substantial Muslim population lives, so the Buddhists chose Dehiwala, a suburb of Colombo where a sizeable Muslim population lives. A giant hoarding in the Sinhala letters was put up depicting Hindu God Lord Shiva astride his celestial vehicle, a bull, proclaiming that 'God bless those of you who don't eat beef'. A newspaper report said that a ban on beef sale had been imposed at Embilipitiya, also a southern town and again with a Muslim population. So, we are faced by the questions: What is all this adding up to? And was all this purely accidental or was there a definite design behind the protests in the north and the south on the same issue by two communities which are not only racially and faith-wise different but also historically confrontationists and had never run a movement together since independence?

Much ado about the abaya

But the beef issue was not the only stick the Tamils had chosen to beat the Muslims with in the mid-2018. Muslim women, who had traditionally dressed themselves in the *sari* in the Sinhalese style, were lately changing over to the Arabic full-length gown-like dress, *abaya,* in consonance with a world-wide trend for Muslim women to dress more conservatively than before, in a reaction to the rising crescendo of anti-Islamic sentiments. One would have thought that Sri Lanka was free of such wanton anti-Islamic sentiments as being seen in the West and in countries like India. For one thing, though Sri Lankan Muslims speak Tamil, they prefer to identify themselves with Arabs whose merchants traded with the island in the medieval period. The truth, however, is slightly different. Sri Lankan Muslims consist of those of Arab-origin, local converts plus Indian Tamil-origin as well as Keralite-origin. In this perspective, Muslim women's growing use of the *abaya* was seen as an outcome of the growing Arabisation and Wahabisation of the community, and may have riled Sinhalese-Buddhists and Tamil Hindus. The development also appeared to be somewhat unnatural as Sri Lankans had traditionally been liberal in the matter of dress, choosing to wear both traditional and western clothes dictated by individual preferences. Nobody could have imagined the outside world intervening in such an intensely personal matter, betraying a stiff dose of conservatism. It would appear that Tamil Hindus may have been disconcerted with the Muslim women identifying themselves with the Arabians, rather than the historical South Asian, culture. A similar thing had occurred in Pakistan after the Partition of India. The newly-created Pakistan sought to replace its South Asian (alias Indian) identity with a Middle Eastern-Central Asian identity, a move which eventually failed because of its unnaturalness (See Aparna Pande, *Explaining Pakistan's Foreign Policy, Escaping India,* Routeledge Imprint, Francis & Kline, Abingdon, Oxon, 2011). Pakistan's confusion was augmented by the George W. Bush administration's unique reading of geography and labelling of Pakistan and Afghanistan as part of a 'Greater Middle East', an intellectually dishonest formulation which remained confined within the US administration. Both Pakistan's desire to earn a Middle Eastern identity and the Bush government's painting all the Muslim countries in parts of Asia and Africa as Middle Eastern were in denial of geography, history and culture encompassing language, dress and cuisine.

Similarly, when Sri Lankan Muslim women preferred to wear an Arabian dress, it was out of sync with their language and culture. But their source of inspiration was a world-wide phenomenon, which itself was a by-product of the rising anti-Islamic rhetoric and action. Therefore, what Sri Lankan Muslim women were doing in the mid-2018 had more substance and was likely to persist.

For the purpose of this book, however, the issue has to be understood from the point of view of the overall political situation in the neighbourhood and possible consequences for a period of stability and development which should interest both India and Sri Lanka. If the Sri Lankan state failed to safeguard Muslim women's choice of dress, the permanently fragile communal relationships between the four religious groups, the Buddhist-Sinhalese, Tamils, Muslims and Christians, might at a future date be jeopardised. In mid-2018, four Muslim teachers of a prominent girls' school in Trincomalee faced serious breaches of their personal freedom on grounds of wearing the abaya. They had to leave the school through no fault of theirs. This was a clear case of injustice. At the same time, the so-called 'RSS connection' was being openly talked about to explain the malevolent turn of events between the Hindus and the Muslims. So the Indian government should be mindful of this relatively new and negative development. Lastly, the Tamil and Muslim leaderships should come forward and take the matter in their hands for reaching an honourable solution to an issue which is essentially a non-issue.

The gravity of the situation, which remained low-key, could be perceived by the fact that both the Hindu Tamils and Muslim Tamils were engaged in a kind of silent competition to gather financial and political muscle, as if to brace for future uncertainties. In Hindu areas, a certain 'North Indian influence' was being talked about and Muslim areas spoke of suffering from a 'sudden attack' of fear psychosis. While Islam was becoming visibly more prominent than before with new mosques springing up and massive educational institutions being set up under political patronage, Hindus were seeking a kind of clandestine Brotherhood of Common Hatred with their traditional nemesis, the Buddhist-Sinhalese, against the Muslims and Christians. A veritable communal cauldron, far more complex than what had been experienced so far, could well be on the boil.[22]

NOTES

1 Tessa Bartholomeusz and Chandra R. de Silva, *Buddhist Fundamentalism and Minority Identities in Sri Lanka,* (Albany, New York State University Press, 1983).

2 Meera Srinivasan, 'Sri Lanka shifts May Day to May 7,' *The Hindu,* 29 March, 2018.

3 www.wikipeda.com, *The Fundamentalism Project, Study Conclusions.*

4 The BJP claims that *Hindutva* represents 'cultural nationalism' and its conception of 'Indian nationhood', but not a religious or theocratic concept. It is 'India's identity', according to the RSS Chief Mohan Bhagawat. However, in today's terminology, 'Hindu' clearly refers to the Hindu religion, not to an Indian nationality. Scholars believe that cultural nationalism is just a euphemism meant to mask the creation of a state with a Hindu religious identity. The Oxford English Dictionary defines the term as originally *Hindutva* is the state or quality of being Hindu or *Hinduness.* In later use, it defines *Hindutva* as an ideology seeking to establish the hegemony of Hindus and the Hindu way of life. According to the Encyclopaedia Britannica, 'Hindutva (Hinduness) [is] an ideology that sought to define Indian culture in terms of Hindu values.' In a 1995 judgment, the Supreme Court of India ruled that 'Ordinarily, Hindutva is understood as a way of life or a state of mind and is

not to be equated with or understood as religious Hindu fundamentalism...it is a fallacy and an error of law to proceed on the assumption...that the use of words Hindutva or Hinduism per se depicts an attitude hostile to all persons practising any religion other than the Hindu religion.... It may well be that these words are used in a speech to promote secularism or to emphasise the way of life of the Indian people and the Indian culture or ethos or to criticise the policy of any political party as discriminatory or intolerant.' RSS leader Vinayak Damodar Savarkar said, 'Hindutva is not a word but a history. Not only the spiritual or religious history of our people as at times it is mistaken to be by being confounded with the other cognate term Hinduism, but a history in full...Hindutva embraces all the departments of thought and activity of the whole being of our Hindu race.' The central concepts of Hindutva are said to be *cultural nationalism, decolonisation,* uniform civil code, and *protection of Hindu interests.* https:// en.wikipedia.org/wiki/Hindutva.

5 Durga Das Basu, *Introduction to the Constitution of India,* 18th, ed., Prentice-Hall of India Pvt. Ltd., New Delhi, 1997, pp. 21, 27 and 111. The Preamble to the Constitution, as amended in 1976, reads as follows: 'We, the People of India, having solemnly resolved to constitute India into a Sovereign, Socialist, Secular, Democratic Republic and to secure to all its citizens: Justice, social, economic and political; Liberty of thought, expression, belief, faith and worship; Equality of status, and of opportunity; and to promote among them all 'Fraternity assuring the dignity of the individual and the unity and the integrity of the Nation...'

6 Steven Kemper, as quoted in Tessa J. Bartholomeusz and Chandra R. de Silva, *op.cit.* p. 2.

7 George Bond, Northwestern University, Conflicts of Identity and Interpretation in Buddhism: The Clash between the Sarvodaya Shramadana Movement and the Government of President Premadasa, in *Buddhist Fundamentalism and Minority Identities in Sri Lanka, op.cit.*

8 Pradeep Jegannathan, *On the anticipation of violence Modernity and identity in Southern Sri Lanka,* contributing chapter to *Buddhist Fundamentalism and Minority Identities in Sri Lanka, op.cit.*

9 Victor de Munck, *Sufi and Reformist Designs: Muslim Identity in Sri Lanka,* chapter in Tessa J. Bartholomeusz and Chandra R. de Silva (ed.) *Buddhist Fundamentalism and Minority Identities in Sri Lanka, op.cit.*

10 Terra J. Bartholomeusz, Sinhala Anglicans and Buddhism in Sri Lanka: When the 'Other' Becomes 'You', a chapter in *Buddhist Fundamentalism and Minority Identities in Sri Lanka, op.cit.*

11 Post-Synodal Apostolic Exhortation Ecclesia in Asia of the Holy Father John Paul II to the Bishops, Priests and Deacons, Men and Women in the Consecrated Life and All the Lay Faithful on Jesus Christ the Saviour and His Mission of Love and Service in Asia, http://www.vatican.va/content/john-paul-ii/en/...eccclesia-in-asia.html/

12 Muttukrishna Sarvananthan, 'Are Religious Conversions Taking Place in Sri Lanka?', www.colombotelegraph.com/index.php/sre-religious-conversions-taking-place-in-sri-,4 November 2016.

13 Ibid.

14 Neil DeVotta, *Engaging Sinhalese Buddhist Majoritarianism and Countering Religious Animus in Sri Lanka: Recommendations for the Incoming U.S. Administration,* 20 June 2016, The Review of Faith & International Affairs: Vol. 14, 2016, Issue 2: Faith, Freedom, and Foreign Policy.

15 Kalana Senaratne, 'Behind a growing social fissure,' *The Hindu,* 22 March 2018.

16 Roshan Peiris, 'Rahula hits back,' *Sunday Times,* 5 May 1996.

17 LankaNewspapers.com, 'Country belongs to the Sinhalese, Minorities cannot demand, says Sarath Fonseka,' 26 September 2008.

18 The Economist, 'Fears of a Religious Strife,' 27 July 2013.

19 The President's Secretariat, Colombo, 25 June 2017.

20 Meera Srinivasan, 'When anti-beef protests reached Sri Lanka,' *The Hindu,* 3 June 2018.

21 'Mosques, shops attacked in anti-Muslim riots in Sri Lanka,' www.newsindian express.com/.../anti-muslim-riots-in-sri-lanka, 8 March 2018 and Anirban Mitra and Debraj Ray, 'Implications of an Economic Theory of Conflict: Hindu-Muslim Violence in India,' *Journal of Political Economy, University of Chicago Press,* Vol. 122, No. 4, Aug., 2014, pp. 719-765, https://www.jstor.org/stable/ 10-1086/676316.

22 Meera Srinivasan, 'Fear of the abaya,' *The Hindu,* 9 June 2018.

3

The Wounded Psyche

SECTION ONE: COLOMBO AND JAFFNA— ONE NATION, TWO WORLDS

One day we too will celebrate our Victory Day.
Not your demolitions and reconstructions,
but our freedom to honour without fear...

—Luxika Nagendriran, *Voice of an Old Woman on Victory Day* (Write to Reconcile II)

COLOMBO is a sun-baked city in the lap of the glistening Indian Ocean, displaying fine civic sense; an efficient municipality; beautiful and manicured roundabouts; wide and clean pavements; well-maintained structures, the Fort exhibiting dazzlingly white colonial office buildings; the slums tucked away and poverty superficially hidden in the back streets. The residents seem to be enjoying their lives, are well-dressed, rushing along the roads; fewer women clad in colourful Sinhalese saris worn in the classical Sinhalese style, easily outnumbered by their sisters clad in smart western dresses and clicking their heels as they walk erect and fast; men still sport ties, perhaps painfully ignoring the oppressive heat, though body odours are discomforting. Tourists from all over the world throng the shopping malls, taking a break from sight-seeing, buying famous handicrafts and dresses, patronising the world-famous Odel departmental store. One can almost hear soft music floating in the evening air.

Residential quarters remain cocooned in enviable greenery, the whiteness of bungalows set off well against lush green lawns, always guarded by high walls and big gates, a relic of the many decades of strangers with cultivated interests and dangerous motives prying around and apparently devoid of honourable motives.

But then the capital city has always been like this, a prosperous and celebratory niche, in an island rocked by a chillingly bloody ethnic strife. This author remembers hectic social life of parties with guests dancing to the tune of lilting *baila* (Sri Lanka's folk music), feasting on mouth-watering western and Sinhalese fare; happily tumbling out well past the midnight hour, drunk in good measure; departing reluctantly and being rudely stopped at security check-points by stern-faced soldiers and policemen searching their vehicles with a fine tooth-comb. There were nights when this rolling *la dolce vita* was peremptorily shattered with huge explosions rocking the city. It was the time to pack up quickly and rush (this applied only to foreign correspondents) to the spot to gather information. Telephone lines would get jammed in a jiffy and one would not be able to verify from the government what had happened or, to put it succinctly, who the latest assassinated notable was.

It was only in the suburbs that the idyllic picture paled a bit, but not a great deal. Green would be more overwhelming; smaller well-maintained bungalows would dot quiet streets and quieter lanes. Different communities lived in apparent peace, putting behind the sickening history of blood-curdling communal riots which had always ended in massacres of minorities. The suburbs and, of course, the southern districts had also lived through two Sinhalese youth rebellions in the 1970s and the 1980s; the ruthless manifestation of state terror to put down frustrated young rebels; the long memories of fiery deaths by boys and men being forced into pyres of burning tyres while still alive and residents discovering the charred bodies the following morning, vainly trying to identify the night's victims. Peace in Colombo was also periodically shattered as and when hidden bombs went off demolishing important buildings, in the process, killing and maiming passers-by. Political assassinations by suicide bombers were ghastly, especially as both the assassins and their victims were blown up, with the mutilated limbs found to be hanging from tree branches or lodged in nearby buildings. But the streets were always carefully washed after the latest atrocity, the tell-tale signs of destruction wiped off and normalcy restored before the day was over. It was like living in a make-believe world at times, making one wonder where reality stood, in the fun-filled five-star hotels or in blood-soaked streets.

A very helpful guide provided by the Foreign Correspondents' Association of Sri Lanka put the situation at the time succinctly, 'Working in Sri Lanka can be an enjoyable experience despite occasional bomb attacks, massacres, military onslaughts and political upheavals if some basic precautions are taken.... Forewarned is definitely forearmed in Sri Lanka, where the military is increasingly becoming edgy.... Nevertheless, Sri Lankans by nature are a friendly people, officials less bureaucratic and telephones work quite well except when a bomb goes off in some part of the capital and everybody tries to call somebody to find out what has happened and nobody is able to get through to anybody.'

A different world

Up in the north, there was no such hide-and-seek game between fun and mayhem, for it was only mayhem and no fun; illegal but regular (almost by the minute) barrel-bombing by air force planes in daytime because that was when civilians and school children would be walking or cycling on the streets; fierce battles raged all around, life was reduced to the bare minimum; living side by side with bombed-out and burnt-out houses; long lines of refugees fleeing the latest battles; hundreds of thousands of residents escaping abroad to live away from a never-ending war. When you look at the raw census data today, it does not tell you why the Tamil population alone had reduced while all the other religious populations had grown. That is why the wounded psyche is more north- and east-centric, and this particular wound is more putrid than anything else.

If the war was carefully shunted out of Colombo except for the aberrations caused by intrepid agents of terror, war was what life had been reduced to in Jaffna or anywhere in the north and the east. It was impossible to escape its reach either in the city or in the towns or in the villages. The last scene of battle between the Tamil Tigers and the Lankan military forces was at Mullivaikkal in the Mullaitivu district. The LTTE was herded into a no-fire-zone earmarked by the army where an unknown number of civilians were already sheltered in the last 72 hours before the war was declared over on 19 May 2009. This village has now become a point of reference for good reasons. Every year on May 18, thousands of Tamil civilians (but no politicians) except the Northern Provincial Chief Minister C.V. Wigneswaran gather at Mullivaikkal to mourn the dead in a silent cry for justice which has eluded them for the last 10 years. During the war years (1983-2009) the spectre of destruction was ever-present everywhere in the north and the east. Even the citizens presented a different picture. If residents in Colombo exuded happiness and well-being, those in Jaffna looked broken, dispirited and hopeless.

Is it any wonder then that Sri Lanka today, 10 long years after the war ended on a bloody note, lives with a wounded psyche? People pulverised by ethnic, religious, economic and societal violence cannot simply hope to possess a psyche that is untouched and untroubled. Happiness seems like an inane emotion in such circumstances.

Visiting the Jaffna city 23 years after my last visit in 1994 (before the forced evacuation of the population by the LTTE), I was constantly caught by surprise. The surprise began after the fabled Yala Devi Express, a brand new train with all the latest technical innovations and a glass-covered luxurious observation coach, flew over the India-laid new track, stopping at or passing by brightly coloured, spic-and-span stations towards the east and then the north. Even the residential houses, glimpsed through thick foliage, looked newly built as indeed they were. All these were fruits of the massive infrastructural reconstruction undertaken by the Rajapaksa government after the end of the war in May 2009.

On all my five visits to the war zone spanning the north and the east of the island, between 1991 and 1995, I always travelled by the A9 highway connecting Colombo and Jaffna or Colombo by other highways to Trincomalee or Ampara or Batticaloa. The railway stations and the tracks in the north-east had long been bombed out by the LTTE to rob the Sri Lankan army of an easy access to the home turf of the Tamil Tigers. The highways, especially in the Jaffna peninsula, were all booby-trapped with landmines, hidden but only meant to explode when an 'enemy' vehicle would be spotted. There was no question of travelling from Colombo to the war zone without the LTTE 'visa', a faxed message from Lawrence Thilagar, manning the international desk of the world's most fearsome guerrilla and terror force, based in Paris (the French capital used to be the most hospitable refuge for the LTTE in the west until Sri Lanka's indefatigable foreign minister Lakhsman Kadirgamar succeeded in persuading the French government to restrain it. He had to pay for this act of 'treachery' to the Tamil cause with his life). One first obtained the army's permission to travel up to the current 'border', implying the end of the government-controlled territory. The army order would also coyly advise the traveller (always a foreigner, otherwise, it was only Tamil Internally Displaced Persons who would travel) that he or she would be proceeding further 'at his or her own risk', thus shaking off any responsibility on the part of the government for an unfortunate turn of events while travelling. Once one crossed into the 'liberated' territory, bamboo poles could be seen on either side of the road at intervals. The poles were to be avoided meticulously as a landmine would be lying dormant just below the surface.

During the daytime those days, Jaffna city and its various locations, such as, the completely demolished railway station, residential and commercial areas, churches and temples, markets, and in fact, the entire peninsula would remain eerily silent with little visible human movement. Of course, schools and colleges functioned, quite a few of them relocated to less risky zones outside the Jaffna city, even including a number of university departments. Similarly, the Jaffna Teaching Hospital functioned, the intrepid doctors and nurses braving swooping bombers to heal the sick. Like doctors and nurses in all war zones, those in Sri Lanka's war zone also shone like angels in a darkened life.

However, the scene would change dramatically as the day yielded place to the evening. The city in particular would spring back to life. Hundreds of bicycles would criss-cross busy streets on errands, bringing home vegetables and carrying students to teachers waiting at tutorial homes. Patients would be taken to doctors, relatives would be dropping in for chats; in short a normal urban life would be humming with a strange urgency, for time was always short.

Recalling my first journey to the peninsula in early 1991, I wrote: While it took an average of about forty hours to travel from Colombo via Vavuniya (only recently taken over by government forces) to Jaffna city, it was the utter deprivation of basics of life that numbed one's senses. A loaf of bread and coffee had to do for meals most of the time, though thanks to the sheer ingenuity of C. Shankaran and his faithful staff at Subhas Hotel, one would at times be treated royally with an actual meal of rice, lentils and a vegetable curry. If nothing was be available in the market, we (no foreign correspondent would travel alone to the war zone; always in twos or threes and even more) would be invited to Shankaran's home for what could only be described as an elaborate meal by the prevailing standards.[1]

As we advanced from Vavuniya into the LTTE-held territory, we were cautioned to take adequate notice of the seemingly innocuous bamboo poles stuck into the surface of the potholed road at regular intervals. We were advised to cross between two potholes, for they indicated the locations of the mines. A little carelessness or foolish bravado would invite instant death or maiming of one's limbs, we were told.

In those days, the peninsula and the entire north lay immobile during the day and woke up in a sudden and astonishing burst of energetic activities throughout the night. Encountering a traveller during the day would be a rarity but the same road would be full of hundreds of people, men, women and children, at night cycling away to urgent destinations and always carrying bundles of daily necessities.

The reason for the day-long hibernation and the night-long flurry of activities was because the dreaded bombers and helicopter gunships of the Sri Lanka Air Force would routinely go and bomb areas and locations identified by the government intelligence agencies as LTTE hideouts, camps and other establishments. What the air force actually bombed in most raids were civilian areas like residences, schools, churches and markets. This was also unavoidable in some cases as the guerrillas lived very much among the people. It was to avoid getting hit by aerial bombardments that the civilian population developed the practice of staying at home during the day (for the planes and helicopter gunships would come only during the day) and carry on its normal activities after dark.

The ubiquitous bicycle became the symbol of the civilian population's determination to maintain a semblance of normal life in the face of the terror from the sky. All petroleum-based fuels were prohibited from entering the LTTE-held territory; motor vehicles of any description were, therefore, out of bounds for civilians (except a few doctors and businessmen who still drove old models of cars, particularly in Jaffna city) who had to fall back upon the bicycle as the only mode of transport, though tyres and tubes were banned as well. The north, however, was not entirely devoid of motor vehicles. The LTTE ran hundreds of vehicles of various descriptions, from the all-purpose Bajaj auto rickshaws, called trishaws or tuk-tuks, to Nissan pick-up vans (in which LTTE fighters and workers generally moved) to LTTE chief Velupillai Prabhakaran's luxurious air-conditioned Pajero for its administrative and military purposes.

The longest moment

Once, travelling in an LTTE auto rickshaw from Jaffna city to Point Pedro to interview ideologue Anton Balasingham, I lived one of the longest moments in my life. I was accompanied by Daya Master, an affable low-level functionary, who in his civilian life was a teacher (hence the pseudonym) and who generally acted as a liaison officer for foreign correspondents in the early days of the Eelam War II. We e were scarcely out of the city when the vehicle stopped at a roadside shrine and the driver got down and offered quick obeisance to the deity.

'Travelling in the day is a bit risky,' explained Daya Master helpfully and translated something that the driver had meanwhile blurted out. 'He says that whenever he travels to Point Pedro, he first offers puja here.' Nothing more was said and we were soon on our lonely way. We did not come across any other vehicle on our way; the whole road lay utterly devoid of traffic.

Soon, a drone could be heard from a distance but the bright sky (one of the bluest I had ever seen, there being virtually no air pollution in the non-industrial area and vehicle-free peninsula) was empty and nothing could be seen. 'The next two kilometres will be crucial,' said Daya Master. 'There is no shelter until we reach Point Pedro.'

The drone had, meanwhile, given way to the steady growl of a bomber; the air force plane had spotted the lone vehicle moving on the deserted road and clearly wanted to have a closer look at it. Before we realised, the plane was over us. Was a bomb going to descend on us? The stifling suspense gave way to a welcome relief as the plane flew over and left us behind, took a curve and went back the way it had come. All this while there was pin-drop silence among the three occupants of the auto rickshaw.

A little while later, as we were talking in Balasingham's bungalow, the drone was heard again. 'Let's go out in the garden and have a look at the plane,' suggested the LTTE spokesman and we along with his Australian wife, Adele, went out. We could see the plane circling in the sky and then moving away into the horizon.

'The plane comes every day around this time,' said Balasingham. 'The air force is looking for my house. They want to bomb it.' I thought of the obvious consequences, since the bungalow was situated in a thickly populated area. 'Oh, they would be least bothered by such considerations,' he dismissed my dismay casually.

The air force made good its intention. For, during my next visit to the peninsula, I found Balasingham living in Jaffna city. 'They bombed my house finally,' he said matter-of-factly, a minor price paid for fighting the government of the country.

On my first visit to Jaffna since the mid-1990s, as I got off the train at the Jaffna railway station one evening in November 2017, I was impressed with the reconstruction in the peninsula. The brightly painted buildings, the newly tarred roads, plenty of new vehicles including the latest models of SUVs, hundreds of auto rickshaws; shops full of the latest merchandise; shops of electronic goods bursting with latest models; shoppers milling around. It was not just a normal urban setting; you could sense money flying around, and aspirational behaviour being flaunted in your face. As I looked around, my memories of people long-deprived living in a wasted city flooded my mind. I just could not reconcile the two.[2]

Over the next few days I moved around the city meeting people of different persuasions, delving into the present and the past, my initial surprise yielded place to a painful realisation that what had dazzled me initially was in fact a mirage, and that the present reality was no less painful. It came as a shock to me that almost no resident, including foreign diplomats (an unthinkable class of people during the war), shared my positive impression of the reconstructed city and the peninsula.

'It's not even skin-deep,' sighed former Vice-Chancellor of the Jaffna University, Prof. Balasundaram Pillay, whom I had met way back in early 1991—at the time working from an electricity deprived office and helped by a single large candle. 'What you are seeing is only the surface. You scratch the surface and the ugly, disappointing reality lies exposed. Eight years have passed since the war ended and peace has since prevailed. There was a good deal of developmental activities under President Mahinda Rajapaksa. International bankers and prospective investors trooped into Jaffna talking of making large investments and changing the war-ravaged face of the north forever.'

Within a short period of time, the hope-generating picture began to pale, and soon enough the popular verdict became remarkably pessimistic and largely negative. Investment in manufacturing has proved to be a red herring. Banks are fighting a losing battle with private finance companies in granting loans to households and recovering them. As the finance companies charge exorbitant rates of interest from their clients, the latter turn to banks to get further loans to repay the finance company loans. A chain reaction has thus set in motion. Debtors get dragged into increasing indebtedness, banks, too, get little or no returns on loans given, leading to low returns causing their profitability to fall. The finances of the indebted are so precarious that the Central Bank was forced to work out a bail-out package.

Agriculture and fishing, the two traditional occupations, show no sign of recovery with most of the cultivable land still under military occupation (the irony being compounded by the fact that military farms are flourishing on the very same land which their lawful owners cannot touch) and an unequal competition from southern fishermen increasingly fishing in the east with liberal licensing by the fisheries ministry has become a serious issue, now being treated by the Tamil leadership as a political issue as well, requiring an immediate solution.

As the provincial government led by chief minister C.V. Wigneswaran and the TNA have failed to concentrate on improving the economy, it is but natural that peacetime has brought only a cosmetic change in the battered former war zone. Bank managers I talked to wondered in unison what on earth had persuaded their managements to open so many retail banking outlets at the same time with scarcely any worthwhile industry, immediately after the government opened up the Northern Province to the outside world. Hotels have proliferated but with unsustainable room occupancy rates. A high-priced hotel in the heritage zone of Nallur offered me concessional rates if I wanted to stay there. Its room occupancy rate was abysmal; only a few foreigners were staying there at the time I visited Jaffna. Incidentally, as far as I could see, the hotel staff right from the manager down to the juniors were non-Tamils and the hotel was owned by a Sinhalese resident in Colombo. 'It's only retail trade that is doing well; as much as 90 per cent of business is with traders,' pointed out a banker. 'The rest of us are just twiddling our thumbs.'

But why is the environment so heavy with a sense of despondency in Jaffna? Why is it that the Northern Provincial government is largely viewed as a failure in bringing about improvement at the grassroots level by identifying, initiating and completing development projects and thereby generally improving the lives of the common people? The Chief Minister shrugs off the complaint, arguing that Colombo is uncooperative. The Opposition claims that he is more interested in ensuring his continuation in office and in this pursuit, his ongoing fight with Colombo is his tool to perpetuate his political space. 'How many times has he talked to Colombo to expedite release of funds since he has been in office?' was a typical question I heard.

The failure to attract investment in the manufacturing sector by foreign direct investors and their Sri Lankan counterparts has led to a situation where no industrial employment is being generated. However, in a remarkable exception, Kargill Food City, a Sinhalese-owned and managed large chain of departmental stores which long dominated in the south has now come to Jaffna. It recently extended its banking operations to the north and east and despite its limited capabilities, has ventured in manufacturing products required by itself and the ingredients procured strictly from local resources and manned by members of families affected by the civil war.

However, banks, hotels and various shop establishments have generated very limited white collar employment opportunities. Thus, high numbers of unemployed youth, who have survived the violent history of Jaffna, are filled with a strong sense of betrayal by both the national and provincial leadership, and this has added to the general atmosphere of despondency in the population. Political activist and analyst Ahilan Kadirgamar pointed out that the educated youth are constantly leaving the peninsula in search of suitable jobs. 'That is no sign of rebuilding of a ravaged economy,' he said. 'Local traders and small-scale industrialists, who had virtually lost everything during the war, are all steeped in loans they cannot service. Few local workshops have been either revived or set up; and therefore, Tamil mechanics and tradesmen like carpenters, plumbers and electricians get few earning opportunities.'[3]

Academic, author and human rights activist Rajan Hoole identified a severe lack of civic sense as a root cause of the Jaffna people's inability to rise and rebuild their future. 'Everybody is keen to take care of himself without caring to see what happens to his neighbour,' he said. 'Members of the diaspora send hefty sums of money to their families who spend it all away on ostentatious festivities. But the roads are unclean; dirt is thrown round, and nobody is bothered. No fellow feeling has been cultivated even though the whole North has suffered so horrendously.'[4]

The dramatic shift from the initial exuberance that followed the end of the war in May 2009 and the despondency that has since descended can be explained by pointing out the hopes for a better present that had arisen among the people, particularly the business class, and their quick realisation that their hopes after all would not be fulfilled. Expectations were initially high for obvious reasons; assuming that the local economy would now grow; based on these hopes, there were large-scale borrowings by businessmen and farmers.[5]

As business did not grow on expected lines, Jaffna businessmen began to default on repayment instalments, soon leading to increased payment frauds and dishonoured cheques. This was clearly one sign of the impending crisis. 'Honour suicides' by businessmen, mostly small traders, began to take place. Bankruptcy had since become almost a given fact of life with failed businessmen abandoning their businesses and running away from facing the consequences. Instead of healing the economic woes inherited civil war, Tamil businessmen gradually came to accept the lingering darkness in their lives.

As we have seen, the proliferation of banks, in an unequal competition with private finance companies in the peninsula after peace was restored, also resorted to reckless granting of loans with little safeguards. The outcome of such a lending policy could not have been any different from what eventually happened, leaving the banks with the burden of unrealised liabilities.

Farmers were also caught in the vortex of high borrowings and inability to repay. They were mostly preyed upon by private finance companies which persuaded them to borrow funds at absurdly high rates of interest in order to buy vehicles, paddy cutting machines and tractors, which they did not really need. Banks also joined in the bandwagon, extending loans to farmers prior to harvesting. Unfortunately, the long period of deprivation followed by a sudden burst of borrowed affluence appeared to have affected them negatively. They splurged money on purchasing expensive consumer goods like TV sets, thus wasting expensive funds. Crops at the same time brought in poor prices; it became difficult for them to make ends meet. Failures to repay the instalments forced them to sell off the goodies they had so lovingly purchased; but a stress-free life still eluded them. They failed to obtain funds necessary for continuing farming and running households. As doors kept closing on the failed farmers, suicides became the only escape route still available to them.

In a shockingly suicide-prone country, the north stands out as particularly affected. According to the Minister for Social Empowerment and Welfare S.B. Dissanayake, in the years after the war, 400 suicides had been reported from the north as also 300 attempted suicides. The reasons for this high rate of suicide were mainly economic; but a deep sense of sorrow at the loss of relatives and friends during the war also drove people, especially women and single parents, to this drastic step. Suicides were chosen more as a relief from an unbearable life than anything else. Unofficial statistics quoted by social activists claim that the average monthly rate of suicide in the north is 30.[6]

The long civil war also brought in its wake a social evil peculiar to the region, that of child marriage. As the LTTE increasingly forced the recruitment of young children into its fighting cadre, many parents often married off their under-age daughters unknowingly facilitating child trafficking and other abuses. The sense of guilt caused by such acts later led to suicides by parents, especially single mothers whose numbers are high in the context of the population.

Bhavanandan's story

At around 5.30 in the morning on a hot day in November last year, when I was waiting at the Jaffna railway station for the Yala Devi express due an hour later, a diminutive, slightly built man came and sat beside me. We soon began to talk.

That was how I met Bhavanandan, a retired Sri Lankan government official who lived in Colombo and was visiting his family members in Jaffna. As was my wont, I asked him to describe his experiences of the war. Readily enough, he began to talk in an affable tone.

'I was working in Colombo and lived there with my family,' he began. 'Therefore, I have no personal experience of the war, except the war-related incidents that happened in the capital. But I can tell you about my family's experience in Jaffna.'

It was sometime after the Indian Peace Keeping Force (IPKF) had arrived in 1987 to fight the LTTE. Indian soldiers were not used to urban guerrilla warfare and were suffering heavy casualties. But they had enormous resources and fought back tenaciously.

Urban guerrilla warfare involved street-fighting, which necessarily meant that civilians were, more often than not, unintended victims of vigorous bursts of shooting, mines going off, fire spreading in congested areas. As a way out, the IPKF had set up refugee camps in closed school buildings. There was one such camp just across the street where Bhavanandan's family lived, his grandmother, father, mother, brother and sister.

On the fateful night, an IPKF troop carrier exploded right in front of his father's house. The night was pitch-dark; nothing was visible. His mother, brother and sister were already sheltered in the camp. Only his grandmother and father remained in the family home.

Seven Indians lay dead right in front. Curious to find out what was happening, his father opened the front door, just a teeny bit. But the light in the room that shone through the chink and it was enough for a soldier to target the father. In a moment he lay dead, with a hole on his forehead and blood oozing out.

His grandmother, hearing the gunshot, had meanwhile rushed into the room, and taking a glance at her dead son, threw open the door and rushed out. A soldier quickly grabbed her, barking, 'Where are you going?' Grandmother understood the question only by the sharpness of the bark, and pointed to the school building. Jerking out her hand from the Indian's grip, she then ran across the street and disappeared into the shelter.

As his narration came to an end, Bhavanandan sat still, looking straight ahead. I sat numbed, the sheer impersonal tone and the staccato style in which he had described his father's terrible death, without a trace of rancour or embellishment, had affected me deeply. He knew very well that I was an Indian and that it was an Indian who had killed his father. The enormity of all this hit me hard.

... and Kannan's

Four feet high at the most, wizened face, white thick hair, clad in the world-famous fast-food chain's Jaffna franchise uniform, a pronouncedly meek man, Arunayagam Kannan wipes the tabletop and serves me my chicken hot dog and coffee. I start talking to him. He readily tells me his name and then as I start probing his background (which I knew for certain would be a tragic one), he clams shut and goes off quickly, leaving me a bit puzzled.

But he comes back soon, accompanied by the suave young man who had taken my order at the spacious counter, who asks me, 'Sir, what did you ask him about?' I explain that as he is an old resident of Jaffna, I would like him to describe his experience of the civil war. Kannan is standing by, listening intently and the young man relays my query. He begins to talk rapidly in Tamil and the young man keeps translating. Kannan had lost his entire family during the militancy and the war; two of his sons were LTTE fighters and died in battles; the third son who survived the war died in a road accident; his wife could not survive the trauma; and today he is left with painful memories; this job and an empty house. Does he have any grievance against anybody, the government, the army, the Tamil Tigers? None, is the reply. He has accepted his fate without any rancour. As he waits on and serves scores of people daily, mostly young boys and girls enjoying their lives, he blesses them for having escaped one of the bitterest histories of mankind. In my mind, I salute Kannan for his humanity.

Massacre at Jaffna Hospital

Just about three weeks ago, the administration, doctors and nurses at the Jaffna Teaching Hospital had observed the 'Remembrance Day', 20-21 October 2017. When I arrived there on an extremely hot November 2017 afternoon, the traces of the commemoration were still there in bits and pieces. The Director was not there, but a staff member of his office readily accompanied me as I wanted to visit the 'Wall and the Staircase'.

What are the wall and the staircase? For answer, I turn the pages of *The War in Sri Lanka: Unending Conflict?* and read, '...a long, dark and unkempt high ceilinged corridor, a large number of rooms opening into it on either side and a cemented path outside; the walls pockmarked with gunshots, but the more compelling sight is of blood splattered on the walls, lots of it, slightly yellowed by the passage of three years. As you look at the walls, kept undisturbed as they became a bloody canvas that fateful day in 1987, the force of the tragedy strikes you hard, very hard indeed. For, while to the Tamils of Jaffna this was the darkest deed by the Indians, to an Indian it was a tragedy of good intentions led astray by a combination of incomprehensible geopolitical factors and the inadequacy of a political leadership.'[7]

In an ironic but historically justifiable twist, the hospital today looks up to India for timely interventions and to its credit New Delhi responds positively. When I was visiting the hospital in November 2017, I was asked if I could pass on a reminder to the Indian consulate in Jaffna for help in procuring a desperately needed machine. When I broached the subject, the consulate informed me that the request had already been conveyed to New Delhi and that the machine would be on its way soon. India has been helping the hospital, the main hospital in the north, in various ways, but the more detailed needs can only be answered by Colombo and therein hangs a tale of delays, such as, filling up vacant posts in vital areas. As is perhaps the wont of most government-run hospitals in developing countries, the Jaffna Teaching Hospital, too, suffers from dearth of doctors, nursing staff and medical equipment.

A wobbly economy

However, while the Tamil leadership remains engrossed in highlighting their political demands, the people in Jaffna recognise their economic woes as the most important of all issues plaguing them. And finding a resolution to these woes is where the provincial government has clearly failed to perform. 'There is a very serious economic crisis; the infrastructure for development does not exist, Jaffna is educationally backward. Even the media do not highlight the economic issues,' Kadirgamar rued. Unemployment is very high and Jaffna urgently requires setting up of small-scale industries. Most small factories were destroyed during the war. Due to the severe dearth of local jobs, young boys were migrating to West Asia and Malaysia. Young girls were going away to Katunayake for jobs in garment factories. Even donors and NGOs were pulling out of the north. The Asian Development Bank had been approached for finance and technical assistance in setting up small industries, but there is nothing on the ground yet.

A tragic manifestation of the continuing economic woes is the exceptional rate of suicide in the north, as noted above. With almost 6,000 people (288 per 100,000 inhabitants) killing themselves every year. Sri Lanka has the fourth highest suicide rate in the world. But the shocking incidence of suicide in the north is clearly a by-product of the long years of the war and its aftermath. People's hopes for a rejuvenated economy lie shattered and suicides are often the tragic result.

The South always wins

What is galling for the northerners is that while the post-war period has brought in considerable investment in infrastructure, new businesses, bank lending and a flourishing retail trade, the benefits of which have almost entirely gone to investors and manufacturers from the south.

The economic assets of the north were almost entirely destroyed during the war; the industrial units were ruined; skilled workers either fled elsewhere or got sucked into the war. But what had truly demolished the hopes for a better life was the obvious discrimination displayed by the government and the commercial and industrial establishment in the south. Many local entrepreneurs continue to feel discriminated against by the state.[8]

They state their experience shows that it is easier for southern firms or even those from overseas to land contracts with the concerned ministries and departments in Colombo. This happens because the government has not introduced a level-playing field for the northern entrepreneurs and businessmen who have suffered so much during the decades of the ethnic strife. Conversely, northern entrepreneurs and businessmen, unless long established in the south, are just a handful, and rarely get to tap the southern market.

Today's situation is in fact a culmination of independent Sri Lanka's historic acts of omission and commission. After the most horrendous 1983 holocaust, it was found that almost all the Tamil-owned business establishments—and at that time, the Tamil business community was a major economic force in the country—had been vandalised. Since then, the Tamil community could never stand up as a dominant force in the south. As a matter fact, not only businessmen who were always easy targets at the time of mob vandalism, but also a large number of professionals, well-established in the south, decided to relocate in the north-east.

Under the circumstances, the economy of Jaffna is necessarily service-oriented with no locally-registered company big enough to be a player in the Colombo Stock Exchange. The circumstances also dictate that local products are more expensive than their southern competitors due to the latter's larger market exposure and concomitant lower prices.

The spectre of PTA

It is clear to any visitor to the north that the continuation of the dreaded and much-abused Prevention of Terrorism Act (PTA) continues to agitate the Tamil mind. While the most visible irritant till recently was the frequent and public presence of soldiers on the streets of Jaffna and elsewhere in the north, it is now much less. But the continuation of the PTA, contrary to the solemn government assurances to abolish it, continues to rankle with the people.

The Northern Province chief minister C.V. Wigneswaran was in the attack mode right from the moment he began answering my questions. 'Politically,' he said, 'there is much confusion. The government leaders are unable to resolve their traditional reservations regarding granting the legitimate rights of the Tamil speaking people, faced with an international community waiting to know the causes for their reluctance. Nearly 10 years after the end of the war, the PTA brought in 1979 is still in force. (The) government gave (the) undertaking to the international community that they would withdraw (it). Still, nothing (so far has been) done.'[9]

Asked about President Sirisena's UN session address in 2017 stating that hasty reconciliation would not yield results, the Chief Minister began on an appreciative mode, 'The present President is a humane person. But he is also conscious of limitations, politically and otherwise.' After 69 years to say hasty steps towards reconciliation would not yield results seemed a hyperbole. He said in reality, no steps had been taken to understand the problem of the Tamils so far and all steps, 'hasty or otherwise', had been in fits and starts lacking cogency and conviction. He felt, the President's UN statement was mouthing of an excuse to delay the reconciliation process. Sinhalese leaders then and now refused to see what went wrong at the beginning when independence was granted. Their hegemonic attitude is still continuing. Without coming out of such an attitude to make statements of this nature only served to confirm their lack of interest in reconciliation, he said.

What, then, should be the right steps towards enabling the reconciliation process? Wigneswaran believes that the Sinhalese leaders must realise that they were unable to 'annex to themselves' all (the) political powers and authorities from the British when they left, since the Britishers and the Tamil leaders believed in the sincerity in the new dispensation.

This was brought out by the last British Governor-General Lord Soulbury when he wrote to a famous author B.H. Farmer following the 1983 anti-Tamil riots in Sri Lanka, to the effect that 'if we had known this would happen, we would have given (to Sri Lanka) a federal constitution'. In other words, neither the Britishers nor the Tamils were aware at the time of independence (1948) of the 'hidden hegemonic aspirations' of the Sinhalese political leaders.

Right from the beginning of independent Ceylon (renamed Sri Lanka in 1972) Sinhalese leaders started working towards a Sinhala-majority polity. They refused to accept that the Tamils had been the 'occupiers' of the north and the east 'from pre-Buddhist' times.

Wigneswaran said, 'In fact, the Sinhala language came into vogue only in the sixth or seventh century A.D. The Tamils had been occupying the north and the east long before that for centuries. In 1919, the then Sinhalese leaders Sir James Peiris and E.A. Samerawickreme accepted the fact that the Tamils had always been the majority community of the north and the east from time immemorial.' So, the first point to remember was that the Sinhalese leaders at the time of independence spoke a different language, but after independence, showed a vicious characteristic unknown to the outside world. As a consequence, the Tamils of the north and the east were deprived of their 'inherent' rights.

Secondly, this meant in the Sri Lankan context that one community arrogated the right to decide for another community. If the Britishers had any inkling of this eventuality, they may have taken steps to protect the Tamils' rights. 'Would they not have done so?' And, thirdly, why could Sri Lanka not rectify its waywardness? The Chief Minister believes that only a federal constitution can amend the historic wrong done to the Tamils.

Another sore point with the Tamils is the issue of return of civilian land taken over by the army even though so many years have passed since the war ended. Unlike most Tamil commentators, however, the Chief Minister is not entirely condemnatory.

'The answer (to the question of the Sinhalese sincerity on the matter) is yes and no,' he says. The present army commander, in his capacity as the commander of the peninsula a few years before, introduced a new culture of empathy for those who were deprived of their lands and assets. This initiative produced results in recent times. However, the pace of return of occupied lands and assets to civilians has been 'very' slow. Responding to this statement in May 2018, the Army Chief Mahesh Senanayake, said that more than 80 per cent of the occupied land had been restored to their owners and that some of the land would not be released as that was required for security purposes *(see below)*. His successor, too, draws praise from the Chief Minister, but ultimately the fact was that 10 years had passed since peace was restored and still over 65,000 acres of northern lands continued to be in military hands. This was the position till November 2017, but in May 2018, the figure stood at about 80 per cent, lower than the 85 per cent figure announced by the President in Parliament. Most of the occupied lands were in the Vanni region which was not under the jurisdiction of the Jaffna commander.

Was the government sincere in this matter? Wigneswaran seemed to have doubts. 'There is more talk and no action...Now the previous Jaffna commander has also come under the influence of the political leadership and I am not sure he would be free to act as he sees fit.'

He explained that it was not just a question of continuing military occupation of land but a much wider spectrum of the resultant loss of livelihoods (such as farming), natural resources including water resources (northern fishermen were for many years not allowed to fish in the adjoining sea), trade, and businesses. Many buildings which previously accommodated government departments and conference halls were still under military occupation. 'Besides, the proximity of the military to 'vulnerable' sections of our community needs to be taken into consideration,' he emphasised.

The women's burden

An authoritative report on how the legacy of the ethnic conflict has impacted on the women in the north and east paints a decidedly grim picture. It finds that the legacy of war continues (in July 2017) to impose hardships, particularly on conflict-afflicted women; lack of information on missing relatives; displacement from their land; economic deprivation; psychological trauma, vulnerability, sexual violence; plus, a militarised environment that reinforces much of the above.[10]

The women had played a leading role during the war braving a powerful military and an authoritarian government to press for (a formal acknowledgement of) truth and consequent accountability, particularly regarding the enforced disappearance of family members.

After the war, their campaigning helped bring Transitional Justice (TJ) issues on to the domestic and international agenda. At the heart of the promised TJ processes are these women's experiences of rape and sexual violence, deaths of family members, forced recruitment and killings by the LTTE, destruction of homes and communities.

However, in a sharp contradiction, the women have been largely ignored in shaping Transitional Justice policies. This is another vital area where the final report of the government-appointed Consultations Task Force on Reconciliation Mechanisms (CTFRM) gathers dust almost eighteen months after it was submitted. Even though both the President and the Prime Minister took keen interest in ensuring that the CTF materialised with a batch of dedicated highly qualified professionals working with a faultless agenda, the government's inexplicable apathy to the business of implementing the recommendations continues to puzzle both the country and the international community. Asked for the reason for this volte face, Chairperson of the CTF and eminent human rights lawyer Manouri Muttetuwegama declined to make a direct comment, but took pains to emphasise that though the CTF team was supposed to submit the report to the President and the Prime Minister in person (which would have recorded its importance as a state-sponsored project), it was eventually presented to former President Chandrika Kumaratunga. At the time, this unexpected development drew considerable public comment, though no clarification was forthcoming from the government. Muttetuwegama, however, expressed her unhappiness at the sudden cold-shouldering of the report by the government, which was expressed in no uncertain terms, and took pains to stress her appreciation of the personal interest and encouragement the team had received from Kumaratunga.[11]

Virtually all accounts of the continuing sufferings of Tamil women identify the issue of bringing a closure to the ultimate fate of those who remain missing as their most urgent demand. The women also insist that the truth and justice they seek must be part of a broader approach to meet their economic, social, psychological and security needs.

Muslim and Sinhalese women were also traumatised by the events in the north and the east at various times (such as those suffering when the LTTE forced the evacuation of Muslims and Sinhalese from the north and the east, and the Sinhalese women in particular when their husbands, sons and daughters, fathers and brothers were killed or maimed fighting during the war) but the Tamils' sufferings were much more widespread involving a far greater number of people. So, the issue of delayed transitional justice carries a much deeper sense of agony for the Tamils.

NOTES

1 Apratim Mukarji, *The War in Sri Lanka: Unending Conflict?* (New Delhi: Har-Anand Publications Pvt. Ltd., (2000), pp.44-47.

2 Apratim Mukarji, 'Changes in Jaffna are cosmetic,' *NewsIn Asia*, 27 November 2017.

3 Interview in Jaffna city, 19 November 2017.

4 Interview in Jaffna city, 23 November 2017.

5 Tomasz Augustyniak, 'Rising from the Embers: The Tamils of Sri Lanka are still stuck between a bloody past and hope,' *Quartz India*, 28 March 2016, https://qz.com/india/642159/the-tamils-of-sri-lanka-are-still-stuck-between-a-bloody-past-and-hope/

6 Quoted in *Sri Lanka Mirror*, 19 October 2017.

7 Apratim Mukarji, *The War in Sri Lanka: Unending Conflict*? p.89, *op. cit.*

8 Tomasz Augustyniak, 'Rising from the Embers: The Tamils of Sri Lanka are still stuck between a bloody past and hope,' *op. cit.*

9 Email interview dated 11 November 2017.

10 International Crisis Group, 'Sri Lanka's Conflict-Affected Women: Dealing with the Legacy of War,' Report N° 289/Asia, 28 July 2017.

11 Interview to the author in Colombo on 14 November 2017.

SECTION TWO: RECONSTRUCTION? WHAT RECONSTRUCTION?

What would you like, little baby
when I return from London?

Only you, Appa.

—Yogarajah Atchuthan, *Please Appa* (Write to Reconcile II)

TEN long years after the civil war ended, the heart-rending cry of Tamil women of the north and the east for a closure on their disappeared family members has not stopped. The human tragedy continues to overshadow the reconstruction and development efforts to rebuild the battered region. But the development agenda seems to be soulless, a mechanical endeavour to bring solace to the accumulated remains of the loss of a once-happy, well-rounded life.

An academic analysis of the political economy of the post-war Sri Lanka concludes that the reconstruction executed so far appears to be a mere technical exercise. Instead of being an inclusive process involving residents from the former war zone, the national government displays great determination and competence on its military strategy to win the war. But five years after the war ended in 2014 (when the stock-taking was being done) the government did not show significant determination to win the peace in the north and the east.[1]

The analysis recommends an immediate and long-lasting political solution to the ethnic conflict transforming the legacy of a violent conflict to peace with a focus on peace-building and ethnic reconciliation through post-war reconstruction efforts should be undertaken. Further, relaxing militarisation and the over-securitisation process primarily in the north would be a strong and effective panacea for sustainable peace. It also recommends improvement in donor-government relationships and government and NGO sector relations saying it would help ease funds inflow and developmental activities. Also, constitutional reforms should be put in place to safeguard the minority rights; improving relationships between western governments and (the) UN on human rights and war crimes concerns so as to address the political, diplomatic and domestic vacuums which still persist and need to be reconciled. Only then the 'soulless' reconstruction efforts would be transformed into a truly national endeavour to unite the north with the rest of the country. However, the former Defence Secretary Gotabaya Rajapaksa, who single-handedly planned and supervised the reconstruction projects in the north-east continues to believe that his government's approach to rebuild the infrastructure first in order to provide economic freedom to the people was right and would be resumed if the Rajapaksas returned to power in 2020 *(see below)*.

Even though the findings of the paper quoted above appear to be dated in the context of the sea-change in the island's political landscape with the national unity government in office for the last three years, some of its recommendations still hold true. Besides, the political upheaval witnessed since February 2018 has put a question-mark over an eventual implementation of some of the measures required to ensure an uninterrupted implementation of the reconstruction and reconciliation process.

Lanka faltering again

Foremost of the questions that have risen since the bitter inter-party feud broke out in the government is over the fate of the transitional justice and reconciliation process. Over the years in power, the Sirisena-Wickremasinghe government now sounds increasingly like the Rajapaksa regime in expressing its opposition to the issue of bringing justice to the Tamils by putting on trial those accused of torture and genocide of Tamil civilians and militants during and after the war. As noted above, the government also appears to have distanced itself from implementing the TJ system by consciously ignoring the recommendations of its own CTFRM regarding the trial of alleged war crimes with at least one foreign judge on each bench. The government, in an eerie echo of the Rajapaksa regime's stand, has shot this recommendation down.

The CTF recommendation, in effect, endorses the United Nations Human Rights Council's demand for a hybrid judicial mechanism consisting of Sri Lankan and foreign judge on each bench to try the alleged war crimes committed by both the Sri Lankan army and the LTTE during the last phase of the war (October 2008-May 2009).

Just as Mahinda Rajapaksa and his government steadfastly refused to honour the UN's call for transitional justice for the victims of the alleged (but widely documented) war crimes, the successor Sirisena-Wickremasinghe government, too, has been refusing to abide by it, thus, arousing international outrage.

Speaking at the UN General Assembly session on 20 September 2017, President Sirisena sounded quite defiant. 'Haste will not yield good results and the slow and steady path is the most suitable one to restore religious and communal harmony so that people of all communities could live in peace and harmony as equal citizens,' he said. Recalling Sri Lanka's 62-year-old association with the United Nations and its adherence to the UN conventions, policies and principles, he urged the world to show 'patience, understanding and support for its slow but steady march to create a peaceful and prosperous country for its people.'

Earlier in 2017, Sirisena in a desperate rear-guard action to ward off increasing attacks by the Rajapaksa-backed Joint Opposition in Parliament for giving in to international pressure, rudely rejected the United Nations' repeated call to appoint foreign (and presumably independent) judges to run war crime tribunals. He also took credit for his defiance of world opinion. 'Two weeks ago, the UN Human Rights Chief had said Sri Lanka must have international judges in the accountability mechanism,' he said addressing his party MPs. 'The following day, I had the guts to dismiss it (the demand).'

That the government had no intention to honour its commitments to the world body was demonstrated time and again. For example, on 6 February 2017, Sirisena revoked a foreign ministry order suspending and recalling an army officer, then posted as Defence Attache in the country's London High Commission, on the grounds that the Foreign Secretary had not followed the due procedure of consulting him (the President) before taking action. 'Brig. (Priyanka) Fernando was suspended and recalled without first conducting an inquiry and also before consulting the President,' sources in the presidential secretariat said. 'The Defence Secretary had also felt that the due process had not been followed. He apologised to the President. And when punitive action was contemplated, the Defence Secretary told the Foreign Secretary about his objection. And yet, the army officer was suspended and recalled,' the sources added, denying that the suspension, recall and revocation of the orders on the officer were connected to the upcoming local body elections.

A so-called UK-based Transitional Government of Tamil Eelam, representing separatist Tamils, urged the British government not to allow the army officer to leave the country, stating that several reports had been published identifying his regiment, Gemunu Watch Battalion of the 59th Division, responsible for war crimes and crimes against humanity during the final months of the war in 2009. According to the UN and other organisations, the 59th Division was the front-line fighting force that committed numerous war crimes including repeated attacks on hospitals, food distribution centres and civilians. 'An alleged war criminal on your soil is the best opportunity for the UK to take actions,' the Tamil body urged. Ironically, the Foreign Secretary initiated disciplinary action followed when a video went viral on social media showing the Brigadier making a throat slitting gesture to protesting crowds outside the Sri Lankan High Commission in London. But then, the imperative of getting the Sinhalese support in the local body elections proved to be much stronger than any call of humanity and the retrograde step by the President followed.

However, the propensity to fly in the face of natural justice and international commitments seems to be much more entrenched in the minds of Sinhalese politicians irrespective of their party affiliations, which helps explain why the country has fallen so badly behind in honouring its solemn pledges.

In his statement to the UN Human Rights Commission in Geneva on 14 September 2015, Sri Lanka's then foreign affairs minister Mangala Samaraweera sounded brave and high-minded, 'As a government that is responsible and accountable to her people, the national unity government remains firm in its resolve to do right by the people of the country, not in the least because of assurances given to the international community at any point in time, but because this is the only path available to ensure justice, remove the causes of terrorism and achieve a durable peace for the long suffering people in our country.'

It is not possible to reconcile this fine expression of high principles with the subsequent backtracking witnessed, sending Tamil leaders to such desperation that they had to publicly declare that they were waiting for a statesman to appear to bring the promised justice to them.

One of the most incomprehensible failures of the Sri Lankan government is in respect of the deeply-hated Prevention of Terrorism Act (PTA). Sri Lanka continues to dishonour its pledge to the international community to abolish it. Its wilful retention has in effect relegated the good governance government in the Tamil imagination to the level of the Rajapaksa regime. In a biting condemnation, the UN Special Rapporteur on Torture and Counter-terrorism, Ben Emmerson said in 2017, that torture of PTA detainees in Sri Lanka was on an 'industrial scale' and 'among the worst in the world'.[2]

Even in October 2016 (almost two years since the present government came into power), there were reports of eighty cases of custodial torture of PTA detainees, quoting a judge who had informed the UN official that as many as 90 per cent of cases brought to his court belonged to this category. Despite the welcome fact that there was a steep fall in PTA cases under the present dispensation, the uncomfortable truth was that even though the government had given an undertaking to abolish the law a little after it assumed power, the PTA continued to remain in the statute book.

Former foreign minister Mangala Samaraweera told the UNHRC on 14 September 2015: 'Additionally, Mr President, the government is committed to strengthening the National Human Rights Commission in line with the Paris Principles; sign and ratify the International Convention for the Protection of All Persons from Enforced Disappearances without delay; maintain the moratorium on the death penalty with a view to its abolition, release previous Presidential Commission reports such as Udalagama and Paranagama by the end of this month; begin issuing Certificates of Absence to the families of the missing as a temporary measure of relief; disengagement of the military from commercial activities; undertake security sector reform; invite a series of Special Rapporteurs to undertake visits to Sri Lanka in 2015 and beyond; issue instructions clearly to all branches of the security forces that torture, rape, sexual violence, other human rights violations are prohibited, and those responsible will be investigated and punished; review and repeal of the Prevention of Terrorism Act and replace it with anti-terrorism legislation in line with contemporary international best practices; review the Public Security Ordinance Act; and review the Victim and Witness Protection Act which was enacted this year.'

He further said, 'Today, we have a government in place which acknowledges the suffering of victims across Sri Lanka's communities, a government which recognises the mistakes of the past and is all too aware of the weaknesses of our institutions.'

Excellent words, but why has the same government turned its face away from taking seriously the recommendation of the CTFRM and meting out justice and succour to the thousands of sufferers, mostly women and single parents?

The curious role of Australia

A leading democracy Australia has reportedly played a major role in facilitating Sri Lanka's undemocratic actions throughout the civil war and thereafter. It is said to have significantly helped Sri Lanka in preventing militants and civilians escaping from Sri Lankan armed forces and taking refuge on Australian soil. All this has been dictated by

Canberra's overwhelming desire to keep illegal migrants (irrespective of their nationalities) off its borders.

A former Australian diplomat once posted in Colombo writes that there was an unholy alliance between Sri Lanka and his country serving mutual interests. Sri Lanka wanted to hunt down Tamil militants and civilians who were escaping by sea and landing in Australia to seek asylum. Australia helped Sri Lanka in this endeavour and turned back asylum seekers or sent them to nearby detention centres beyond its borders for which it has received international criticism. In this context, Bruce Haigh, a commentator and former Australian diplomat posted in Sri Lanka has said, 'returning asylum seekers and refugees to a place of danger is an act considered illegal under international law and attracts a strong legal sanction known as *sur place*, and in this instance makes Australia directly implicit in the crime of genocide.' Sri Lanka stands accused of committing genocide in the final days of the civil war.[3]

He further says that the Rajapaksa government received support and assistance from Australia in prosecuting its policy of genocide against the Tamil population. 'An Australian Federal Police (AFP) contingent is posted in Colombo to assist the local police and the navy to stop boats,' he writes. There are allegations that the AFP contingent is aware that Tamils returned illegally from Australian custody have been tortured in detention.

The former diplomat points out that Australia supplied patrol boats to the Sri Lankan navy for the express purpose of turning back boats, despite it becoming public knowledge that President Rajapaksa's brother, the then defence minister, was 'involved in the chain of people smuggling'. He describes the then Australian Prime Minister Tony Abbott saying on a Sri Lanka visit in 2013 that under certain circumstances torture could be justified, which was and 'remains an extraordinary statement'. This refers to the remark that Abbott made after returning from the CHOGM summit on 16 November 2013 that 'Obviously the Australian government deplores any use of torture. We deplore that wherever it might take place, but we accept that sometimes in difficult circumstances difficult things happen.' This statement drew an enormous amount of flak for the Prime

Minister who was asked repeatedly to explain it both in and out of Australian Parliament.

Australia's eagerness to side with the Colombo regime manifested itself in various other ways, too. For example the then foreign minister Bob Carr referred to Tamil asylum seekers as economic migrants instead of political asylum seekers. Julie Bishop, who succeeded him in the office, followed his rhetoric. 'Australian governments,' writes Haigh, 'have adopted the fiction that the minority Tamils were the aggressors in the civil war. Their position is that (the) Sinhalese won the war, peace has been restored, and the Tamils must accept it and get on with life; which consists of a military occupation of the north, confiscation of their land, desecration of their cemeteries, rape of the women, and marginalisation from economic activity; all against a background of bribery, cruelty and corruption.'

Apart from consistently supporting Colombo on the issue, Canberra has never joined the United Nations and the international community in demanding that Sri Lanka face the reality of a genocide squarely and bring justice to its own people. Eighteen months after coming into power, the Sirisena-Wickremasinghe dispensation ensured that Australia turned back Tamil asylum seekers who had been trying to reach the Australian shore.

NOTES

1 Rosanna Ampere, 'The Political Economy of Post War Economic Development in Sri Lanka,' *International Journal of Business and Social Research*, Vol. 94, Issue 12, 2014.

2 NewsIn Asia, 'Torture in Sri Lanka among the "worst in the world", says UN Special Rapporteur,' 14 July 2017.

3 Bruce Haigh, 'The Sri Lankan war crimes swept under the carpet,' *The Sydney Morning Herald,* 3 February 2017, https://www.smh.com.au/opinion/the-sri-lankan-war-crimes-swept-under-the-carpet-20170203-gu59yy.html

SECTION THREE: THE WAR MAY BE OVER BUT THE WOUNDS DO NOT HEAL

Not even ellaikal left,
we languish,
robbed of any trace that tell us
our place.
(Ellaikal—a stone used to identify the boundary of a piece of land)
—Kandiah Shrikarunaakaran, *Ellaikal* (Write to Reconcile II)

BY 2019, as many as 10 years had passed since the end of the civil war in May 2009. While civil liberties had been restored and the 'shadow state' of yore did not exist on the streets, shades of dark deeds still constituted parts of the public discourse. More alarmingly, the political stability and democratic governance which had been ushered in the country were now yielding place to political uncertainty and concomitant consequences.

In a disturbing development, Sri Lanka has emerged as still continuing with serious cases of human rights violations. The *Associated Press* reported on 8 November 2017, that it had reviewed 32 medical and psychological evaluations and interviewed twenty men who said that they were accused by the government of trying to revive a rebel group on the losing side of Sri Lanka's civil war (the LTTE).

After the publication of the report, the Sri Lankan government faced increasing pressure to answer for alleged human rights violations following a recent war crime lawsuit and allegations from over fifty men who said that they were raped, branded or tortured as recently as 2017.[1]

'Someone has to do something about this,' the report quoted Frank Arnold, one of the several doctors who wrote to the UN Human Rights Chief Zeid Raad Al Hussein and called for an independent investigation into the torture allegations. 'As forensic experts, we have seen many hundreds of Sri Lankans who have fled their country following torture over the years,' the letter from the physicians said. 'We continue to receive a worrying number of cases from Sri Lanka despite the change of government.'

One of the men investigated by the *Associated Press* said that he was held for 21 days in a small room where he was sexually assaulted twelve times, burned with cigarettes, beaten with iron rods and hung upside down. Another man described being abducted from home by five men, driven to a prison, taken to a 'torture room' pocked with blood splatters on the wall. Most of them said that their captors identified themselves as members of the Criminal Investigation Department, a police unit that investigates serious crimes. Some, however, said it appeared that their interrogators were soldiers.

In an assessment of the human rights situation in the island, the Human Rights Watch report said that the 'general openness' for media and civil society groups that had emerged after the electoral defeat of the Mahinda Rajapaksa government in 2015 continued till 2017. 'However, action stalled in 2017, on Sri Lanka's October 2015 pledge to the UN Human Rights Council (UNHRC), to address accountability and political reconciliation emerging from the long-drawn civil war.'[2]

Despite a presidential pledge to release names of people in government custody, particularly those who forcibly disappeared since the war's final months in 2009, the list was not yet been produced. The government enacted a law to give effect to the International Convention for the Protection of All Persons from Enforced Disappearance, but made clear that the law would not be retroactive (rendering it meaningless in the Sri Lankan context).

The Human Rights Watch said that the religious minorities also remained at risk. In June 2017, then justice minister Wijedasa Rajapakshe, publicly threatened a lawyer who criticised the government's failure to protect minorities. In September, the authorities took 31 Rohingya Muslim refugees into protective custody following threats by Buddhist extremists (who had openly vowed to push the Muslims out of the island and the government had declared that it would ensure their quick departure). There were further flare-ups of violence in Galle and Vavuniya in November between Muslims and other communities, with allegations of mobs attacking Muslim homes and businesses. In March 2018, a more serious human rights violation occurred in the Kandy district with anti-Muslim riots spreading and continuing even after a nation-wide curfew was imposed, inviting international condemnation and the UN Secretary-General calling for an immediate stoppage of the riots, dealt with in detail elsewhere in this book.

UN Resolution a non-entity?

In October 2015, the UNHRC adopted a consensus resolution in which Sri Lanka pledged to undertake several human rights reforms, including transitional justice demands arising from the civil war, and to establish four transitional justice mechanisms, including a judicial mechanism with 'participation of international judges, prosecutors, lawyers and investigators' with an independent investigative and prosecuting body.

Civil society leaders, appointed by the government, conducted nation-wide consultations in 2016 and handed a comprehensive report to the government in January 2017. It contained strong recommendations, including for a hybrid justice mechanism, acknowledging the need for independent international participation to ensure justice for victims of war crimes and other grave human rights abuses by all sides (meaning the LTTE). The report included the need for justice for all victims of the long conflict, regardless of ethnicity, religion or political persuasion.

As already noted above, neither the President nor the Prime Minister received the report publicly and it has since languished, with scant government attention. The government's response to the report since January 2017 had also been disappointing. Senior cabinet ministers explicitly rejected the recommendation that foreign nationals participate in the special court. Both the President and the Prime Minister publicly reiterated the point, and further emphasised that the government would not allow 'war heroes' to be prosecuted. Perhaps the most glaring failure of the government was its suspect conduct over the promised repeal of the truly dreadful Prevention of Terrorism Act (PTA). The two versions of a substitute law circulated for study by various UN organisations included 'troubling' provisions, such as, overly broad definitions of terrorist offences stretchable to peaceful political protesting—a fundamental right in a democracy. Symptomatic of the unacceptable nature of the draft anti-terrorism law to the Tamils (the main sufferers of the PTA) was the stiff resistance put up by the TNA, which ran the Northern Provincial government. The TNA said on 5 May 2017, that the proposed definition of terrorism would extend far beyond activities defined internationally as terrorism, replicating restrictions on free speech that had previously been used to punish dissenting voices of politicians and journalists, including the editor of *North Eastern Monthly* magazine, J. S. Tissainayagam. 'The definitions of acts of terrorism are also exceedingly vague and indeterminate and would have a chilling effect on advocacy in favour of greater diversity in Sri Lanka. We are shocked by the extent to which the draft framework curtails civil liberties, erode judicial control over the state security apparatus, and the staggering potential for abuse and torture,' the TNA said. What in particular seemed to have alarmed the Tamil leadership was the presentation of a *fait accompli*, an act which simply ignored official assurances given earlier, such as, safeguards essential to prevent torture like elimination of confessions (always extracted by force). 'The present framework envisages the admissibility of confessions which are deeply inadequate to prevent torture and abuse given the widespread and continuing practice of torture in Sri Lanka,' the TNA said.

Just as the Tamils and human rights activists were expressing their dismay and opposition to the draft bill, further expression of opposition came from a different quarter altogether but which nevertheless would have appeared to have played an important role in strengthening the government's resolve to dishonour its own commitment to the people and the world at large. The National War Heroes Front, an organisation of former and present defence services officers and blessed by Rajapaksa who glorified the officers for winning the war, issued a statement which poured pure venom on the CTFRM and the TNA and accused them of being on the payroll of Tamil separatists. Its president, Rear Admiral (retd.) Sarath Weerasekera said, 'It is a lowly and contemptuous attempt by (the) CTFRM together with (the) TNA and GTF, to seek punishment and bring discredit to the war heroes who survived. How much money has been paid officially/unofficially to the 11 members of the CTFRM by the separatist Tamil diaspora is not known, for no one with an iota of patriotism would present a report based purely on the evidence of the people instigated by the separatist TNA. The former head of the UNHRC Zeid Raad Al Hussein had also welcomed the recommendations of the CTFRM....So a report that could bring a grin on to the face of Zeid Hussein would also be one of such nature, and hence should be rejected *in toto*.' The 'war heroes' also specifically opposed the proposal to include foreign judges in trial courts to be set up for the purpose, the very point of reference on which the entire government led by the President has since agreed. As is well-known, no government can survive in Sri Lanka without bowing down to the wishes of the Sinhalese. So, the otherwise strange behaviour of the government to its own creation, the CTFRM report, is not really a surprise after all.

Yet, transitional justice lay at the root of post-war reconciliation and reconstruction of the former war zone; and the failure to advance from preparing a comprehensive and satisfactory action plan to its implementation clearly dented the government's credibility. Either insincerity or political compulsions dictated this volte-face.

An analysis suggests that Sri Lanka's search for transitional justice, arising out of the blood and ashes of the 30-year-long conflict, was destined to be confronted by different world views born of different nationalisms within the nation, Sinhala-Buddhist, Tamil and Muslim. Dissenting views dominated national discourses, rendering convergence of view a difficult, if not an impossible goal. As we have seen above, the Tamils and the Sinhala-Buddhists looked at the whole issue of reconciliation and reconstruction from completely different angles. One community was victimised by the war while the other community was widely and correctly regarded as the perpetrators of physical and political domination over the victims. It was but natural that in the post-war scenario, the communities would continue to spar with each other over the festering wounds coupled with an unsparing urge to seek justice. For Buddhist-Sinhalese, what made all this more galling was the role played by the international community which kept on insisting on a fair trial and the necessity of administering justice to the victims and punish the guilty. The fact that the international community empathised with the war victims, rendered any move to seek transitional justice all the more unacceptable to the dominant community. The problem lay precisely in such clear-cut definitions of guilt and victimhood.

The 2017 UN reports noted that barring a few highly visible cases, the police were not held accountable for routine torture and ill-treatment in custody. Both the 2017 reports by the UN Special Rapporteur on Torture and the UN Special Rapporteur on Counter-terrorism and Human Rights, submitted to the UNHRC, spoke of Colombo's failure to conduct credible investigations into cases of torture and corroborated accounts of continuing torture, including sexual abuse. However, the report noted that Sri Lanka's Human Rights Commission had access to alleged victims of custodial abuses. It noted some progress in ensuring women's rights in respect of trafficking, sexual and other violence. Further on the positive side, the report noted Colombo's continuing engagement with international organisations, though at times the government seemed 'unable or unwilling' to answer questions of concern that the CEDAW (Convention on the Elimination of All Forms of Discrimination Against Women) committee members put to the government delegation.

A wayward army?

In an undisguised flouting of international norms, the Sri Lankan army sent a batch of 49 soldiers to Lebanon on UN peacekeeping operations in February 2018. All the UN member-states are obliged to get their defence services personnel vetted by their national human rights commissions. In this case, the Sri Lankan army simply chose to ignore the requirement, inviting a strong protest from the Human Rights Commission of Sri Lanka (HRCSL).

In a letter to President Sirisena, HRCSL chairperson Deepika Udagama, said that the commission was astonished over the failure to seek its clearance. 'Further', she wrote, 'the commission was not informed that the said group of 49 personnel had to be deployed in Lebanon early. Deploying soldiers who have not undergone the vetting process is a complete violation of the agreement made with the Human Rights Commission.'[3]

The UN member-states which nominate or provide personnel to serve with the organisation must 'screen and certify' that such personnel have not committed criminal offences and/or violations of international human rights law and international humanitarian law. Those who seek to serve with the UN must attest such certificates and, where necessary, provide relevant information. The processes by which this can be done are outlined in Decision 2012/18 of the UN Secretary-General's Policy Committee.

Sri Lanka happens to be the first member-country to have obtained the opportunity to vet military personnel for peacekeeping operations by a national human rights commission. Completing this process with a high degree of credibility is essential to enhance the recognition given to Sri Lankan peacekeeping operation troops.

However, what clearly shocked the HRCSL was that it had learned of the *fait accompli* deployment of the 49 soldiers in Lebanon through a media report, a fact later confirmed by the army. As a result, none of the soldiers was cleared by the commission.

Even more shocking was the revelation that this was not the first occasion when a wilful defiance of the international norm occurred. Granted the vetting right by the UN in June 2016, the first violation was recorded the very first time Sri Lankan soldiers were sent on a peacekeeping mission in February 2017. While the HRCSL was still busy with the vetting process for a 200-strong contingent, it was informed by the army that the soldiers had already been vetted by the UN and, therefore, further vetting was not necessary.

Following the confusion thus created, vetting was suspended and later resumed after discussions between the government and the armed forces, including the police. In December 2017 the HRCSL received a list of 204 more soldiers destined for Lebanon. Before vetting, however, the soldiers were dispatched. In truth, though, the commission was scheduled to receive the relevant documents only on 19 March 2016. The full documents had not reached the HRCSL even by the first week of April 2018.

The army's response to the HRCSL's complaint was frankly evasive, talking of the high standards expected of its soldiers and deliberately avoiding any commitment on its part and answering the commission's specific concerns. This entire episode should be viewed against an unsatisfactory background, in which Sri Lankan personnel had failed in the past to maintain the behavioural standards expected of them, inviting disciplinary action. The army's conduct is difficult to explain because at this very juncture Sri Lanka was seeking to enhance and expand its participation in UN peacekeeping operations, and the army's acceptance of HRCSL's involvement was 'the most appropriate way forward with respect to screening of personnel.'

It was in October 2015, that Sri Lanka announced its decision to contribute more troops for UN peacekeeping operations, inviting immediate international concerns over the clouded antecedents of its armed forces during the civil war. Incidentally, the announcement almost coincided with the world body's investigation into human rights abuses in the island and subsequent confirmation of 'gross violations of international human rights law, serious violations of international humanitarian law, and international crimes in the context of the civil war.' 'Perpetrators of such violations', a report said, 'have enjoyed near-total impunity over many decades, as the Sri Lankan judicial system has failed to hold them accountable.'[4]

There is evidence, the report says, that this 'climate of impunity' affected the actions of Sri Lankan soldiers deployed abroad. In 2007, for example the UN Office of Internal Oversight Services (UNOIOS) investigated serious allegations of sexual exploitation and abuse of children committed by Sri Lankan peacekeepers within the United Nations Stabilisation Mission in Haiti. The investigation concluded that 'acts of sexual exploitation and abuse were frequent, occurred usually at night, and at virtually every location where the contingent personnel were deployed. In exchange for sex, the children received small amounts of money, food and sometimes mobile phones. Indeed, Haitian lawyers accused Sri Lankan peacekeepers of 'systematically raping Haitian women and girls, some as young as seven years old.' The damning findings led the Sri Lankan authorities to repatriate 111 soldiers, one Lt Colonel and two Majors on disciplinary grounds. ''This expulsion from Haiti constituted the single largest troop repatriation in UN peacekeeping history,' the report noted. Twenty-three soldiers were subsequently convicted of sexual exploitation and abuse, and were discharged, demoted, formally reprimanded or otherwise punished. But the report pointed out that these were merely disciplinary actions, where the severity of the allegations clearly suggested a need for criminal investigation and prosecution. No evidence emerged suggesting that any of the soldiers was ever prosecuted.

As scandals continued to rock various national armies deployed on UN peacekeeping operations, the United Nations was obliged to strengthen its vetting mechanism. However, it is pertinent to note that the latest UNOIOS report carried recommendations endemic to Sri Lanka. The report called upon the international community to ensure that no member of the Sri Lankan security forces was sent on a UN peacekeeping without vetting to establish that the individuals, including commanders, had not in any way been involved in human rights violations or criminal acts. Any allegations of abuse by Sri Lankan peacekeepers while on peacekeeping duties must be fully investigated by the authorities.

When one listens to the Commander of the Sri Lankan Army Lt Gen Mahesh Senanayake, one realises why the Sri Lankan army continues to suffer the legacies of its rather inglorious past. Senanayake speaks proudly of the fact that 'Sri Lanka is the only country that has eradicated terrorism.' But when he is asked about the charge of genocide and the continuing international pressure to go for a credible investigation into the allegation, he seeks to fob it off by a glib counter-argument, 'If we were listening to only what the international community was saying, not only Sri Lanka, any other country will not prosper. We would have not won the war. The peace that everybody enjoys today, irrespective of whether you are a Sinhalese or Tamil, north or south, would have never been there. So, at that time, with political will and public support, all armed forces, everybody got together and we finished that. Now we face allegations, those are baseless. No war was fought with zero casualty. If accusations against anyone are proved in the courts, there will be no sympathy from our side. We want to maintain discipline, so we are ready to face any inquiry, but within the legal framework of Sri Lanka.'[5]

'I live in fear...'

Sri Lanka Campaign for Peace and Justice came out with perhaps the most damaging indictment of the *Yahapalanaya* government in February 2018. Based on interviews with 27 war-affected individuals and human rights activists from northern Sri Lanka, the organisation found that despite 'some significant improvements' in the ground situation since the beginning of 2015, much remained to be done to break with the legacy of authoritarianism. The findings reinforced the view that the climate of fear that was once pervasive in Sri Lanka had not lifted evenly or consistently over the past three years, with Tamils living in war-affected areas continuing to bear the brunt of oppressive state practices. These practices would pose a serious threat to any prospect of building sustainable peace; by eroding the kind of trust within the minority communities that would be needed to achieve lasting reconciliation, it would revive issues at the root of the ethnic conflict and raise the possibility of future crackdowns against those who had spoken out in recent times. '...measures adopted by the Sri Lankan security agencies in the name of preventing violence may in fact be hastening its return,' the report cautioned.

NOTES

1 AP, 'Sri Lanka faces fresh charges of human rights violations eight years after civil war came to an end,' *Firstpost*, 11 November 2017, https://www.firstpost.com/world/sri-lanka-faces-fresh-charges-of-human-rights-violations-eight-years-after-civil-war-came-to-an-end-4204397.html

2 Human Rights Watch, World Report 2018: Sri Lanka: Events of 2017, https://www.hrw.org/world-report/2018/country-chapters/sri-lanka

3 The Sunday Times, 'HRCSL complains to President: 49 peacekeeping soldiers sent to Lebanon without its vetting,' 8 April 2018.

4 Sri Lanka Campaign for Peace and Justice, 'Impunity without borders: UN Peacekeeping and the Sri Lankan Military,' 5 November 2015, https://www.srilankacampaign.org/impunity-without-borders-un-peacekeeping-and-the-sri-lankan-military/

5 Meera Srinivasan, 'Sri Lanka is the only country that has eradicated terrorism', *The Hindu*, 16 May 2018.

SECTION FOUR: SRI LANKA'S NEW DEMON – ISLAMOPHOBIA

Demonisation of Muslims has to end.

—Rauf Hakeem

(Do not) leave room for a Muslim Prabhakaran to be born.

—Maithripala Sirisena

SEEMS like its violent past has returned to haunt the island nation after a decade of relative calm. When the Easter Sunday of 2019 dawned in Sri Lanka, it was a normal holiday morning, allowing for a leisurely day to be spent in convivial circumstances. But within the first few hours, the world turned upside down. Huge bomb blasts and suicide-bombing ripped through the Capital and a few other towns in the west and east, and by afternoon and in the next few days, as many 250 people—both Sri Lankans and foreigners including Indians—lay dead. There was no iota of doubt any longer. Rabid 'Salafist' jihadism, on the one hand, and Islamophobia, on the other hand, were poised to devour Sri Lanka—the latest demon the island nation had to deal with. The impact of the infamous Easter Sunday and subsequent bomb outrages, followed in quick succession by widespread and, at times seemingly unstoppable, anti-Muslim counter-attacks mounted by fundamentalist Buddhists and, at least in one or two instances by Christians, had shaken up the country to an unprecedented extent.

The qualitative adjective 'unprecedented' is not usually applicable with ease in the case of Sri Lanka. For as this narrative amply establishes, this country has witnessed a long list of truly unprecedented incidents/ developments that have few international parallels. Why then the use of this word in the instant case? The principal reason seems to be the uniqueness and extent of Salafi jihadism in the Sri Lankan context, which in the popular perception was considered to be safely far away from any such contamination. As we will see, this was a terrible misconception bred purely by ignorance, for the Muslim community had been under the influence of this extreme ideology for several decades. As for the fundamentalist Buddhist onslaughts, this was by no means unprecedented, for ever since 2013-14, Sri Lanka had been witnessing sporadic and, at times prolonged, anti-Muslim attacks and riots carried out by Buddhist-Sinhalese monks and mobs, mainly in the Central and South-Western Provinces. Those violent activities by the majoritarian community did not altogether cease, as would be evident from the following statement that the United Nations issued on 3 November 2018. Under-Secretary-General for Political Affairs, Jeffrey Feltman condemned the anti-Muslim violence that had targeted mosques and businesses in Sri Lanka. While still in the midst of his visit to the country, he urged the government to bring the perpetrators of the violence and hate speech to justice. Feltman, who met with Muslim leaders to show solidarity during the visit, 'condemned the breakdown in law and order and the attacks against Muslims and their property', a UN statement said. At that time, the country was being rocked by a week of violent riots by Buddhist-Sinhalese mobs that had attacked 11 mosques and at least 200 Muslim-owned businesses, prompting the government to declare a state of Emergency. Feltman urged 'swift and full implementation of the government's commitment to bring the perpetrators of the violence and hate speech to justice, to take measures to prevent recurrence, and to enforce non-discriminatory rule of law.[1]

The UN official also met with the government leaders, conveyed his organisation's growing concerns over the issues of good governance, democratic reforms, full implementation of its commitments to the different communities in particular, minorities and received reassurances of Colombo's oft-repeated shibboleths. But, as the events five months later exposed, the government had failed to honour a single commitment in this regard.

What is clearly a major governance failure is the realisation, available since the Easter massacre, that several governments in succession had failed to read the writing on the wall even as political Islam in its worst form, the Salafi jihadism, was taking root in the Muslim community, particularly that which was concentrated in the eastern town of Kattankudy region in the Batticaloa district and among the young generation, mostly who were professionally advanced. In this particular distinction, the Sri Lankan case does not differ from those found in various Western countries where jihadists were mostly from young and professionally well-endowed Muslims.[2] Now that the microscope has been turned on the community, all these facts are coming to the fore. At the same time, it has become clear that the government of the day, too, remained ignorant of this fact, and that speaks a lot about a country which otherwise boasts, with reason, about its expertise in fighting terrorism.

Before we proceed further, it is necessary to get a glimpse of the driving force behind the hydra-headed Salafist jihadism that has taken apparently deep roots in Sri Lanka. It was in 2014 that the world first heard about the Islamic State of Iraq and the Levant (ISIL) or ISIS (Islamic State of Iraq and Syria). Its head turned out to be one Ibrahim Awwad Ibrahim Ali al-Badri al-Samarrai *alias* Abu Bakr al-Baghdadi. But, as was subsequently learned, this terrorist outfit was a by-product of the earlier Al-Qaeda, the brainchild of Saudi Arabian Osama bin Laden and his Jordanian deputy Abu Musab al-Zarqawi, which kind of ended with the defeat of the Taliban government in Afghanistan in 2001. Bin Laden, along with the leadership and fighters of the Taliban–Al-Qaeda, took shelter in Pakistan. Bin Laden and al-*Zarqawi* were killed in separate US operations, in 2011 and 2006, respectively. After Osama, Salafi jihadism took a back seat, and it looked like the world could breathe once again with ease.

In 2014, a new frightening name came up for ISIL or ISIS. This third name, *known as Daesh* or *Daish*, which stands for *al-Dawla al-Islamiya fi al-Iraq wa al-Sham* in Arabic, is a transnational Sunni insurgent group operating primarily in Western Iraq and Eastern Syria, and is now being used increasingly, particularly in the context of the present-day Afghanistan. The roots of the ISIS can be traced to 2003 when the US invaded Iraq. The ISIS participated in the war. However, the second name has stuck because Syria was where this ultra-cruel Islamist group took its last desperate stand to make up for its already shattered dream of setting up the fabled Caliphate, to which 'true' Muslims in every country were invited to join and live together. This call to migrate to the promised heaven continues to reverberate in the minds of many Muslims and some Sri Lankan Muslims have fallen prey to this seductive idea, as became apparent when the Easter bombings took place.

In their preliminary inquiries into the bombings, Sri Lankan intelligence and security forces thought that this was the work of a local Islamist outfit. But, with the ISIS chief al-Baghdadi's claim that his organisation was linked to the Sri Lankan attacks, not just the Sri Lankan state but also the whole world sat up and began to treat the conspiracy with necessary seriousness. On 29 April, seven days after the Easter Sunday attacks, al-Baghdadi (till then considered to have died in a bombing at least five years ago) announced in a video that his followers in Sri Lanka had taken revenge for the defeat of the ISIS in the last stronghold in Syria and that a long hard battle lay ahead.

As the investigations advanced, more shocking revelations came to the fore. For example, multiple sources of intelligence, which were ignored at the official levels not just once or twice but every time, came to light. All that the highest authorities could do was to inform the world of their frustration. As did President Maithripala Sirisena as late as on 29 May 2019, after he attended the inauguration of the Indian Prime Minister Narendra Modi's second stint in office. He lamented, as he had done quite a few times before along with his Prime Minister Ranil Wickremasinghe, that he was never informed of the crucial intelligence and that had he known, he could have immediately taken effective action to prevent the conspiracy from coming to fruition.

What were the 'intelligence inputs' available to the Sri Lankan intelligence services and police? The presidential pardon of the firebrand, rabid anti-minorities Buddhist monk Galagoda Aththe Gnanasara Thero on 22 May 2019, was officially in appreciation of the consistent intelligence provided by this monk to the authorities about jihadist activities in Sri Lanka. More relevantly, the government decided to heed the strong appeal made by moderate Muslims for his release for his services in this specific regard. When the President met the monk at his detention centre in the Welikada prison, the latter narrated to him in detail the information available with him.

What became clear was that the monk had kept passing on accurate information about jihadist activities from time to time, and that the matter got bogged down by red tape and did not proceed any further. The intense blame game that followed this revelation also led to a peculiar and difficult-to-appreciate situation wherein severe punishment was meted out to efficient intelligence officers by the present government. Following the end of the civil war and the Tamil campaign against officers for their alleged anti-Tamil crimes had led to a widespread 'demoralisation' among the ranks of military and civil intelligence personnel. That this is no idle popular misconception is borne out by the subsequent sharing of this view by important Opposition leaders in Parliament (all members of the Rajapaksa-led coalition).

But consider the wilful frittering away by the authorities of the tremendous advantage they enjoyed vis-à-vis moderate Muslim sections who had regularly cautioned them against unwarranted jihadist influences spreading among the young, affluent and westernised members of their community. The authenticity of these inputs was well borne out when investigations revealed the involvement of one of the richest Muslim families in Sri Lanka, not just young sons but also of the parents and women in the family.[3] Zahran Hashim, the mastermind of the conspiracy, had long been marked out for his rabid Islamist preaching and hate-mongering but he was never arrested. He managed to escape the dragnet each time, indicating that his own intelligence network worked better than the official ones. Thus, the effort of the Muslim community leaders to help the police nab him failed due to official apathy. Besides, ever since January 2019, the police had been stumbling upon secret hiding places for large quantities of explosives in Puttalam district on the west coast and other evidence of a rising anti-Buddhist sentiment among Muslims, such as, systematic and periodic attacks on statues of the Lord Buddha. Three months later, nine Islamist terrorists blew themselves up in Colombo, Negombo and Batticaloa—killing more than 250 people and destroying properties extensively.[4]

While Sri Lanka recovered and regained its state authority to a large extent in few weeks' time, having mastered the initial period of sheer panic and helplessness, an inevitable and totally predictable aftermath followed an unsurprisingly familiar script. Buddhist-Sinhalese mobs went on a prolonged revenge campaign against Muslims, demonising them, targeting businesses, religious and educational institutions. As a news report published on 13 May 2019 described, 'The incidents point to an escalation targeting Sri Lanka's Muslim community, following the Easter terror attacks that the government attributed to the local Islamist radical groups ... The cluster of villages in Kurunegala—Kuliapitiya, Kobeigane, Rasnayakapura, Hettipola, Bingiriya, Dummalasuriya—witnessed much destruction, according to local sources. "It began in the afternoon today, it was like they (the mob) had planned to move from one village to the next, attacking our homes and property," said a community leader in the area, who asked not to be named. Even as violence persisted, despite the curfew, "a group of men are still on the motorbikes, making a big noise while villagers are either indoors, or hiding in the nearby jungles in fear," he told *The Hindu*. At least three mosques were attacked late on Sunday (12 May 2019) in nearby Kiniyama, sources said. 'One mosque has been almost fully destroyed. It will take us millions to rebuild it,' a source from the village said.'[5]

The government, too, supported the above contention. 'These are organised attacks on Muslim business houses and premises,' said Navin Dissanyake, Minister of Plantation Industries on 15 May 2019.[6] Asked who were organising the attacks, he said, 'I think that these organisations that Amith Weerasinge, Dan Priyasad, and Namal Kumara (are heading)', referring to the three Buddhist extremists arrested on 14 May. Local media reported the following day that Priyasad had been released on bail on

Wednesday while Weerasinghe was remanded to custody until 28 May 2019. The status of Kumara was not made clear.

Besides the immediate formal linkage of the attacks with Buddhist groups, the developments in the aftermath of the jihadist attacks have laid bare two other unforeseen factors—a suspected army connection to the attacks and a political angle to the otherwise seemingly racial and communal disharmony and inter-communal tension. Speaking along with Minister Dissanayake, Minister for Public Administration Ranjith Madduma Bandara said the 'group(s) behind the attacks had "political aims". (These groups) are trying to tarnish the government's image and show the government is unable to handle the situation.'[7] It might be of some import to note that Kurunegala is the former President and present Opposition leader in Parliament, Mahinda Rajapaksa's constituency and that his party is the principal political force in the district. Apart from this district, another nearby district, Gampaha also witnessed organised anti-Muslim attacks around the same time, where too, Rajapaksa is the main political force to reckon with. Immediately following the jihadist attacks and the anti-Muslim backlash, Rajapaksa and his party were vociferous in condemning the government's failure to respond quickly to the emergency. They also lambasted the government and the ruling coalition for the obvious cracks in the government over tackling the crisis.

The Sri Lankan army itself stated at the time that it was investigating the various allegations and the evidence that had surfaced over the alleged involvement of soldiers in the riots. Among the evidence being examined was a video showing a man wearing what appeared to be an army uniform walking away seconds before an anti-Muslim mob attacked a building in the third week of May 2019 in the 'general area of Thunmodara', said an army statement. Reuters reported that a mosque and some Muslim-owned shops were attacked at Thunmodara. In several reports, Muslims in Kurunegala alleged that the attacks took place 'despite the presence of security forces'. Later, the police claimed that they lacked resources to tackle such widespread riots effectively.[8]

A Forensic Analysis

Before we resume our narration of the developments since 21 April 2019, and where they have pushed the country to, it would do well to pause and consider the minority view of what may have gone wrong with Sri Lanka. According to Tamil National Alliance MP M.A. Sumanthiran, the prolonged peace since 2009 had lulled the people into believing that this blissful period would last for quite some time and that everything was fine. But the Easter Sunday massacre and the subsequent anti-Muslim riots had shattered this belief and the people had been jolted back to a rude reality. The illusion of peace was itself the result of a deliberate refusal to look at reality and the continued belief that the people were being administered justly with the government taking care of the grievances and demands of every community.

Such an attack would have happened one day because the country had not laid 'the foundation for peaceful co-existence'. 'What we saw was a false edifice. And we were quite glad to carry on with that. Three decades of violent conflict that emanated from the North and the East kept us on our toes and those days we actually saw the need to address those issues in a very deep and meaningful way,' Sumanthiran said. Once the civil war was brought to a conclusion in May 2009, those responsible assumed that there was no need to address those issues. They continued to pay lip service, adding that 'whenever issues were raised, they said they must resolve those issues. But deep down, they didn't feel those issues had to be addressed... Unless we agree on those basic issues (of peaceful co-existence), we are doomed,' he said. He emphasised equality was one of the key issues that Sri Lanka must address without further ado.

Equality as a key virtue could only be enshrined for all the Sri Lankan communities through a new all-inclusive Constitution, 'a written social contract', which itself remains an unfulfilled objective for the country four years after the present government assumed office. This coalition had come to power on the promise of bringing in precisely such a statute to the book. Moreover, a principal election pledge of the coalition manifesto was to bring about a new Constitution that would meet the political aspirations of all the communities. Regrettably, even in 2019 that work remains far from complete. It is important to remember that the Tamils have not 'yet' agreed to live in a united country as that question remained open even if the war had ended. 'The most significant minority community has not yet given (its) consent to live together as one country because they had not agreed to that social contract. They were not party to that social contract,' Sumanthiran said. The very fact that the Sri Lankan Constitution traditionally and automatically accords a superior role to Buddhism without giving an opportunity to non-Buddhists to argue their case, renders a consensus on the basic values issue a non-starter. It is a contradiction in terms that while the society is multipolar, its Constitution is unitary.[9]

In a scholarly analysis of the jihadist upsurge (which initially appeared to have been sudden) in Sri Lanka, Professor Jayadeva Uyangoda of Colombo University argues that the 'so-called' terrorist attacks do not take place in isolation. They usually take place in the context of larger political crises. 'For the past few months, the political instability in Sri Lanka was very much visible to the outside world. For that, the President, the Prime Minister and his cabinet are all equally responsible. Therefore, we see a serious crisis not only in governance but also in the state structure of the country. The "power" crisis we experienced in March and early April was also a manifestation of state paralysis. But, beneath that paralysis has been an infinitely more serious paralysis, that which had gripped the security apparatus, which is the core of state power. This has to be rectified immediately. In order to do this, restoration of the democratic government, with a President who is accountable to Parliament and responsible to the cabinet are crucial. While the two sides are blaming each other for this failure, they seem to have developed a consensus on sacrificing heads of the police and intelligence for their own political failure ... As citizens, we see that this is not just an intelligence failure but a failure at the highest level of managing the state and security by the political leadership.'[10]

A right-wing turn

Judging by the subsequent state, popular and political responses to the jihadist attacks of 21 April, it would appear that Sri Lanka has already decided to follow an intrinsically undemocratic and repressive regime of governance in order to counter Islamist jihadism with an iron hand. This would necessarily entail a sharp shrinkage of the still-recovering human rights situation in the name of protecting national security, a phenomenon being witnessed in various countries, such as, the United States of America, South American, certain European, Asian and Africa countries, in a seemingly united global effort to contain political and extremist Islamism and Leftist movements. Analysts like Uyangoda believe that this trend must be effectively countered by the Sri Lankan government as also the other governments in a similar situation.

In Sri Lanka's case, an equally debilitating factor has proved to be the sordid lack of coordination in the top echelons of government. Several acknowledgements of this fact have emanated from the very quarters involved in running the state machinery. It was, therefore, little surprise that the sacked police chief, who had to be forced out of his chair, lost no time in squarely pointing an accusing finger back at the President who had removed him from his job in the first instance. In an explosive statement (2 June 2019), Pujith Jayasundara alleged that Sri Lanka's premier spy agency, the State Intelligence Service (SIS), which functions directly under the President, had ordered him last year to drop investigations against jihadist elements. What the SIS wanted was to put an immediate stop the job being done by the Terrorist Investigation Department (TID) of the Sri Lankan Police, which functioned under him. Most significantly, the TID was asked to stop investigations at a time when it was fully engaged in tracking and collecting evidence against the jihadist outfit, National Thowheeth Jamath (NTJ), which subsequently emerged as the one responsible for the Easter Sunday massacre. Jayasundara also made it clear that the authentic intelligence shared by India did not help the recipient agency because the SIS paid little heed to it. Yet, President Sirisena put the blame squarely on the former police chief and rebuked him publicly for not passing on this intelligence to him. Still, Jayasundara claimed to have initiated action on the NTJ but did not hear anything further from the SIS, especially regarding the information passed on by the Indian intelligence agencies. In a detailed petition to the Supreme Court, he also alleged that Sirisena sought to shut him up by offering him a diplomatic post if he were to take the fall and own complete responsibility for the government's failure to discipline the NTJ in time. He said when he declined the offer, the one-sided blame game ensued.[11]

The seriousness of the situation was soon brought home when all the nine Ministers (including four cabinet-ranking) Muslim Ministers and two provincial Governors—both Muslims—resigned in unison in a protest against the witch-hunt launched in the country. Their collective stand was against the 'demonising' of the entire Muslim community for the extremist attacks that had enveloped the country. Leader of the Sri Lanka Muslim Congress (SLMC), Rauf Hakeem told media that the unprecedented move would provide the authorities 'space and time' to probe the allegations linking Muslim politicians to the terror suspects. Mincing no words, he said, 'Either they (the authorities) should apprehend and punish any of us found guilty or they must vindicate us. We hope they will look into this in a month's time and bring some closure to this. The survival of the government will depend on the manner in which it handles the probe and deals with hate speech, racial violence and impunity,' he added. 'Innocent Muslims are at the receiving end.... they are being victimised despite the community unequivocally condemning the heinous terror attacks.'[12]

Western province Governor Azath Salley and Eastern province Governor M.L.A.M. Hizbulla stepped down from their posts after a Buddhist monk started a fast demanding their resignation in connection with the Easter Sunday bombings killing over 250 victims. The monk, Athuraliye Rathana Thero, an MP of the ruling United National Party led by Prime Minister Ranil Wickremasinghe, specifically accused the two Governors and Minister Rishad Bathiudeen of maintaining links with the terror suspects, a charge the politicians denied vehemently.

The matter came to a head when President Sirisena chose to deliver an alarming speech warning the people against breeding a 'Muslim Prabhakaran'. Pat was a sharp rejoinder from one of the most senior Muslim leaders of the country and among those who had resigned in protest against singling out of their community after the bombings, Rauf Hakeem. Sirisena made this statement on 8 June, while speaking to a Tamil audience in Mullaitivu district, that while the Easter Sunday killings had left the country 'divided', the people should not 'leave room for a Muslim Prabhakaran to be born'.[13] Two days later, on 10 June, Hakeem made his powerful plea not to demonise his community because the nine suicide-bombers were Muslim. The president of the Sri Lanka Muslim League called for an end to the 'continuous demonisation' of Sri Lanka's Muslim community. He told senior journalists in Chennai that in the aftermath of the blasts, the community was in 'a serious introspection mode'. He assured that the jihadists had 'absolutely no sympathy' among the community and that they had been 'isolated' in the community few years ago.[14]

Yet, Hakeem maintained, the Muslims, be they politicians or professionals, were being 'targeted' for allegations. 'If one allegation cannot be proved, you will be taken into custody on some other pretext,' he said. It was for the purpose of halting the trend of 'continuous outburst by xenophobic elements' that the mass resignation (by the Muslim Ministers and Governors) took place. 'We (the Ministers and Governors) have put the community at ease by collectively taking the decision (to quit positions),' he added. This alone, however, was not sufficient. The focus had to be turned away from the Muslim community. 'We have started talking to political leaders, representatives of (the) international community, religious groups and civil society,' he said, emphasising the need for reaching out to all, mindful of 'extremist preaching, hate-mongering and hate speech'. The resignations could be seen as 'an attempt to divide the country further', Hakeem conceded. 'It is the opposite we want. We want reconciliation and a healthy dialogue to promote co-existence.' Referring to the presidential election likely later this year, the SLMC leader said that the 'personality' of candidates to be put up by the two major parties in Sri Lanka would also matter. They must be seen as unifying figures and not divisive, he added.

PSC exposes Govt ineptitude

True to the Sri Lankan penchant for politicisation of any and every issue, the jihadist attacks have also been converted into the latest chapter of the Sirisena-Wickremasinghe tussle for power. The tussle broke out in the open after Parliament set up a select committee to investigate the intelligence failure prior to the bombings and the hearings were publicly telecast. Right from the first telecast, it became crystal clear that the onus of failure to act in time despite a 10-day advance warning, lay with President Sirisena since all vital intelligence inputs had eventually ended up on his desk, as did the inputs in this particular case. As the whole country began to berate him for his failure, he found no other recourse but to first bar serving police officers from deposing before the Parliamentary Select Committee (PSC) and then to stop its public telecast and finally, the hearings itself. However, as we have seen, Speaker Karu Jayasuriya hit back, warning him not to interfere with the PSC's work saying it was beyond the President's jurisdiction, and declaring that the Committee's hearings would continue. In a curious countermove, the President had also set up a separate investigation team comprising members of his choice (including a serving Supreme Court judge) which submitted its final report in record time to him. It goes without saying that the people would, in course of time, heed the PSC report alone and shun the Presidential inquiry report.

As a corollary of the conflicting nature of the President-Prime Minister equation, the latter lost no time in setting up a Parliamentary Select Committee to probe the Easter Sunday jihadist attacks. Right from its first sitting, the hearings began to unravel the sorry state of affairs in state intelligence and governmental alertness necessary to tackle terrorism. These facts were made available by statements and replies made by the two senior-most officials who paid the price for not keeping the President informed of the intelligence inputs received well in time from foreign intelligence services.

On 11 June, Parliament formalised its rejection of the President's order and resumed its investigation into the alleged security lapses in respect of the jihadist attacks. The latest political crisis ballooned into a first-rate frontal battle. The PSC hearings were resumed after a recess with Muslim leaders apprising the MPs of the events leading to the bombings. The leaders claimed in their testimony that they had repeatedly alerted the authorities about the steady and dangerous radicalisation of the younger generation of the community. On the same day, the Opposition Sri Lanka *Podujana Peramuna* (Sri Lanka People's Front) castigated the state for non-governance prevailing in the country and blamed the 'continuing stand-off' between the President and the Prime Minister for this sorry state of affairs in the country. 'The current stand-off effectively means that there is no government in Sri Lanka from today,' SLPP leader Gamini Lakhsman Peiris told media. A cabinet meeting scheduled on the day (11 June) was cancelled without any explanation from the offices of either the President or the Prime Minister. Barring the unprecedented element of the jihadist attacks, what was happening in June 2019 was an almost exact replica of what happened for over two months from last October. The intense rivalry between the two highest political officers of the state had once again spilled over on to the streets, so to speak.

Both former Defence Secretary Hemasiri Fernando and former Inspector General of Police Pujith Jayasundara had categorically denied any lapse on their part in conveying this particular intelligence to the President. But, more significantly, they lay bare how the favouritism indulged in by the President had weakened the intelligence apparatus to a dangerous extent. As we have already seen, Jayasundara described how his wings were clipped. Since no state of emergency was in force, he had no power to declare a curfew and he could not have done so all by himself. As probable evidence of him not having messed up on the intelligence front, Jayasundara claimed that the President offered him an ambassadorial post if he owned up, even while assuring him that the Presidential commission to investigate the terror attacks would manoeuvre to absolve him (Jayasundara) of any responsibility in the matter. But, as he told the MPs, he declined the offer and had instead sought the Supreme Court's intervention to get justice. [15]

Defence Secretary Fernando's testimony to the PSC added to the Opposition's arsenal. He revealed that President Sirisena's favourite officer Nilantha Jayawardena, Chief of the State Intelligence Service (SIS), functioned in a style that led to deliberate sidelining of other senior officials in the organisation and creating a sense of disaffection among the operatives. Fernando informed that Jayawardena had rung him up on the morning of the Easter Sunday (21 April 21) and asked him the number of Methodist churches in the capital city. This was because he had heard that terrorists might attack Methodist churches and not Catholic churches. In reality, however, it was the Catholic churches that were attacked and destroyed with highest rate of casualty.

It would be beyond the scope of this book to cover the entire proceedings of the PSC, but judging by the trend witnessed till mid-June 2019, it seemed as if many more skeletons would have tumbled out of the President's cupboard. In yet another revelation (yet to be ascertained for veracity), former Governor Azath Salley claimed that as far as he knew, the military intelligence unit of the Defence Ministry under the Mahinda Rajapaksa government, had regularly funded jihadists, and he was quite specific about the head of a splinter group of the NTJ, K.Abdul Razik of the Ceylon Towheed Jamath (CTJ) in this respect. According to him, the MI of the Defence Ministry had regularly funded Razik and the Bodu Bala Sena, the ultra-nationalist Sinhalese-Buddhist organisation that was largely responsible for anti-Muslim riots which had rocked the country at intervals since 2014.[16] The following day, M.L.A.M. Hizbullah, the other Muslim Governor who had resigned along with Salley, told the PSC that the Easter Sunday attacks mastermind Zahran Hashim had campaigned for the then dark horse Maithripala Sirisena during the January 2015 presidential election. A fellow-resident of the Kattankudy town along with Hashim, he told the PSC, 'I campaigned for Mahinda Rajapaksa at that time, while Zahran supported and actively campaigned for Sirisena.' He said in response to a question that Hashim had about 2,000 followers and any politician would see the need to cultivate him.

Like many other politicians, he too, knew him. 'Zahran Hashim is a terrorist now, but until 2017 he was considered a religious leader who was drawing many Muslim youth with his sharp debates on religion. Sometime later, he seems to have come in contact with the IS (Islamic State) or some other group,' Hizbullah said in his testimony. While the controversy around him grew for his fiery and uncompromising sermons and speeches attacking his co-religionists who practiced moderate Islam, the police and administration continue to effectively support him by never refusing permission for his meetings, along with facilitating availability of loudspeakers and other accessories.

Universally castigated

The external world had, right from the beginning, caught on to the extreme seriousness of the situation in the aftermath of the Easter Sunday jihadi attacks, as the volatility of Sri Lankan politics has long been studied with considerable concern. True to its apprehensions, politicians in the country, especially those in the Opposition, lost little time in targeting their Muslim counterparts—an obvious ploy to endear themselves to their majority electorate. Interestingly, most of them were careful not to profile an entire community in a bad light but instead, chose individual leaders as targets. For example, Muslim politicians, MPs and Ministers have been singled out for attacks by the politicians from other communities. An analyst feels that this tactic has been used to show that the government of the day has been partial to a particular minority community, pampering its leaders to absurd lengths and the latter taking full advantage thereof. The analyst mentions the Eastern Province Governor M.L.A.M. Hizbullah (who, as we have seen, subsequently resigned under pressure) in this connection, referring to the allegations against him that he was a conduit for Saudi money for a grandiose project to establish a Sharia university, which could presumably be a 'breeding ground' for rabid Islamists. What came handy at the time was the *discovery* of a secret cache of swords and other weapons and ammunition in a Muslim leader's property.[17] The analysis also mentions how the President jumped into the fray, trying to take credit when the country was swaying with trenchant criticism of the inefficiency of the government to combat jihadis, in a desperate bid to project himself as a man of stern resolve and action. For high drama, he even claimed that he was ready to sacrifice his life in order to protect his country from terrorists.[18]

However, under the hyperbolic official and private responses, typical of a dominant majoritarian and nationalistic background, lay a number of facts which were read quickly and correctly by the international community. The United States, followed by the United Nations and the European Union, were quick to caution Sri Lanka against excessive repression in the name of fighting terrorism. American Ambassador to Sri Lanka, Alaina B. Teplitz said in a statement issued six days after the bombings, that 'These terrible attacks are the work of a few individuals and not of an entire community. Sri Lankans of all backgrounds and faiths have come together to condemn these atrocities. Unity is the most powerful answer to terrorism. While we work together to bring the perpetrators of these heinous crimes to justice, we must remain vigilant in defending the democratic ideals that form the pillars of a strong society. And we must do so without destroying communities of peaceful, innocent people who share the faith of the attackers, but not their warped ideology. We must always respect the wonderful diversity of Sri Lanka and fortify the culture of unity that needs to thrive,' she emphasised.[19]

As violent manifestations of Islamophobia, however, continued, representatives of Muslim-majority countries began to speak. The Organisation of Islamic Cooperation (OIC) cautioned the Sri Lankan government of taking 'every measure necessary' to prevent such incidents. Speaking on the issue on 4 June, one day after the Muslim Governors and Ministers had resigned from their constitutional posts in protest, envoys of the Jeddah-based group stated: 'The developing situation over the past few days has been extremely worrying with regards to the safety and protection of the Sri Lankan Muslim community, including some foreign Muslim refugees. The lives and livelihoods of Muslims, including their local stores and large business establishments, are threatened by the prevailing conditions with unforeseen, dangerous consequences.' They also sought 'swift and stern judicial action' against perpetrators of communal violence, regardless of their 'religious and political influence' in Sri Lankan society.[20]

However, unlike in the earlier years, a satisfactory explanation of what once again went wrong with the island 'where every prospect pleases, only man is vile' cannot be had any more, for the reason that for the first time, a global problem had reared its head in the distant Indian Ocean outpost. The questions, why and how Islamic terrorism reached Sri Lanka are now fairly explainable, helped by the confirmed facts and authoritative analyses. The Parliamentary Select Committee, on the conclusion of its work, was expected to add further clarity to the situation. It is perhaps time to turn our attention to broader issues: Why is it that the bright and rich Muslim youth are increasingly forsaking their assured future in the known world and opting to sneak into the nether world of hate, revenge and 'supreme' self-sacrifice? What are they searching for? Peace and proximity to God in Heaven? But that is hardly comprehensible.

What is Jihadism: Explained

Instead of seeking an answer to the question why jihadism succeeds in inducting new recruits from all over the world and, not necessarily from Muslim countries, we may turn to one of the finest Muslim scholars of the problem, Prof Mahmood Mamdani Columbia University, for a broader approach. Mamdani begins by quoting critics of American bombing of Afghanistan who have argued if it is a sound policy to automatically classify terrorism as criminal. He seeks to answer the question by saying that while it sounds appealing, 'but if terrorism were simply a crime, it would not be a political problem.' The distinction between terror and crime is that the former makes an open bid for public support. Unlike the criminal, the political terrorist is not easily deterred by punishment. Whatever we may think of their methods, terrorists have not only a need to be heard, more often than not, a cause to champion.[21]

He brushes aside Salman Rushdie's formulation that terrorists are nothing but nihilists who wrap themselves with objectives but actually have none and that society and the state must remorselessly attack them, and adding that one needs to recognise that 'terrorism has no military solution'. Even a successful military confrontation with terrorists requires their political isolation, precisely by addressing the issues they raise. That is why America's bombing campaign in Afghanistan is more likely to be remembered as a 'combination of blood revenge and medieval-type exorcism than as a search for solution to terrorism'. Mamdani wrote this in 2003. Sixteen years later, as we discuss his assessment of political Islam and jihadism, the United States is half-way through surrendering Afghanistan lock, stock and barrel to the Taliban—just to get out of the God-forsaken country. Today, his words, that terrorism has no military solution, seem prophetic. Drawing attention to the official nomenclature that the United States and its Western allies chose for their response to the 9/11 attacks, the 'War on Terror', Mamdani argues that few would fail to notice 'the growing common ground between the perpetrators of 9/11 and the official response to it... Both sides deny the possibility of a middle ground, calling for a war to the finish. Both rally forces in the name of justice but understand justice as revenge'. If the perpetrators of 9/11 refuse to distinguish between official America and the American people, target and victim, the 'War on Terror' has proceeded by dishing out collective punishment, with callous disregard for either 'collateral damage' or legitimate grievances. Both practices are likely to nurture the spirit of revenge.

But, what about choosing a different path of response to terrorism altogether: one of opening up a dialogue, of debate; in other words, choosing the democratic way of debate and discussion? Can we, for example, turn the moment of injury into a moment of freedom of choice? Grief for victims should not obscure the fact that there is no choice without a debate and no democracy without the right to choose... Can we then fit this formulation into the Sri Lankan case of the Easter Sunday jihadist attacks and the state's response and the accompanying Islamophobia witnessed so far? Is the Sri Lankan state likely to yield positive results by hunting down suspected jihadists and thus be able to eradicate terrorism for ever from its soil? If every other country beginning with the United States has failed so far to achieve such a satisfactory result, would Sri

Lanka be able to break out of the pattern? Sri Lankans can possibly point out their state's apparent success in tackling the Tamil terrorism by waging an all-out war against the Liberation Tigers of Tamil Eelam (LTTE). Truly, the country had lived in peace since May 2009 until 21 April 2019, when the jihadist attacks took place. We would like to draw the reader's attention at this stage to the earlier quotation from the Tamil National Alliance MP M.A. Sumanthiran's call for the final settlement of the Tamil question, without which, as he succinctly observed, no permanent peace could prevail in Sri Lanka. Should this not be taken into account when making the claim that the Tamil question is buried for ever. For that is not the case at all. Any observer of Sri Lanka would know that the embers can still be ignited if conducive conditions prevail at an unforeseeable future.

We now come to the all-important question: despite terrible fates awaiting them, why do highly educated young Muslims—mostly from affluent families and living in high-income nations—get attracted to jihadist groups? Apparently, this seemingly intriguing question has so far attracted a plethora of scholars to delve deep into the subject, as a result of which we have a wide choice of learned findings to choose from. One such intriguing finding is that a highly disproportionate percentage of terrorists happen to be engineers or, otherwise technologically qualified graduates, from renowned institutions. This seems to be easily explainable. According to one study, as high as 44 per cent of the militants, whose educational background after high school was verifiable, were engineering graduates.[22]

The database of Sociologist Diego Gambetta and political scientist Steffen Hertog has since kept growing as violent extremism or terrorism in its plainest form gathers new victims and exposes new adherents. However, a very important fact unearthed by them should be given due importance. This fact points out that terrorists are not exclusively Muslim; they are also white Christians. 'As this list suggests, this phenomenon is not confined to Muslims or Middle Easterners. In fact, thinking in terms of religion, nation and class has failed to explain why, for example, out of thousands of normal-acting sons of middle-class, moderate Muslim families from Nigeria, apparently only Umar Farouk Abdulmutallab (confessed Al Qaeda operative and engineering student) who tried to blow up an airline over Detroit in late-2009. But the satire was rooted in a statistical fact: in the ranks of captured and confessed terrorists, engineers and engineering students are significantly over represented. Maybe that's a numerological accident,'[23] As for non-Muslim terrorists captured alive or dead, there was Joseph Andrew Stack, a software engineer who crashed his plane into the Internal Revenue Service offices in Austin, Texas, in February 2010. In March 2010, John Patrick Bedell, an engineering graduate student, opened fire at an entrance to the Pentagon.

Gambetta and Hertog also argue, in a paper published in *The European Journal of Sociology* (2009), that the engineer-terrorist connection is part of the answer to the question: what are we missing when one out of thousands of normal young people suddenly emerge as a deadly terrorist? They say that the engineer-terrorist connection is only part of the answer: it is a new window onto what Gambetta calls the 'hidden logic' of society. Though the difference in susceptibility is very small, 'it's like saying the probability that you will be struck by lightning is one in a million, and the lightning is four in a million'. It is also enlightening that the researchers found engineers 'only in right-wing groups'—the ones that claim to fight for the pious past of Islamic fundamentalists or the white-supremacy (fanatics in America) subscribing to the Aryan Nations (founded by Richard Butler, an engineer) or the minimal pre-modern US government that Stack and Bedell extolled. Among communists, anarchists and other organisations mastered the same technical skills as the right-wingers.[24] The engineer mindset might be a mix of emotional conservatism and intellectual habits that prefer clear answers to ambiguous questions—'the combination of a sharp mind with a loyal acceptance of authority. Does this formulation fit into the Sri Lankan jihadist found in April 2019? Do the known educational backgrounds of the terrorists killed in the Easter Sunday attacks and thereafter match the findings of Gambetta and Hertog? This first lot of Sri Lankan jihadist suicide-bombers was a mixed lot consisting of both foreign-educated graduates from rich families to middle and lower-income family-born locally and poorly educated young men sharing the common thread of religious fervour. Zahran Hashim, later identified as the mastermind, himself was rusticated from school after his extra-curricular activities attracted attention of his teachers and when he failed to change despite repeated warnings. But this man was able to bring into his fanatic fold two highly-educated brothers and another relative from one of the richest Muslim families in the country. Reports revealed that Hashim utilised chat rooms to converse secretly with his would-be recruits who obviously included Ilham Ahmed Mohamed Ibrahim and his elder brother Inshaf Ahmed. The fourth bomber was Mohamed Azzam Mubarak Mohamed (his wife was later arrested as a suspect in the conspiracy). The others were Ahmed Muaz (his brother was later arrested); Mohamed Hasthun; Mohamed Nasser Mohamed Asad; Abdul Latheef (who had studied in Britain and Australia); and Fathima Ilham, wife of Ilham. The younger of the two brothers who bombed hotels in Colombo, had blasted explosives strapped to her body, killing not just herself but her two children and three police officers who had rushed to the family home in Colombo.

It was the brutality of the woman's death that truly shocked the country. But there was much more to the story. In an evocative description, Joanna Slater and Amantha Perera wrote, 'Inside the sprawling home with a white BMW parked outside, there was a terrifying secret. At least three of the suicide bombers who struck Sri Lanka on Easter belonged to the same extended family, police said. The patriarch is one of the country's most successful spice traders. Two of his sons carried out attacks early Sunday morning... That afternoon, as police entered the family residence,... his daughter-in-law detonated explosives, killing herself and three officers. The role played by the family in the devastating attacks that killed over 250 people was one of several new details about the plot that emerged, as Sri Lanka continued to bury its dead and investigators raced to understand whether the perpetrators had received help from abroad... Neighbours (at Dematagoda, a suburb of Colombo), a quiet neighbourhood lined with spacious homes, sits the three-story residence belonging to a businessman known professionally as Y. M. Ibrahim and whom police refers to simply as Ibrahim. The house where he lives with his extended family takes up much of a block and was cordoned off with police tape. Its façade is painted white and dotted with metal balconies. Neighbours spoke fondly of Ibrahim, whom they described as a man from a modest background who rose to become a wealthy exporter of spices. Ibrahim was one of at least 60 people arrested in the wake of the attacks.'[25]

The India connection

On the very day that the Easter bombings struck a languid Sri Lanka which was enjoying a hard-earned holiday, and rudely interrupting the serendipity prevailing in the hot, humid climate with foreign and local tourists making merry on the sun-baked beaches and breakfasting leisurely in the air-conditioned five-star hotels, the Indian connection became one single pole to cling to. Within hours the country came to know that at least 10 days earlier, around 10 April, Indian intelligence services had passed on a vital input to its Sri Lankan counterpart to the effect that terrorists were likely to strike at three prominent places in Colombo, taking advantage of the holidays. As we have seen above, a major part of the post-jihadist attacks centred around this aspect of the story, that the Sri Lankan government surprisingly refrained from initiating appropriate action after receiving the information from India. Moreover, the Indian input was supported by the United States and the United Kingdom.

Soon after, the two countries got in touch with each other in double quick time. The Sri Lankan President attended Prime Minister Narendra Modi's second inaugural in the Indian capital with apparent promptness. On that occasion, the two leaders resolved to firm up their security cooperation further, and also spoke about fighting global terrorism together. This dialogue continued on an expanded form when Modi visited the Maldives and Sri Lanka on his first foreign trip since winning the 2019 general election. The five-hour crowded Colombo visit allowed the two leaders to reiterate the urgency of fighting terrorism 'together'.

This purely symbolic visit fitted perfectly into the prevailing environment in Sri Lanka at the time. Its emphasis on a joint fight, which also includes other global powers, was essentially a message to jihadists like Hashim and his followers, warning them against any future intention to disrupt life in Sri Lanka. Unspoken publicly but acknowledged is the point that it is imperative to follow up intelligence inputs and for sharing of intelligence. This, however, is only the first part of the exercise and has to be followed by concrete and appropriate action. Otherwise, bilateral and international cooperation in fighting global terrorism would continue to be buffeted by inefficiency and internal politicking, a lesson for Sri Lanka in particular.

The Indian Prime Minister also met a delegation of the TNA which urged him to take up with the Lankan government the stalled new constitution project. The TNA followed this up with a visit to New Delhi where the details of the present stalemate in this regard were further discussed, indicating that the Indian government had begun to exert considerable pressure on a reluctant government in Colombo. In more than one sense, the sudden deterioration of the Sinhalese-Muslim relations was not isolated from the long-simmering disaffection between the Sinhalese and the Tamils. This state of affairs also reflected the all-round disaffection leaving every minority community in Sri Lanka dissatisfied with the majoritarian rule with a warped mindset, which is by every account a potentially dangerous situation for a tightly-held unitary state with a very diverse religious, cultural and economic environment. In mid-2019, and looking forward to yet another presidential election by the year-end, high-voltage disruptions are widely anticipated. With the new demon of Islamophobia to deal with, Sri Lanka appears to be in a desperate need of far more self-assurance and open-mindedness in governance. The performance of the Sinhalese leadership so far does not inspire much confidence in such a scenario. The need for 'peaceful coexistence' may never be heeded.

NOTES

1 Pulse Nigeria, *UN condemns anti-Muslim attacks*, https://www.pulsena/in-sri-lanka-un-condemns-anti-muslim-ttacks/....

2 Columbia University Professor Mahmood Mamdani is the author of *Good Muslim, Bad Muslim, America, and the Roots of Terror* (New York: Pantheon Books, 2004). Mamdani traces the growing Western intolerance of Muslims, against both American, British and other European Muslims and Muslims migrants, especially illegal migrants who came in a flood of desperate, overcrowded ocean-crossings in the wake of the Western invasions in various Muslim countries in West Asia and Afghanistan. While Western governments and populations blamed the flood of migrants to rising curves of crime, the Muslims blamed the Westerners' 'in-born' intolerance of Islam. His analysis of this phenomenon is considered one of the most satisfying of its genre.

3 NewsIn Asia, 'Family networks behind Sri Lanka bombings,' 11 May 2019, https://newsin.asia/family-networks-behind-sri-lanka-bombings/

4 Ibid.

5 Meera Srinivasan, 'Mosques, shops come under attack Police impose curfew across Sri Lanka amid fears of an escalation in 6violence, social networks blocked,' *The Hindu*, May 15, 2019.

6 Reuters, 'Sri Lanka says hardline Buddhist groups likely to blame for anti-Muslim attacks,' May 16, 2019.

7 Ibid.

8 Ibid

9 Shamindra Ferdinando, 'TNA blames Easter Sunday massacres on Sri Lanka's failure to address grievances of minorities,' 1 May 2019, https://www.onlanka.com/news/tna-blames-easter-sunday-massacres-on-sri-lankas-failure-to-address-grievances-of-minorities.html

10 Anuradha Kodagoda, 'Collective responsibility, vital to address issues', Sunday Observer, 12 May 2019, http://www.sundayobserver.lk/2019/04/28/news-features/%E2%80%98collective-responsibility-vital-address-issues%E2%80%99`)

11 Meera Srinivasan, 'Suspended police chief blames Sirisena over terror attacks,' *The Hindu*, 2 June 2019)

12 Meera Sirinivasan, '9 Muslim Ministers, 2 Guvs. step down in SL,' *The Hindu*, 4 June 2019.

13 Colombo Gazette, 'Don't leave room for Muslim Prabhakran: Sri Lanka President,' 9 June 2019.

14 T. Ramakrishnan, 'Demonisation of Muslims has to end: Sri Lanka's ex-minister,' *The Hindu*, 11 June 2019.

15 Meera Srinivsan, 'Former Sri Lankan officials points to fissures within govt,' *The Hindu*, 7 June 2019.

16 Meera Srinivasan, 'Easter suspects were funded by Rajapaksa-era intelligence unit,' *The Hindu*, 13 June 2019.

17 P.K. Balachandran, 'Impact of Easter Sunday blasts on Lanka's external and internal affairs,' *NewsIn Asia*, 2 May 2019, reprinted from the *Daily Express*.

18 NewsIn Asia, 'Lankan President vows to crush terrorism even risking his life. Promises action against errant officials,' https://newsin.asia/lankan-president-vows-to-crush-terrorism-even-risking-his-life-promises-action-against-errant-officials/

19 U.S. Embassy in Sri Lanka, 'U.S. Cooperation to Enhance Safety in Sri Lanka,'27 April 2019, https://lk.usembassy.gov/u-s-cooperation-to-enhance-safety-in-sri-lanka/

20 Meera Srinivasan, 'Sri Lankan situation 'extremely worrying', say OIC envoys,' *The Hindu*, 5 June 2019.

21 Mahmood Mamdani, *Good Muslim, Bad Muslim*… op. cit.

22 Diego Gambetta and Steffen Hertog, *Engineers of Jihad: The Curious Connection between Violent Extremism and Education*, New Jersey: Princeton University Press, 2016.

23 David Berreby, 'Engineering Terror,' The *New York Times*, 10 September 2010.

24 Ibid

25 Joanna Slater and Amantha Perera, 'Sri Lankan spice tycoon's sons and daughter-in-law were suicide bombers in Easter Attacks,' *The Washington Post*, April 25, 2019).

4

Reconciliation: Hopes Fading Away

From the morning, when we eat,
until night when we sleep
I am ever floating
—Fathima Nusaira, *Afloat* (Write to Reconcile II)

AS you read, more than 10 years have passed by since the war was won and peace restored. Thousands of missing persons—majority of them Tamils—are yet to be accounted for. Their parents (mostly mothers), wives, brothers (few), and in most cases, sisters keep vigil, and now that at long last the Office of Missing Persons (OMP)[1] is functioning, the people who have been at the end of their tether will now be required to queue up there in the fading hope of getting some official word about what has happened to their missing family members since the civil war began 35 years ago. Members of the Lankan-Tamil diaspora keep corresponding and visiting the north and the east to get some kind of news, some closure. But as the OMP would be obliged to reply, the task is vast; at least 64,000 and may be many more remain untraceable; the job is certainly complex.

It took nearly three years for the national unity government (which had by then qualified to be renamed as the national disunity government) to come out with budgetary provisions for the setting up and functioning of the OMP, one of the most important demands of the ethnic Tamils. While President Sirisena initiated the move to set up the OMP in July 2017, another seven months elapsed before the commissioners could be appointed. And this did in no way mean that the OMP was functioning. It would take another three months for the OMP to move out and begin recording the cases of missing persons. As time was wasted, frustration mounted and the Opposition criticism of the tardiness displayed by Colombo peaked. International pressure also increased and the UNHRC grilled the government to find out its actual intentions. The suspense was finally over when Finance Minister Mangala Samaraweera presented his 2018 Budget, including a provision for $63 million for a variety of socially relevant projects in the Northern Province. Commissioners were appointed in February-end in some haste, as the UNHRC was in session in Geneva at the time, and as much as two years had passed without any action since the government's 2015 commitment to the UN body.

However, there was a catch, a rather thorny one, to which a Tamil civil rights organisation, took immediate exception. The contentious issue was the appointment of a retired army Major General Mohanti Antoinette Peiris, who was the Director (Legal) of the army and the army's senior legal adviser for humanitarian law and human rights. During the armed conflict, she assisted the government in countering LTTE propaganda.[2]

There was confusion and consternation when the government clarified in Parliament, in the wake of protests from Buddhist nationalists like the JVP about the OMP's jurisdiction over the past cases of enforced disappearance, that the OMP would only take up 'future' cases and not cases relating to the last war. The Tamils were eventually reassured when the OMP Chairman Saliya Pieris gave a counter-clarification on March 20 saying: 'The mandate of the OMP is not limited to a particular area, community or time period and also covers those of the Sri Lankan forces Missing in Action (MiA). Regrettably, the contents of the letter (appointing the office) are teeming with inaccuracies and distortions, not (the) least on the law relating to the OMP. The OMP reiterates that the definition of Missing Persons in the OMP Act is not limited to those missing or who disappeared during the conflict in the north and east and its aftermath, but also covers missing and disappeared as a result of enforced disappearances as well as other political and civil disturbances in every part of the country.'

'The OMP is not a quasi-judicial body and its objective is to trace the missing and disappeared and to inform the relatives of those persons, the circumstances of the disappearances and the fate of their loved ones. The findings of the OMP do not give rise to criminal or civil liability. While the work of the OMP is confidential in nature, it is as it is in every situation in our country, subject to the jurisdiction of the Supreme Court in the exercise of its Fundamental Rights and Writ jurisdiction.' This was followed by a surprisingly political statement vouchsafing that 'None of the members of the OMP have ever advocated the cause of separatism and all members of the OMP unequivocally support and believe in a united Sri Lanka and are convinced that a strong domestic mechanism will be useful to establish the credibility of the country in granting relief to the loved ones of the missing and disappeared.'[3] Does this not convey the impression that the government is more interested in obviating any scope for an international role in respect of any human rights violation than in finding out the culprits for such violations and meting out justice in such cases?

Needs correctly identified

Finance Minister Samaraweera also said at the time of the budget that the OMP should be functional by January 2018. An amount of $4.8 million had been made available for constructing 50,000 brick and mortar houses, aimed at substantially alleviating a key housing problem for the applicants for OMP help. Along with an equal number of houses being built by India, the acute housing shortage should be mitigated to a substantive extent. A European company, Arcelor Mittal owned by the Indian NRI Lakshmi Mittal which had won a contract for building 65,000 houses in the north, had for some strange reason, opted for building steel (the Mittal group is also the world's largest producer of steel) houses rather than brick and mortar houses. The decision raised a storm of protest as the extremely hot weather in the region would surely render such houses uninhabitable; and TNA MP M.A. Sumanthiran went to the Supreme Court for redress. The matter currently rests there.

But the Tamils were overall happy with the direction of the budget provisions for the north. Sumanthiran said, 'The amount is small, but the targetting or identification of the projects for the allocation of funds shows that it is a well-thought out budget. The government has not only chosen the right areas for concentration but has also taken a long-term view. The issues and projects identified in the north and the east are those which the TNA had drawn attention to.'[4]

Since opportunities for livelihood have been poor in the north because of the war and its aftermath, especially for women (in most cases left alone without an adult male member), and since infrastructure had not developed in the war years, $17.9 million was allocated for all-round development, which includes homes for disabled women in the north. Housing for disabled women is a peculiar problem since in many cases their own families turn them out and they have nowhere to go. The demand was for one home per family (or whatever is left of it), and the budget bravely tried to provide for it. As it is, post-war reconstruction of damaged houses and other properties has proved to be too expensive forcing people into incurring large debts which they could not service as they have little income. The budget provided $6.5 million to help such people rebuild their homes in the Northern and the North Central Provinces.

Admirably, the budget also provided $162,760, to help develop entrepreneurship skills among the former LTTE cadre and another equal amount to give formal educational certificates to those of 12,600 rehabilitated cadre who were already skilled but lacked formal training, education or officially recognised certificates. This would enable the skilled cadre to get jobs and a clientele. In addition, $1.6 million was provided for distribution among private firms which would employ at least five such people. This would be in the form of subsidies with the maximum of LKR10,000 towards the salary of each such employee.

These steps were welcomed by the people and the TNA, for the former fighters were truly passing through a very bad patch. They had had to live through hostile responses from society and were avoided by local employers, thus effectively leaving them on their own. Consequently, armed robberies and highway hold-ups were occurring regularly. During my November 2017 visit to the north, both civilians and the police cautioned me about venturing out at night lest I came across armed desperadoes.

The government clearly thought through the problems and zeroed in on effective measures. For example, its munificence was not restricted to the Tamils but also extended to the Muslims of Mannar district who had returned from self-imposed exile after peace was restored. These people, mostly traders and small and medium-scale entrepreneurs, had suffered for 19 years after having been expelled by the LTTE and forced to leave all their wealth behind.

Other areas where immediate development was necessary and budgeted for were food processing plants, irrigation and water management, rebuilding of the Myliddy harbour as a fishing harbour, subsidised electricity for industries in the north, and modern economic centres in Jaffna and Dambulla (in the North Central Province). Besides, funds were also allocated for promoting Tamil as an official language and bolstering the functioning of the Secretariat for Coordinating Reconciliation Mechanism (SCRM).

Is time running out?

Unfortunately, despite honest intentions to mete out justice to a wronged people, the government had not been able to deliver results; most of the tasks undertaken to facilitate societal reconciliation remain either delayed or incomplete. The OMP was established after more than two years of delay; the budgetary provisions were made in November 2017; and finally the commissioners, too, were appointed in March 2018. But by the first week of May, when I tried to find out if it had actually started functioning, checking against the minister's assurance in Parliament that it would start functioning in January 2018, the report was that it was yet to start. It finally began its work by visiting war-affected zones by the end of May; and informed sources said that the OMP would merely replicate the work done earlier—during the Rajapaksa regime—by similar commissions which listed the missing cases and passed these on to the police and the army. If their cynical assessment was anything to go by, the OMP was intended to be nothing like a single-window grievance redressal mechanism that the thousands of families of the missing were waiting so long for. The police stations were the first place that the families had gone to for some information about their lost relatives. And that was where they were being asked to go again.

A rudimentary glimpse into the numbing extent of desperation such families may be suffering from can be had in the following excerpt from a short story written on the subject, based on a combination of several real-life events.

'In February 2012, six years since the day she was abducted, Arathi revisited what remained of her family or house. Nature had taken over—it was now fallow land, with awkwardly placed blocks of cement. *If only the trees could talk*, she thought to herself, *they saw everything, they can tell me what happened.* She stooped to pick up a round stone to take as a memento of her first visit back in all these years.... Despondent, she walked away, clutching the stone tightly. As she walked away, she recalled, as if they were talismans, Shiva's dimpled face, Selvi's mischievous smile, Gajan's way of wrinkling his forehead when he was amused, Kalai's deft fingers braiding her hair. She would continue her search, she would never give up.' (Janani Balasubramaniam, *Snapshots of Loss*, Write to Reconcile II)

> 'I have forgotten how to smile after my son's disappearance.' —Missing person's mother
>
> 'Just because the war is over and he has not come back home, I can't believe that my husband is not alive. I did not see his body. I believe he might be alive somewhere. Then again it has almost been eight years since his disappearance. Sometimes I feel if he were alive, he would have returned.' —Missing person's wife
>
> 'I strongly believe my husband is alive. Many people saw him surrendering to the army. Many villagers also told me that he was

> taken by the army to identify LTTE members. Those who had surrendered to the army were released later. So he too should be alive somewhere in a secret detention. Besides, his picture was published in the newspaper, too, he is standing in front of the Katchchari. I am sure he is alive.' —Missing person's wife
>
> 'I have not seen my son's body. There is no proof he is dead. I also heard rumours about security forces kept in detention by the LTTE in India. My son must be there. He must be alive.' —Missing person's mother
>
> 'Neighbours stigmatise me saying I am a widow and they don't like to see my face because I bring bad luck.' —Missing person's wife

(All quoted from interviews conducted with families of missing persons, contained in *Living with Uncertainty: Needs of the Families of Missing Persons in Sri Lanka*, International Committee of the Red Cross, 26 July 2016, https://www.icrc.org/en/document/sri-lanka-families-missing-persons.)

Colombo responds

As the *Yahapalanaya* government struggled to retain and strengthen its control over a threatened dismantlement, President Sirisena struck the right note when he told Parliament on 8 May 2018, 'The foundation of a stable country is national reconciliation. It is important to introduce a structure for taking political decisions based on equality for achieving meaningful reconciliation. I believe, it is a dire need of the day to strengthen the existing provincial council system in order to achieve these objectives.'[5]

Trust deficit

Reconciliation of two communities—different in race, religion, language and culture, and separated by myth, history, popular conception and social media—and politics would be difficult in any country. In Sri Lanka's case, the job is doubly arduous because there is a very serious trust deficit between the communities. As we have seen above, there is no dearth of good intentions on the part of the government. But reiteration of these is no longer strong enough to bridge the trust deficit that has come about since the Sirisena-Wickremasinghe regime took office.

In an assessment of the reconciliation situation, it was urged that without wasting further time, the government should launch a programme of action to 'expedite' the realisation of its promises made in 2015 on constitutional reform, transitional justice and governance. This must be a 'truly national' programme capitalising on the unique features of the victorious coalition of 2015. This design and execution of the programme of action should be treated as a matter of the utmost national priority with the support and participation of the public galvanising activity. Further, despite the rhetoric of reconciliation, the government was yet to engage with a cross-section of society. In doing so it would be confronted with and hopefully comprehend the 'complexities and challenges' associated with it. 'Reconciliation is a long and messy process', the assessment warned.[6]

Easily, Sri Lanka's tragedy is that its national unity government has wasted the enormous goodwill that it had generated initially. The people, both in the north and the south but, with much more poignancy in the north, were full of hope that better days were ahead. They had extended their wholehearted support to the new coalition with a singular aim, that of getting rid of Mahinda Rajapaksa. They had continued to repose their faith in the coalition ignoring the frailties in governance that began to be exposed as time passed, clinging to their hope that this government must not fail. The south was the first to be disenchanted and withdrew its support to the government, which was brutally reflected in the results of the local government elections on 10 February 2018. The north continued to stick by the government and the coalition—by then distended and hydra-headed and an object of ridicule. But, for this act of loyalty, the TNA had to pay a heavy price, as ethnic Tamils were no longer enamoured of the joint UNP-SLFP venture and had begun to look for an alternative to the dreaded return of the Rajapaksas.

It would be advisable at this stage of the narrative to pause and take a look back at the Rajapaksa regime.

Reconciliation not an isolated issue

In a sense, ethnic reconciliation was fated to fail in the aftermath of the war and peacetime. This statement might seem strange and illogical but it is quite valid in the Sri Lankan case. Reconciliation could not have materialised in a vacuum, without addressing the concomitant issues, such as, bringing a closure on the lives of thousands of Tamils; rebuilding the shattered lives of many more thousands and helping them regain a sense of purpose in living. The situation has been seriously compromised by the rise of Sinhala-Buddhist fundamentalism in the south; admittedly, it is the Muslims and Christians who are the main victims but Tamils cannot feel reassured when they see a re-enactment of their fate in the context of the other two religious communities. Without these simultaneous inputs and a satisfactory and complete suppression of the rising religious fundamentalism, how can there be a true reconciliation between the two communities which are looked at as victors and victims? There is no ethnic reconciliation yet because the two communities are not equal to each other. One is strong and the other weak.

Today's situation itself was part of the historical process through which the island was passing at the time. While the Rajapaksa regime lasted, the Sinhalese also suffered enormously and they were also victims, not the victors of today. A painstaking study of November 2013 noted that devolution in the north—intimately linked with the entire gamut of the ethnic issue—was unlikely to make real progress while the rest of the country suffered from democratic deficit. It advised the TNA to frame its struggle for demilitarisation, security and democratic rights in both the north and the east in ways that resonated with growing unhappiness elsewhere in the country. Increasing numbers of Sinhalese were questioning the high cost of living, corruption, economic mismanagement, land grab and apparently political connected violence. Faced with popular discontent and protests on a range of social and economic issues, the government had frequently responded with repression and violence, using the Anti-Terrorism Act to jail critics and the army to attack protesters. This had led to unprecedented public criticism of the army, police and ruling family. There was also evidence of serious discontent within the President's own party and Cabinet.[7]

The disaffection between the Sinhalese and the Tamils was also present when it came to relations between the Sinhalese on the one hand and the Muslims and Christians on the other. All these boiled down to an entirely disaffected nation, definitely not a fertile soil for cultivating ethnic reconciliation after a protracted period of violence, repression and reprisal.

The very first recommendation that the International Crisis Group (ICG) made in its report spoke about the government enabling an 'effective' Northern Provincial council by giving it an adequate budget and allowing it to receive international development assistance through the national treasury; refraining from using the President's and the Governor's powers 'to block or delay', enabling legislation for Council Ministries; appointing a provincial governor who has the Council's confidence and a provincial chief secretary chosen by the majority and ensuring that the provincial administration is adequately staffed with competent professionals; establishing the national land commission or similar mechanism to lead an inclusive national dialogue on land use and land rights; reduce the number of troops and military camps in the northern province, remove the military from involvement in civilian administration and return all 'arbitrarily' seized land; and implement the 13th Amendment 'fully' and abandon plans to reduce provincial powers and resume talks with the TNA on constitutional reforms for 'meaningful' self-rule: in the north and the east with adequate protections for the Muslims and the Sinhalese.

In hindsight, it is easy to see why several of these recommendations could not have been implemented even if the government also thought on similar lines. Despite the fact that the LTTE has been thoroughly and convincingly defeated and crushed out of existence, the Sinhalese mind continues to genuinely fear a future revival of separatist sentiments among ethnic Tamils. In short, the trust deficit on this particular point is very deep and seemingly unbeatable, and therefore, a potential spoiler for any sincere attempt at reconciliation. Unarguably, the most debilitating feature of the post-war situation is that the constitutionally enshrined devolution of power to the provinces is yet to materialise. In the ultimate analysis, every crucial goal that Sri Lanka must achieve is intricately linked to the issue of federalism as far as the provinces are concerned. In other words, it is a debate between unitary and federal state, and in the Sri Lankan context, federalism has little chance of winning the debate because Sri Lankan diversity is in denial.

But why so? Unitary is in this context synonymous with unity, and therefore, federalism spells nothing but catastrophe for a unitary and united Sri Lanka. How can the Sinhalese, who are the (self-appointed) protectors of Sri Lankan heritage, history, culture and overall unity, compromise themselves by agreeing to devolve more power (and eventually power to segregate) to other communities who may not be as committed as they are to the country's unity and integrity?

This is the crux of the perennial tussle between the national question and its solution.

From the above, it might appear that the majority community is solely responsible for the national mess. Reality, however, is never uni-dimensional. Sri Lanka's woes would never go away as long as ethnic Tamils in particular also continue to be in denial. As this book endeavours to establish, they have also been responsible, if not equally, definitely substantially, for this. The Tamil leadership, both political and militant, had failed at various stages of modern history to rise to the occasion and do their bit. The political leadership's failure to fight for federalism when the ground was ripe has been mentioned earlier. The Sri Lankan society was a highly divided and deliberately segregated based on caste and class parameters. One example cited in this book is the caste composition of the fighters of the LTTE and other militant outfits, who were from the lowest castes. Velupillai Prabhakaran and many other top LTTE leaders came from the fishermen community which was also low-caste but financially and politically the most dominant caste.

However, when Tamil militancy broke out in the north-east, one of the vehicles it chose to ride upon was the caste system.

Why Tigers fought casteism

A rigid caste system, intimately connected with the land-owning system and pattern in Tamil areas in Sri Lanka, was a historical legacy, perpetuated under the Jaffna kingdom. Under it, the *Vallala* caste groups consisting of various sub-castes, dominated the land-owning pattern and subjected lower castes who were the majority in numbers to oppression. When the Dutch colonialists codified the traditional law system, they not only retained the Vallala superiority over others but also allowed slavery. This helped the already oppressive land-owning and caste system to gain further strength, and the Tamil society grew more repressive and feudal. It eventually became a fledgling capitalist society based on the twin pillars of slavery and the caste system. It was only in the second half of the twentieth century that the British abolished slavery.[8]

But the society continued to remain extremely unequal in social, economic and political spheres. As is customary in such societies, gender inequality, too, was inbred. Till the 1960s the Tamil society remained cocooned in a set-up which was as feudal and regressive as before and the leadership had little interaction with the lowest strata of society. The land-owning class in the Jaffna peninsula at the time constituted 50 per cent of the population and retained its supremacy over politics, society, education and economy. The Vallalas controlled land, epistemology, capital and bureaucracy. This condition continued until, in consonance with the extent of repression that the Sinhalese-run state began to exert on the Tamils, the rigid traditions of societal norms began to break down as victims of such majoritarianism embraced all the classes of Tamils. Realities of life thus proved to be an effective teacher for the uninitiated.

It was at this juncture that for the first time in Tamil society, the caste system was challenged. The *Olduvai Resolution* of May 1976 adopted by the Tamil United Liberation Front (TULF), announced a movement against the caste system and called for its abolition. The resolution in part said, '...in the State of Tamil Eelam caste shall be abolished and the observation of pernicious practices of untouchability or inequality of any type based on both shall be totally eradicated and the observance of any form punished by law.' While all militant groups fought casteism, the LLTE was the most effective in fighting it. During the fifteen years of its rule over the north-east, it introduced re-distribution of land as an important part of its societal reform as also ensuring gender equality. Induction of women cadre into the militant outfit and placing them at important positions within the organisation was another part of this reform process, all elaborated in a pamphlet entitled 'Socialist Tamil Eelam', published in 1980. The LTTE judicial system, which generally drew ridicule in Sri Lanka and elsewhere, played a role in challenging, for the first time in the history of Sri Lankan Tamils, the *Thesawalamai*, the ancient sanction for legalising the landowning class's traditional privileges which were class-biased and inherently antagonistic to poorer classes and lower castes.

This societal landscape highlights the infirmities which confronted ethnic Tamils when they could not take any more the injustices being heaped on them by the state. Therefore, the journey from democratic protest to armed insurrection was not a straightforward escalation of a conflict. At every stage, the process had to go through the necessity of bringing about societal reformation before all sections of Tamils could gather and fight together. In its own perspective, it was a heroic struggle. It was another matter that the liberation movement deteriorated into terrorism and turned as much against the Tamils themselves as it did against the Sinhalese state. It was not strong enough to withstand the onslaught of this deterioration.

There was an aspect of the recent history that deserves to be reiterated at this stage. The November 2013 elections to the Northern Provincial Council were held in extraordinary circumstances. Sri Lankan soldiers actively campaigned among the voters against voting for the TNA candidates. They threatened the electorate of dire consequences if they voted otherwise. 'Political control asserted by the army and the state security forces runs deep in the Tamil areas in the north and, to a lesser extent, the east,' the ICG said in its report. 'Since the end of the war, the military has directly monitored civilian activities, including through information-gathering visits to homes and to the meetings and offices of community and non-governmental organisations and activists suspected of sharing information with journalists, diplomats and human rights bodies are targetted for harassment.' The military also used Tamils employed on army-run farms for information-gathering activities. I had heard, during an earlier visit to Sri Lanka, that even marriages, funerals and other religious and social functions could be held only with the army's permission and under physical supervision of army officers and soldiers. A member of the Tamil diaspora at the time alleged that Tamils were in effect being forced to live in 'an open jail'. Speaking nearly three years after the war ended, he said that 'it is an open jail for the Tamilian people in Sri Lanka. They cannot speak or relate to a human being normally. We want foreign governments to do something about it.'[9] This seemingly maximalist condemnation, nevertheless, presented a raw portrait of the reality in the north prevailing at the time. There has been substantive amelioration of the situation since then, after the Rajapaksa regime was bid goodbye and a humanistic period began. But the topic has regained currency in an unsuspected turn of events and Sri Lanka may be witnessing a return of the retrograde majoritarianism experienced earlier.

At the root of the island slipping back to negativism, as already mentioned, lies the Sinhalese community's pathological distrust of the Tamils. Of the many instances of this particular mind-set colouring the contemporary history, one should be fairly representative, the Sirisena-Wickremasinghe government's panicky reaction to the separation movement in distant Catalonia.

'The Government of Sri Lanka', a foreign ministry statement said, 'unequivocally supports the sovereignty and territorial integrity of the Kingdom of Spain, and considers Catalonia as an integral part of Spain. The Government of Sri Lanka urges the pursuit of dialogue for a united Spain in accordance with the rule of law and within the Spain constitutional framework.'[10]

The government and the Sinhalese would point out an actual incident of unilateral declaration of independence experienced earlier in the island's history. In 1990, a hopelessly adventurist chief minister of the

North-Eastern Province, Annamalai Varadarajaperumal, issued an Unilateral Declaration of Independence and fled to India after his Tamil National Army was defeated by the LTTE, supported by the Sri Lankan army. Even now, given the Tamils' demand for a federal constitution for Sri Lanka, the fear of secession continues to bug the country's Sinhalese majority community. Almost all Sinhalese-dominated political parties and Sinhala-Buddhist interest groups in Sri Lanka, oppose federalism and even devolution of power to a Tamil-dominated province (beyond the powers already vested), all because of the fear of separatism.

Logically, as the Sinhalese argue, one success story of separatism anywhere in the world would light a flicker of hope among die-hard Tamils who, they genuinely believe, have not really given up on the idea of a separate state. Catalonia, therefore, must remain a part of Spain.

As a matter of fact, the fear of Tamil secession is endemic to the Sinhalese way of thinking, and it is expressed in diverse ways. A good example is the proposed new constitution for Sri Lanka, which reveals how deeply entrenched it is. The interim report of the steering committee of the Constituent Assembly (CA), submitted in September 2017 contained several stringent measures to counter secession. The interim report had encapsulated the issues to be addressed by the CA and the extent of consensus or any lack of it already thrashed out among the members on some of the issues. The members, as is the parliamentary custom, represented all the political parties in Parliament. It is pertinent to note that the TNA had campaigned with all passion at its command for gifting the country a federal constitution within 'an undivided and indivisible Sri Lanka'. And what was the fate of its campaign? It was well expected that the demand for federalism would be immediately equated with secessionist sentiments. The steering committee, chaired by the Prime Minister, finally achieved a sort of compromise and succeeded in avoiding the fearsome word 'federalism', opting instead for a Sri Lanka which would be 'undivided and indivisible with maximum devolution of power' to the provinces. Even then the spectre of separation haunted the MPs and, therefore, they hit upon a further safeguard, agreeing that there should be special provisions to prevent secession.[11] It must, however, be noted that the fear of Tamil separatism was born to an extent by the TNA's history which, during the LTTE's rule, was associated with the militants. At that time, the LTTE considered the TNA as an adjunct, expecting it to behave as it was bidden to R. Sampanthan was very much part of the scene as the TNA leader. His reputation is proving to be a deadly legacy though his acceptance today as a democratic leader is well-established. Still, the Sinhalese suspicion not only about his ideology and that of other Tamil leaders, including the Chief Minister for Sri Lanka's Tamil-dominated Northern Province C.V. Wigneswaran's, but also of the general Tamil population, is not likely to pale soon as it is grounded on certain facts of life. The entire TNA election campaign in 2013 leaned on the Jaffna people's pent-up anger and frustration at the military rule they were living under at the time, and that paid it the dividend of a hands-down win. The south was scandalised and agitated over these developments and publicly criticised the Tamil leaders for harbouring secessionist sentiments. Wigneswaran in particular made it a point to praise Prabhakaran for his struggle for a Tamil homeland where the Tamils would be able to live honourably. He also called the LTTE leader a 'freedom fighter' who may have been brutal at times but 'so is the government'.[12] His nomination, for which Sampanthan and his close associate M.A. Sumanthiran had to perspire for acceptance by the TNA, nevertheless, experienced a concerted in-house opposition mainly because of his Colombo connection (though born in Jaffna, he spent his professional life mostly in Colombo). It is a moot point if the military were withdrawn at the time of the election allowing a truly free atmosphere, the TNA leadership would have found it necessary and profitable to invoke the LTTE 'martyrs'. While, both the TNA and Wigneswaran, defended their frequent invocation of the LTTE as a vote-catcher, the sum-total was further consolidation of the Sinhalese composite identification of devolution as eventual secession.

It was more out of a desire to make its point than anything else that led the TNA members to propose a 'secular' constituency and as in the case of federalism, so in this case, too, the state's prime religion Buddhism won the day with ease. Thus, there was no tinkering with Chapter II which accorded the 'foremost place' to Buddhism and guaranteed to 'protect and foster' the Buddha *Sasana* (an omnibus term embracing the precepts, including the behavioural virtues and remedies for non-compliance, etc.) and assured to all (other) religions the rights granted by Articles 10 and 14(1) and (e) and guaranteed to treat them "with honour and dignity without discrimination."

But there was yet another bogey for the Sinhalese to encounter and that was the long-standing Tamil demand for a reunification of the Northern and Eastern Provinces. The SLFP led by President Sirisena was all for it with the rider that the two provinces—which were once united—could be re-united provided a referendum was conducted among the people living there. As is well-known, the Eastern Province, once a Tamil-majority area, had long since become a home for all the three principal religious communities, that is the Tamils, Sinhalese and Muslims, now more or less equal in number. Besides, to go by allegations by the Tamils, in the post-war period large numbers of Sinhalese settlers had come to live in the province. While the Muslims might not object to a unified province, the Sinhalese surely would. However, the proposal was stoutly opposed by the Rajapaksa-led Joint Opposition which cried that a unified province would be nothing but a step towards strengthening the Tamils and an eventual move towards secession.

One progressive proposal in the interim report spoke of abolishing the Concurrent List which, it was felt, was usually exploited by the central government to interfere in and curb the powers devolved to the provinces. However, the proposal still allowed the centre to legislate on a province-specific area but always in consultation with the concerned provincial council. The SLFP pitched for a small but well-defined Concurrent List to facilitate the implementation of national policies and priorities.

The fear of secession again reared its head over the ever-contentious issue of devolution of powers over land and policing to the provinces. While the interim report favoured dealing with this question by following the 13th Amendment, the ultra-nationalist and Buddhist Jathika Hela Urumaya (JHU) strongly opposed it on grounds of granting too much power to the provinces on land and policing and paving the way for secession. It challenged the concepts of a provincial police force and a provincial police commission on the same grounds. The interim report was quite vague equivocal on the issue of abolition of executive presidency. The interim council also dwelt on the concept of a second chamber to represent the provinces and while it gained support, at least one party felt that it would be a wasteful and unnecessary addition.

Since the steering committee was deliberating on a new constitution well past the time when Mahinda Rajapaksa had already emerged as the most formidable challenge to the ruling coalition, the success or failure of drafting a new statute book relied entirely on this new factor. Taking an overall view of the progress made in this regard at the time, the JO judged it to be a clear agenda to destroy the unitary character of the state and turn it into a federal state.

One of the several enduring mysteries of Sri Lankan politics is the never-ending tussle between progress and regress. One would have expected Sri Lankans to have learned the most important lesson from the civil war was that no nation can survive for long without caring for all of its inhabitants irrespective of their race, religion and language. Even at this late stage, the majority community sticks to its age-old concept that as the majority, they have the inalienable right to lord over the other communities. In their perception, even the enormously debilitating costs of the war in terms of the killings, physical destruction and shattering of thousands of lives and damage to property do not qualify to make them rethink of Sri Lanka in a new light, a country of happiness and living as one people. They appear to be mighty pleased with the way things have turned out, that is the complete defeat of the Tamil separatist movement.

In November 2013, the International Crisis Group (ICG) made the following comment in its report, *Sri Lanka's Potemkin Peace: Democracy Under Fire*: 'What many Sinhalese miss is that the Tamil polity's move away from separatist language and dreams will necessarily be slow and require a government in Colombo open to compromise and meaningful dialogue. The TNA leadership needs to be seen as an ally in this process. Over the past eight years, however, the Sinhala public has heard from its leaders a relentless discourse not only opposed to federalism or even modest devolution, but also denying the existence of an ethnic conflict in need of a political solution. Sinhalese opinion has hardened as a result.'

In mid-2018, the above quotation may not be correct in its entirety, but it does to a large extent. The truth of this assertion lies in the Constituent Assembly steering committee's interim report and the determined opposition offered by the Joint Opposition to the very carefully drafted proposals for a compromise between the Sinhalese and Tamil polity's contrary stands on the issue of devolution of power to the provinces.

If the Rajapaksas win the 2020 presidential and parliamentary elections, even that compromise formula would be thrown out lock, stock and barrel. All that would be left for the Sinhalese to do then would be to ensure that the Tamils never raise their heads again. But is this the right way to run a country? Throughout this book, efforts have been made to find a satisfactory answer to this question. However, the answer remained elusive till the end.

NOTES

1 Variously spelt in government documents (usually Office on Missing Persons) but popularly referred as the Office of Missing Persons, which has been followed here.

2 NewsIn Asia, 'With UNHRC in session,Sri Lanka appoints Commissioners for Office of Missing Persons,' 9 March 2018.

3 NewsIn Asia, 'Manadate of Lankan Office of Missing Persons not limited to a particular time period,' 20 March 2018.

4 P.K. Balachandran, 'First ever Sri Lankan Budget to Address Post-war Reconciliation Issues,' *The Citizen*, 11 November 2017, https://www.thecitizen.in/index.php/en/NewsDetail/index/5/12224/First-ever-Sri-Lankan-Budget-to-Address-Post-war-Reconciliation-Issues

5 NewsIn Asia, 'Lankan President stresses need to strengthen Provincial Councils for national reconciliation,' 9 May 2018.

6 Centre for Policy Alternative, Colombo, 'The need to reboot reconciliation in the post-war Sri Lanka,' 19 May 2017.

7 International Crisis Group, 'Sri Lanka's Potemkin Peace: Democracy Under Fire,' Asia Report N° 253, 13 November 2013, https://www.crisisgroup.org/asia/south-asia/sri-lanka/sri-lanka-s-potemkin-peace-democracy-under-fire

8 Athithan Jayapalan, 'The LTTE and the Annihilation of Caste,' *Round Table India*, 15 May 2014, https://roundtableindia.co.in/~roundta3/index.php?option=com_content&view=article&id=7464:ltte-and-the-annihilation-of-caste&catid=119&Itemid=132

9 Shanmuganathan Kaviraj in an interview to *The Statesman*, Kolkata ed., 18 February 2012.

10 NewsIn Asia, 'Lanka opposes Unilateral Declaration of Independence by Catalonia,' 28 October 2017, https://newsin.asia/lanka-opposes-unilateral-declaration-independence-catalonia/

11 NewsIn Asia, 'Lanka's constitutional proposals reveal concern about threat of secession,' 21 September 2017, https://newsin.asia/lankas-constitutional-proposals-reveal-concern-threat-secession/

12 Karthick S., 'Lanka Tamil party's CM nominee wants India to take part in Commonwealth Heads of Government Meeting,' *The Times of India*, 20 September 2013.

5

Human Rights: The Dark Age and Thereafter

IN mid-2018, discussions on Sri Lanka invariably veered around to the possibility of the Rajapaksa brothers returning to power in the 2020 presidential elections. Apart from the sharp contrast to the euphoria and optimism for a better future—that was so palpable in the wake of the victory of the 'rainbow' coalition in January 2015—the forebodings about a negative turnaround in such a short time indicates the visceral malady from which Sri Lankan democracy suffers.

The extent of apprehensions caused by just a possibility of such a development cannot be dismissed as lopsided. In fact, if one listened to the Rajapaksas—speaking with an astonishing degree of confidence and a complete lack of sense of guilt for their record in office—following the upset results of the local government elections held on 10 February 2018, their possible emergence as the rulers looks reasonably certain. There are two aspects of the brothers' statements following their win. They seem to be convinced that the people (meaning, of course, the majority of the Sinhalese community; 55 per cent of such voters opted for Mahinda Rajapaksa in the January 2015 election), would definitely vote for them whenever the next presidential poll is held. They also acknowledge the technical 'hitch' that would prevent the former President from contesting a third time, but that could be circumvented by nominating his brother Gotabaya to the post.

This would bring the second aspect of their public posture, available at the time, to the fore and therein lies a cause for alarm. For, in interviews to national and foreign media, Gotabaya Rajapaksa laid bare his concept of how the next President should be conducting business and whatever else could be said, surely his ideas could not be described as suitable for a democracy. So, let us first hear him expand on his favourite theme.

Question: Many believe that you have blood on your hands. That as Defence Secretary during the war, you defeated the LTTE, but were also behind the killing of thousands of civilians. What do you say to these charges? And how did the war affect you personally?

Answer: I know I have not done anything wrong. I know I have done the correct thing. My conscience says that. When you ask about civilian killings, you must understand that war is not a rosy thing. Whether it is in Sri Lanka, Afghanistan, India, Pakistan or Iraq, war is not a good thing. But in Sri Lanka, I didn't create the war. I ended the war. Ending the war was much better than what it was. Our country is a better place without the LTTE. Today, the President of Sri Lanka can go to Jaffna and speak there. Today it (Jaffna) is a free country. It is not only soldiers but also innocent people who died due to terrorism. Bombs do not understand who is enemy and who is friend or if it is a civilian or military van. So I do not regret. I used to sleep everyday during the war, too.[1]

In another interview, Gotabaya Rajapaksa was asked, '...you have this projected image of being an evil human rights violator. Don't you think it is going to affect you if you contest the next presidential election?'

His answer was a lengthy one, but it apparently brings out his true self: 'I was a military officer and then I was away from this country for some time. I came to limelight after becoming the Defence Secretary. My main challenge at that time was to defeat terrorism which was prevailing in this country for almost three decades. Most of the sections of this country as well as the international community thought there is no military solution for this problem and that terrorism cannot be defeated militarily. Somebody told me—I still have not read that book though—that it was mentioned in Eric Solheim's (Norwegian diplomat who monitored the Oslo peace talks with the LTTE in 2002) book that nobody, not even military strategists or even the President at the time, (believed) that the LTTE could be defeated except Secretary Defence Gotabaya Rajapaksa. Even then there were these NGOs and various groups with various viewpoints, be it liberal or whatever you call them, who thought anybody who talks about war is evil. But, when you are at a certain position with a definite focus on achieving a certain target, you have to do everything possible. You have to talk, you have to act and you have to think to achieve that target, and this does not differ when it comes to ending the war. That is why I was projected as an evil person. The LTTE had a network in the southern parts of the country and they had infiltrated various areas during the ceasefire period. Their suicide bombs did not take into consideration whether it is going to kill Sinhalese, Tamils or Muslims. Even those who are criticising me as a human rights violator could have been a target. Those who (were) involved in the operations had to profile and identify terrorists. Even though we (were) aware of the fact that all Tamils (were) not terrorists, unfortunately, 99 per cent of the terrorists were Tamils. Actions we took against terrorism were projected as things done against Tamils… Unfortunately, I have not done anything to earn that evil image. I have done whatever I have done with conviction. And I would always say, "Yes, I have done everything possible to end the war." I take pride in that and I think the majority respect me for that.'[2]

A critical analysis argues that Gotabaya Rajapaksa redefined the power dynamics of his brother's presidency. He did it with a 'triad' of image engineers that spawned a new oligarchy that is today committed to this presidential bid. How did he do it? Defeating the LTTE, killing (the LTTE chief Velupillai) Prabhakaran, and the restoration of normalcy were impossible tasks. The Rajapaksa regime made the 'impossible' possible. The means employed to achieve the impossible was, therefore, unpunishable.[3]

On the top of all this, as already related, in the summer of 2018, the possibility of an eventual return of the Rajapaksas to power indeed looked quite real. And in case this actually happened, the gains of Sri Lankan democracy in the last three years might well be lost. The gains were substantial; since January 2015, the island had travelled a long way in terms of individual freedom. The native's argumentative nature had been resurrected; the Sri Lankans always had opinions and in the post-Rajapaksa period they were actually arguing about their opinions.

That was not so before 2015 when dissent was not expressly prohibited but emphatically discouraged. Then the Sri Lankans kept their opinions to themselves, knowing well that dissent was tracked, collated and presented to the great grandee who decided the fate of those who dared to opine. Sri Lanka must not allow the 'monster' to return.

Gotabaya's prescription

Even though President Sirisena had ridiculed the Rajapaksas for 'day-dreaming' about their victory in the 2020 election[4], Gotabaya Rajapaksa—about whose clear conscience for his alleged involvement in the bloody ending of the civil war we have already been apprised—was ready with a detailed advice of what the next President should do during his tenure.

In the interview to Weerakoon, quoted above, he first explained why he qualifies for contesting the next presidential election. 'I have served this country as a military officer for 21 years and a major part of my career was under (the) UNP regimes. I have won many gallantry awards under three UNP Presidents, J.R. Jayewardene, R. Premadasa and D.B. Wijetunga, while my family was mainly engaged in SLFP politics. So you cannot say those were political awards. I think I have proved to this country that I deliver what I promise. I am not an ordinary politician who would only talk but would not work. Instead, I am vice versa. I have proved that I am effective, productive and will not give up until the objectives are achieved. I have proved I can work and I can bring results. I have a way of working and I have my policies. My main aim is producing results. You can have visions and dreams. This country will not go any further unless those talks, vision and dreams are implemented.'

He then elaborates on his plans and intentions. Asked if he were to be next President, would he go for a political solution to the North and East. He replied: 'I don't understand this word 'political solution' and that is my problem. There was terrorism and I believed that it could only be defeated militarily as all these so-called political solutions have been tried. My basic idea is that every citizen should be able to live with dignity in this country and every individual should be able to have the same freedom everywhere in this country. I think for that what is necessary is having economic freedom. Whether you are in the north or south you can live a dignified life if you have economic freedom. All other things are secondary. So my aim is to give economic freedom.'

These utterances—directed towards the people—show that the speaker has maintained his militaristic attitude towards what is euphemistically described as the national question, an out and out political issue, which he rather spectacularly demonstrated by orchestrating the defeat of the LTTE. It might even be inferred that in his mind he equates the Tamil community with the defeated Tamil rebels, though well aware of this implication, he prepares an escape route. More dangerously, he refuses to recognise the necessity of a political solution to the ethnic question and believes that the singular failure of all the political solutions tried so far proves beyond doubt that those were wrong assumptions. The only way forward, in his view, is securing economic freedom to all the communities. This was in complete negation of the Tamils' repeated assertion that without political emancipation, economic freedom was impossible to achieve. Further, the failure of the economy in the north to pick up after the infrastructural development, had amply proved the correctness of their assertion. Even though he was the Defence Secretary, he continued to be engaged with the former war zone along with his defence forces even after the war was won. This was a major departure from the past practices when rebellions were put down and the security forces were sent back to the barracks. This did not happen after May 2009.

The Defence Secretary was allowed to initiate, undertake and supervise the reconstruction work in the war-devastated northern and eastern regions. Whatever was happening in the post-war period was under his complete control. Civilian rule was allowed to be restored only in 2013 after the northern provincial elections were held when a new, popularly elected government assumed office.

Still, it was by no means a normal civilian rule. The governor continued to be a former military officer. The army was omnipresent, right from the street in front of your house to bazaars to educational institutions to hospitals, anywhere where civilians would be obliged to gather as part of their lives. It was only after the new elected dispensation took office that the intimidating presence of the military began reducing, that too, in fits and starts; and the remnants still make their presence felt all over the peninsula.

The extraordinary role handed over to Gotabaya by Mahinda Rajapaksa in the post-conflict north-east cannot be explained in a rational way, since Sri Lanka remained constitutionally democratic all the while. Even though President Rajapaksa interfered with the business of each and everyone, he did not meddle in what Gotabaya did. It could have been not only because the latter was his favourite sibling but also because the special role the brother undertook in the military victory at great risk. The President's policy on Gotabaya appeared to have been to allow him to carry on without any interference. This seemed to have bestowed enormous power on the Defence Secretary without any control. And, this in the ultimate analysis, was akin to his becoming the 'grave digger' not only of his brothers but also of the government's.[5]

However, a new element entered the narrative in mid-May 2018, when it was revealed that another brother was harbouring presidential ambitions. Basil, who always played second fiddle to his other brothers, and built up the rural vote base for the Paraphrases which eventually made possible the show-stopping performance in the local government elections in February 2018, laid claim to his suitability as a presidential candidate. He based his claim on the substantive grounds that it was he who had built up the SLPP all by himself and that he had proved his political prowess. This was where he apparently hoped to score over Gotabaya who lacked political experience. As the familial ambitions clashed, some outsiders allied with the SLPP hopefully suggested a relatively neutral and politically experienced person, Chamal.

On the top of all these came the news that Mahinda himself was still hopeful of contesting the 2020 poll provided the Sirisena-Wickremasinghe government managed to revoke the two-term constitutional bar. The 19th Amendment to the Constitution not only curtailed the presidential term of office from six years to five years but also prevented the same President bidding for a third term. At this time President Sirisena was openly talking about his wish to continue to be in politics after his term would end in January 2020. This was necessitated after his plan to continue into the sixth year was rejected by the Supreme Court. Apparently alarmed by all these developments, Gotabaya did not wait for a signal from Mahinda and launched a virtual election campaign in Colombo on 15 May 2018. However, he sweetened his open challenge with the coating of a sophisticated alias, his 2030 Vision for Sri Lanka and calling for the establishment of a 'socialist market-economy', certainly a sufficiently mysterious signboard![6] He still had a major hurdle to cross. The 19th Amendment also barred him from contesting an election because of his dual citizenship.

Earlier in the year, Gotabaya, however, had expressed his readiness to give up his US citizenship if he was nominated to by the party as a presidential candidate. In the event the amendment was revoked, it would pave the way not only for Sirisena and Mahinda but also for Gotabaya to throw their hats into the ring. There was, nevertheless, scepticism in the public mind about Gotabaya's real intentions as far as renouncing his dual citizenship was concerned. According to t sceptics, his US citizenship could act as a shield against any state attempt to prosecute him provided he got advance intelligence and had time to flee the country. Not an improbability if one took account of the desperation of the ruling coalition not to allow more leeway to the Rajapaksas to return to power. But, as has already been noted, such a scenario would arise only if the investigations into the criminal cases registered against him and were currently progressing could be wound up before the next presidential election. Therefore, the capacity of the CID to wind up its work in reasonable time would be the crucial factor.

Selective memory

The Sinhalese community's spontaneous embrace of the military as the 'war heroes' after May 2009, (the entire process of installing the military on the pedestal of hero-worship was designed and executed by the Defence Secretary) was also a significant departure from tradition, as was the continuing military control over the former war zone after peace had been restored.[7]

It is important to note at this juncture that the civil war was not the first *internal* rebellion to be crushed by the security forces; it was in fact the third. It had been preceded by the 1971 and 1987 JVP rebellions. It is equally significant to note that while the first two internal rebellions were led by the Sinhalese, the third was led by the Tamils.

The same security forces were involved in the defeat of all the three uprisings, yet there were no 'war heroes' at the end of the JVP rebellions. The obvious conclusion could be that it was their ethnic identity that made the vital difference. In the JVP rebellions, both the victors and the defeated were Sinhalese, and therefore there was no room for rejoicing over their cruel end. In fact, the opposite happened. Even though the people desired a quick end to the rebellions, they opposed vehemently the cruel manner in which they were put down, like burning people alive on street-corners so that the nearby members of the public could witness the scene. But it was the Tamils who were defeated in 2009 and, therefore, there was every reason why this difference in behaviour occurred.

The obvious conclusion could only be the difference in ethnicity involved in the three uprisings. Because it was the minority Tamils who were defeated in 2009, the victory of the security forces over them deserved to be celebrated. And the celebration had not stopped with the 10 years which had meanwhile passed by. Part of the ongoing celebration was the national unity government's toeing the Rajapaksa line of denying international access to justice over the genocide charges. Not surprisingly, politicians close to the Rajapaksa brothers were harsh on the security forces in respect of the JVP rebellions but led the country in honouring the same forces over the LTTE's defeat. This dichotomy in behaviour could only be explained by noting a vital difference in the attitudes of the three governments under whose care the three rebellions took place.

President Ranasinghe Premadasa was conscious of the people's dislike of the security forces, and that was why he withdrew them from the temporary military camps set up across the south after the second JVP rebellion was crushed. At another level, Mrs Bandaranaike did not hesitate to prosecute military officers who were found involved in the sensational murder of the beauty queen Somawathie Manamperi during the 1971 rebellion. Did this act of justice defame and demoralise the military? On the contrary, the army could clear its name while the officers were given the maximum punishment under the law.

By fiercely protecting the military from facing charges of the excesses committed during the civil war, Gotabaya, had in fact inflicted severe damage on the image and behavioural pattern of security force personnel. This had affected, as we have seen, even the deployment of Sri Lankan forces on global peacekeeping operations, a field of activity which the government had later identified as of special interest to the country. Each such personnel now requires a certificate from the national human rights body clearing him or her of any misconduct on account of human rights violation and only then they can be recruited for international duty.

Gotabaya's 'evil' contribution also encompasses two other criminal features of the Sri Lankan state: use of security forces in extrajudicial killings and what has been christened as *barracksification.*[8] Under this system, military officers were extensively engaged in civil administration and activities, which is a normal feature only in a military dictatorship. Even the diplomatic service was encroached upon, in a remnant of which President Sirisena recently had to whisk away a military officer from facing criminal charges in a foreign country.

When asked to comment on the extensive politicisation of the Sri Lankan armed forces, the present army chief Lt Gen Mahesh Senanayake admitted it, but added, 'In the past, extra politicisation was there. Of course, the war is an extension of politics, we do know and understand that. But today, with the change of government in 2015, we are proud to say that we are not under pressure. As an army commander I am not under pressure from my minister, the President or the Prime Minister. That means, politicisation of the armed forces has been curtailed or is very minimal.'[9] The army chief also defended the extensive militarisation of civil administration and services, including education after the end of the civil war, arguing that as the prolonged civil war had denuded the state machinery in the war zone extensively, the military was the only state entity that could fill up the gaps efficiently and adequately. But, as normalcy was gradually restored, the military personnel were withdrawn from civilian duties and responsibilities. 'Thirty years of war have left our community in the north at a disadvantage. The government machinery was not functioning for decades. There was a big gap and our services are needed to address it. The armed forces deployed in the north are the only organisation who have the capacity to perform. I have been discussing this with the (northern) Chief Minister, requesting him to use our capacity. Some can look at our presence negatively but the majority will accept it. Then there is the question of security itself. By that I mean security concerns from non-traditional threats (like drugs and drug abuse)...Our Tamil population has never experienced this threat in history, and that is why there is a security requirement as of today, until the police do policing correctly. There is a gap in policing, law and order. The day the Sri Lankan police does proper policing, we will be the happiest to go inside a camp and play cricket or come back to the south.'

Lasantha Wickrematunge murder

While the score sheet of dark deeds committed under the patronage of the Rajapaksas kept piling up, perhaps the most sensational was the murder of journalist Lasantha Wickrematunge, editor of *The Sunday Leader*, after he had publicly accused the President of plotting his assassination.

In a letter addressed to President Mahinda Rajapaksa and released to the public, Wickrematunge wrote, 'It is well-known that I was on two occasions brutally assaulted, while on another my house was sprayed with machine-gun fire. Despite the government's sanctimonious assurances, there was never a serious police inquiry into the perpetrators of these attacks, and the attackers were never apprehended. In all these cases, I have reason to believe (that) the attacks were inspired by the government. When finally I am killed, it will be the government that kills me...In the wake of my death I know you will make all the usual sanctimonious noises and call upon the police to hold a swift and thorough inquiry. But like all the inquiries you have ordered in the past, nothing will come of this one, too. For truth be told, we both know who will be behind my death, but dare not call his name. Not just my life, but yours too, depends on it...In the name of patriotism you have trampled upon human rights, nurtured unbridled corruption and squandered public money like no other President before you.'[10]

In a searing indictment, Wickrematunge's widow and journalist Sonali Samarasinghe, wrote to Mahinda Rajapaksa, 'As you are aware, on the morning of 8 January 2009 my husband, Lasantha Wickrematunge, one of Sri Lanka's best-known journalists...was brutally slain as he travelled to work. It is no secret that Lasantha and I were the biggest irritants to your government. While you were still Prime Minister in 2005, I exposed the Helping Hambantota scandal, in which millions of rupees donated to the government for tsunami relief had mysteriously found their way into a private bank account controlled by you. Shortly after that exposé our presses were attacked and severely damaged. The perpetrators of this crime were never brought to book and there was never a serious police investigation.

'In September 2005, we reported a suspected plot to attack our newspaper office following an incident in which a group of thugs entered the premises of the press and recorded the number plates of vehicles parked in it. Lasantha lodged a complaint at the Mount Lavinia police station and also informed the Inspector General of Police of the incident. No action was taken. On the morning of 11 January 2006, you were quoted publicly as having threatened Lasantha's life. The words alleged to have been used by you in a telephone conversation recorded by him (in addition to the statements propriety prevents me from quoting here), included the following: "I will show you what it is to be scared. I will rest only once I have destroyed you. You wait and see. You don't know who Mahinda Rajapaksa is. I will finish you. I treated you well all this while. Now I will destroy you. You don't know who Mahinda Rajapaksa is. You watch what I will do to you." ...Indeed, it is no secret that your administration is prosecuting an undeclared war of terror on the independent media, and in the eyes of many, you and our brothers have blood on their (your) hands.'[11]

She continued, 'In an interview with the BBC's Chris Morris, your brother, Defence Secretary Gotabaya Rajapaksa, giggled hysterically when asked about my husband's murder and made very clear that he was "not concerned" by the killing. Your brother also famously asked, "Who is Lasantha?" Why is he so important in contrast to those killed by the LTTE? "He was just someone writing to a tabloid." These are words uttered, Mr President, by the man under whose purview your entire police operates. (He) dismissed Lasantha's killing stating that anyone could have killed him given that he picked up a number of enemies in the course of his career as a journalist. What is implied by this oft-repeated statement of your brother is that journalists who criticise abuse of power by the state should accept their fate without protest...Indeed, your brother has made it a habit publicly to brand as 'tiger terrorists' or 'traitors' journalists whom he perceives as critical of your administration...he confirmed the free media's worst fears by admitting that the defence ministry considered dissent during war time was tantamount to treason and, thereby, presumably punishable with death.'

As predicted by Lasantha, there was no progress in the murder investigation as long as Mahinda Rajapaksa remained in office. When the new government came in, one of the first campaign pledges that was honoured was the reopening of the case and the inquiry to be conducted by the Crime Investigation Department (CID). And results began to come in fairly fast. In contrast to the earlier detentions of alleged suspects leading nowhere and the investigation by the police virtually abandoned, the CID appeared to have made a breakthrough and had since advanced step by step towards a possible conclusion.

Gotabaya-Fonseka tussle

Meanwhile, an unsavoury exchange of accusations and barbs broke out between the former Defence Secretary and Field Marshal Sarath Fonseka, the man who led the army to the victory over the LTTE. The intense tussle erupted after reports indicated that the CID investigation into the 2009 murder of journalist Wickrematunge and the 2008 abduction and assault on another journalist Keith Noyahr was pointing towards the involvement of Gotabaya Rajapaksa in both the crimes.

Gotabaya sought to ward off the accusation by redirecting the arrow of suspicion onto Fonseka, who at the end of the war was hailed as the leader of the 'war heroes' and promoted to the rank of four star General and shortly thereafter elevated to the post of Chief of Defence Staff. So far so good, but what was unknown at the time was his budding political ambitions. His fate may well have been sealed when he contested the presidential election as an Opposition-backed candidate in January 2010 and was soundly defeated by the incumbent President Mahinda Rajapaksa. Soon he was thrown into prison on various charges. His restitution could only come about with the emergence of the Sirisena-Wickremasinghe government which not only pardoned him and restored his rank and everything else but also made him an MP and subsequently a minister. Thus, the bad blood between the Rajapaksa family and Sri Lanka's first and only Field Marshal is of vintage lineage and will not wash away easily.

After claiming that the CID was only unearthing evidence which were already in the files of the Colombo police, Gotabaya alleged that the so-called fresh investigations were actually a plan hatched by the government and Fonseka to malign him. 'They have found nothing', he said. 'These are all what we found. They are manipulating evidence we found.' Even though it was he who had ordered the investigations, the evidence gathered at that time was now being presented to the court as new evidence and the CID was coercing those who had been arrested to implicate him. 'They are arresting them and telling them that if you say Gotabaya Rajapaksa's name then you can get out,' he said. Those arrested were all from military intelligence, both serving and retired.

He was also quoted saying, even though 'I knew, definitely, that Sarath Fonseka was behind the crimes,' and the finger of accusation was firmly fixed on him, he still allowed the investigations to continue and did not initiate any action against him in order to not gain any political advantage (which would have accrued to him by arresting the top war hero).

In response, Fonseka was understandably acerbic, 'If Gotabaya Rajapaksa is a self-respecting person, he should come out and reveal the truth and make available the information he has to the CID instead of levelling wild allegations against me in the media. When the police are closing in on him, this is what he does. Rather than defending himself he sends his lawyers running to the Supreme Court to get rulings preventing him from being arrested. The day I am accused, I will defend myself like a lion, not like a coward.' Anyone in the country could understand that if the Rajapaksa government had any evidence implicating him in any of the attacks on journalists, he would have been dragged to the prison in chains after the 2010 presidential election (in which Fonseka contested against Mahinda Rajapaksa) by the Defence Secretary without a thought being spared for the criminal justice system and for no other reason than to fulfil a political vendetta. It is a moot point what may happen if the investigations into Lasantha Wickrematunge's murder and Keith Noyahr's abduction and assault, apart from a host of other serious crimes committed against independent journalists (even state-owned media personnel were not spared) and consequent trials were not concluded before the Rajapaksas make a comeback to power in January 2020.

New evidence of civilian killings

As the noise over the charge of genocide committed by the Sri Lankan armed forces in the last days of the war was slowly dying down with Colombo staunchly denying the allegation and stiffly opposing an international-national hybrid court, the claim of fresh evidence emerged in May 2018. The International Truth and Justice Project (ITJP), a human rights group, said that nearly 280 Tamils, including 29 children, who had surrendered before the army on the final day of the war, 18 May 2009, had gone missing. 'This is the largest single group of enforced disappearances in Sri Lanka's history, hundreds of people disappearing at the same time and place with multiple eyewitnesses both inside and outside the country,' the ITJP executive director Yasmin Sooka said in a press release: 'On the final day of the war, the Sri Lankan army made loudspeaker announcements urging Tamils to surrender promising them an amnesty.' The Sri Lankan civil society in one voice demanded to know the plight of the 29 children, last seen with their families in the custody of the army on or around 18 May 2009, ITJP said. The rights body asked Sri Lanka's Office on Missing Persons (OMP) to question the military commanders if it wanted to unearth the truth about these cases, adding that the commanders had even shaken hands with the LTTE leaders who had surrendered and were alleged to have been executed. 'Nine long years have gone by and their grandmothers and mothers should not be left alone to stand on the roadside demanding the truth while exposed to intimidation and threats from the security forces,' the ITJP said.

Disputes over the allegation of genocide have not died out even if the spotlight is no longer on it because there are plenty of proofs of wartime excesses against both the security forces and the LTTE. Since the Tamil militants are no longer in existence to answer the genocide charges, only Sri Lanka's armed forces can be brought to book over the same allegations. This development seems to have reinforced Sri Lanka's majority community's belief that the international community has unjustifiably put the entire responsibility for civilian killings on the security forces. The same logic keeps the Sinhalese and Tamils from achieving any kind of reconciliation. What appears to be a minor deviation from normal human behaviour (but unavoidable in the exigencies of war) to the Sinhalese is nothing short of one of the worst genocides in world history. The distance between the two views is apparently too wide to allow any kind of understanding.

In this seemingly perennially grim scenario, a sane voice was heard in May 2018 when a Muslim leader appealed to the two communities to work proactively for the future of Sri Lanka even as they remember and commemorate their war dead. In a *Facebook* post, Sri Lanka's Deputy Minister of National Unity and Reconciliation (a key ministry today if allowed to function satisfactorily) Seyed Ali Zahir Moulana, said that 'hateful attitudes of the past should not be sustained because these were only pushing the Tamils, who were once held hostage by the militants, into immortalising the undesirable political agendas of the past'. Commenting on the 18 May 2018 commemoration of the mass-scale deaths of civilians trapped between the army and the LTTE at Mullivaikkal, Mullaitivu district, on the eve of the end of the war, when Northern Province Chief Minister Wigneswaran called for observing the day as the 'Tamil Genocide Day', he wrote: 'As an individual who very nearly paid the ultimate sacrifice for my country, and thereby contributing to what is now known as one of the key turning points in our civil conflict, I am of the fervent opinion (that) the significance of May 18, 2009, should never be forgotten. For nine years, sentiments have echoed from both sides of the divide, remembering and honouring whom they lost and paying tribute to the bravery and courage of those who fought on their behalf. As an elected representative of what was once a war-ravaged area, to this day I am witness to the fact that the decades of war and strife have left deep scars in our beautiful countryside, and ingrained into our beautiful people. Further, I also witness that while each side remembers and triumphs, it is also important to take into account the innocent civilians who were once held hostage by barbed wire and machine-gun fire, are now today victims to hateful discourse which continues to immortalise the undesirable political agendas of the past. But now, as someone who has experienced these challenges first hand from its inception to conclusion, I must state that it is now time to go further. While we honour and remember the fallen, let us work proactively forward. Let us use the significance of May 18th as a way to reflect on our nation's past, and build a stable, peaceful and prosperous future. Let us work fervently to reconcile on our differences, and unite harmoniously with pride in our diversity as citizens of a singular, sovereign and free Sri Lanka.'[12]

Sensible advice, but will Sri Lanka listen to it? Especially when political instability is rising and sworn political enemies are rattling their sabres before jumping into renewed adversity? It would not take long to find out the difference between a war hero and a terrorist. The Chief Minister added that there were groups which sowed extremism in the south as well as in the north and it was the duty of all citizens to understand this reality and work in a responsible manner. The current President has been paying the customary tribute to the 'war heroes' but he never mourns for the dead Tamil civilians, a point that has been duly noted by the minority community. The Moulana mentions extremist groups in the south, by which he most likely means the Rajapaksas. Sirisena and Moulana were certainly speaking in two different voices.

NOTES

1 Arun Janardhanan, 'Modi govt officials look at Sri Lanka differently...without understanding: Gotabaya Rajapaksa,' *The Indian Express*, Kolkata ed., 25 March 2018.

2 Gagani Weerakoon, 'Former Defence Secretary Gotabaya Rajapaksa Discloses His Readiness to Give Up His US Citizenship and Contest Elections If Selected as a Presidential Candidate' (Interview), posted in *DBSJeyaraj.com* on Facebook, 11 March 2018.

3 Sarath de Alwis, 'Gotabaya Rajapaksa Re-defined the Power Dynamics of Mahinda Rajapaksa With a "Triad" of Image Engineers,' *Sunday Observer*, posted in DBS.Jeyraj.com on Facebook, 6 May 2018.

4 At a May Day rally (held on May 7, instead of the First of May) 2018, in the Eastern Province.

5 Victor Ivan, 'The Shadow of Gotabaya,' *Sri Lanka Guardian Columns*, 8 July 2014, http://www.srilankaguardian.org/2014/07/the-shadow-of-gotabhaya.html

6 NewsIn Asia, 'Sri Lanka's ex-defence chief launches election bid,' 15 May 2018, https://newsin.asia/sri-lankas-ex-defence-chief-launches-election-bid/

7 Victor Ivan, *op. cit.*

8 Victor Ivan, *op. cit.*

9 Meera Srinivasan, 'Sri Lanka is the only country that has eradicated terrorism,' *The Hindu*, 16 May 2018.

10 Steve Coll, 'Letter from the Grave,' *The New Yorker*, 12 January 2009.

11 Sampsonia Way, 'Sonali Samarasinghe Confronts Sri Lanka's President,' 3 April 2013, https://www.sampsoniaway.org/blog/2013/04/03/sonali-samarasinghe-confronts-sri-lankas-president/

12 NewsIn Asia, 'Remember the war dead, but also work for the future, pleads Lanka's Deputy Minister for Reconciliation,' 19 May 2018.

6

India and Sri Lanka: Fruits and Curses of Neigbourliness

Is India stepmotherly?

—A Sri Lankan Perspective From Vijayvaani.com

IN November 2017, there was considerable curiosity in Sri Lanka about the need to demystify the Indian mind, as indeed there always is. Looking at India from the Sri Lankan point of view, the northern neighbour looks so truly gigantic that such an all-occupying curiosity appears to be quite justified. Depending on one's predilections, the giant is instantly metamorphosed into a menace or a much-valued friend in need. But the average reading seems to be: better be on the safe side, be patient and wary. If one talks to current ruling coalition members in Sri Lanka, India presents a benevolent face. Responses from the Opposition are understandably opposite and disturbingly negative. The Opposition is quite openly unhappy at the presumed advancement India has made, since the national unity government came into being, in pursuing a policy of interference and influence in Sri Lankan domestic and foreign policy.

Academics try to present a balanced assessment. In their view, India and Sri Lanka cannot remain detached from each other for long and are compelled by geopolitics and changing circumstances as well as domestic compulsions to interact constantly and intimately with each other in order to extract the maximum benefit for their own countries. They cite the instance of New Delhi finally abandoning its hands-off policy adopted and followed assiduously in the aftermath of the IPKF misadventure as a prime illustration of this symbiotic relationship. The second major chink in the relationship occurred when New Delhi joined ranks with the international community to condemn the brutalities perpetrated by Colombo's armed forces on the ethnic Tamils and began to support the UNHRC's devastating indictment of President Rajapaksa's policies. The latter brushed aside his gratitude for New Delhi's substantive help during the last phase of the civil war and repeatedly branded India as one of his country's worst enemies. He seems to be pursuing the same strand of Indophobia into his current role of the leader of the Opposition in Parliament. However, there is a distinct change in his attitude towards India. He now praises New Delhi for supporting him in the later stage of the civil war and in the recent years in the UNHCR annual sessions. At the same time, both he and his brother Gotabaya talk openly about the chasm with the present Indian government. Mahinda Rajapaksa, nevertheless, is hopeful that with more time the two sides can arrive at an understanding. He is hinting at the strong possibility of his return to power, if not as the next President but as the power behind the throne.

However, as far as the national unity government is concerned, the relations could not have been better. Barring minor obstacles, New Delhi and Colombo are seen to be sailing on a calm sea.

India was visibly upset when, after its initial blustering and hasty steps to punish the aggressively interfering China, the Sri Lankan government suddenly surrendered and decided to pursue the pro-China policy initiated and implemented vigorously by Rajapaksa. To a shocked New Delhi, this was considered unacceptable and it tried reapplying its time-honoured practice of browbeating Colombo for being so openly and aggressively pro-China in its various dealings and pronouncements. The efforts were clearly ill-advised and failed in their objective, as Sri Lanka reiterated in unequivocal terms its firm decision to pursue the same policy toward China. Colombo's ruffled feelings were eloquently expressed by a minister who was quoted saying at the time, 'India should desist from dictating to us what our China policy should be'. It would appear that New Delhi has now come to accept the reality, namely, that it can never match Beijing in wooing developing countries in its so-called area of influence, the Indian Ocean Region (IOR, see *Conclusion*). It is not just accidental that Prime Minister Wickremasinghe, who is believed to be genuinely pro-India, is also a loud votary of the need of his country to be an enthusiastic member-state of the Chinese mooted One Belt One Road (OBOR) Initiative (or BRI-Belt and Road Initiative) that seeks to link Asian countries to those in Indo-Pacific region and Europe. Apart from reiterating his government's policy in this regard, he does not shy away from advising India to fall in line with his country in the matter.

For good reasons, India's tendency to take for granted the concurrence of its neighbours with its own views on various issues seems to rankle Sri Lankan academics. The latter advised a hard re-thinking by India on what its relationship should be with their country. Professor Jayadeva Uyangoda puts his formulation quite succinctly, 'There is no proper evaluation of India-Sri Lanka relations by India. The MEA seems to be going by the old, familiar stereotyped policies without taking into account vitally changed circumstances.'[1]

This view is reciprocated time and again by other Sri Lankans. A Cabinet minister, Patali Champika Ranawaka, believes that India is unable to see his country 'as a whole' and should no longer restrict its perspective through the prism of the Tamil-majority Northern Province. 'That India is a guarantor of the northern Tamil people's rights should now be a thing of the past,' he said referring to New Delhi's constant push for the devolution of powers to the Northern Provincial Council (NPC) under the 13th Amendment to the Constitution, enacted following the 1987 India-Sri Lanka Accord.[2] However, Ranawka's strong indictment of Indian policy for his country, deliberately bereft of any diplomatic nicety, is explained by his political affiliation. He belongs to the nationalist Jathika Hela Urumaya (National Heritage Party, led mainly by radical Buddhist monks), earlier a constituent of the Rajapaksa government and thereafter a switch-over to the Sirisena-Wickremasinghe government. His extreme view about India is not necessarily shared by the UNP and SLFP (Sirisena faction) and other constituents of the government. However, this does not detract from the general feeling of resentment at India's perceived interference in what are essentially domestic issues.

To quote the Minister further, 'The Sri Lankan Tamils have to cooperate with the existing government to settle their problems without dragging India in'.

Has India also grown weary of northern Tamils' almost pathological dependence on it for support on every issue that crops up between them and their government? And is there a re-thinking in New Delhi about selectively disengaging itself from its close and traditional ties with those people?

Indian diplomats are chary of discussing an obviously touchy subject but they leave little doubt that the matter has been thought through and a decision taken. The decision is to make northern Tamils realise that they can no longer take India's traditional, unstinted support for their positions on every issue for granted.

The overhauling in policy brought about by Prime Minister Modi may well be described as a tectonic shift. It has been formulated under two persisting issues: one related to Sri Lanka's India policy and the other dictated by geopolitics in the Indian Ocean Region. Indian government sources say that India has 'consciously adopted a new policy approach not willing (any more) to be seen as solely committed to the north-east Sri Lanka but also equally keen to help the south (dominated by the Sinhalese)'. This would be evident from the decision to hold a public meeting in Hambantota (in the deep south where the Rajapaksas hold sway), just a week after Mahinda Rajapaksa's eldest son and the MP for Hambantota Namal 'attacked' the Indian consulate in October 2017 in the guise of leading a 'popular' demonstration against India's alleged dominance in the island. But the large gathering in the Indian Consulate-organised meeting proved that the people did not share the Opposition party's anti-India movement.[3]

Seven years earlier, it was the Rajapaksa regime which had agreed to allow India to open missions in Hambantota and Jaffna after the countries exchanged notes on 21 August 2016, under a reciprocatory agreement, that allowed Sri Lanka to open a fourth consulate in India in addition to the existing High Commission in New Delhi, a Deputy High commission in Chennai and a Consulate in Mumbai. This agreement was followed by another agreement signed on the same day allowing India to upgrade the coastal rail line network in the south between Galle and Matara and between Colombo and Matara. At the same time, Indian funds and assistance were also requisitioned for the reconstruction of the railway infrastructure, disrupted by the Liberation Tigers of Tamil Eelam (LTTE) during the civil war. Seven years later, Namal Rajapaksa led his father's supporters in a violent demonstration to the same Indian consulate which was set up during his father's regime. The demonstration was ostensibly against the government's decision to study an Indian proposal to 'operate, manage, maintain and develop' the Chinese-built airport in Mattala near Hambantota.

China had already built a port at Hambantota and had a major stake in its ownership. Even though both the port and the airport were built by Chinese companies under Rajapaksa, the latter's supporters were now opposing them on the grounds that Colombo was allowing 'foreign entities to own national assets'. This issue alone was enough of an example to understand how India's Sri Lanka policy is beholden forever to the domestic politics of both the countries. In its policy overhauling, New Delhi made at least an honest attempt to break out of the shackles of India's domestic politics but it is powerless as far as Sri Lanka's own domestic politics is concerned. Its decision to decisively move away from the debilitating identity of an ethnic Tamil-oriented mind-set also logically led it to turn attention, apart from the Sinhalese, to the India-origin Tamils as well, a community which had never experienced fraternal relationships with ethnic Tamils. Therefore, when the Indian government decided to build houses for the plantation Tamils of Indian origin living in the Central Province, it was considered a signal to northern ethnic Tamils that other Sri Lankans were equally important for India.

To reinforce its newly-found engagement with the Sinhalese in the south, a special ceremony was held at the Nonagama Cultural Centre, Ambalantota, Sri Lanka's Minister of Fisheries and the Indian High Commissioner Taranjit Singh Sandhu jointly launched a project in April 2018 to provide livelihood to nearly 70,000 people from the farming and fishing communities in the Hambantota district. The project envisaged supporting livelihood activities by providing useful tools and equipment to the beneficiaries. In particular, 7000 bicycles, 1000 sewing machines and 60,000 grub hoes were disbursed to beneficiaries. With India's grant of $887,340 it was expected that close to 70,000 persons or families would be able to improve their incomes and enhance their livelihood.

Speaking on the occasion, Sandhu emphasised the importance of capacity building as reflected in 'numerous' projects being implemented 'all over Sri Lanka' with Indian assistance. He reiterated India's readiness to continue to assist Sri Lanka 'wherever possible and whenever needed'. At the time, India's 'overall commitment' for development assistance to Sri Lanka stood at $2.9 billion, out of which $545 million was 'pure' grant assistance.[4]

The Indian government appeared well-settled in assiduously following its reoriented Sri Lankan policy to a logical conclusion, namely, to be known as a regional power disposed to in equal measures to the various communities in Sri Lanka. In a way, this change in policy was expected to neutralise, at least to some extent, the deeply entrenched belief in the majority community that India would always tilt in favour of ethnic Tamils irrespective of the merits and demerits of any dispute between the two communities.

However, a new wave of expectation of Indian help rose in the north-east in May 2018 after the 2017 annual report of the Central Bank of Sri Lanka (CBSL) was released. The report revealed the poor stage of economic development in the former war zone, with the Northern and Eastern Provinces showing a very low contribution to the GDP of the country, 4.2 per cent and 5.7 per cent respectively. This set the political and civil society circles in the Tamil region linking the relative importance of the region in the national economy to the stepmotherly treatment being meted out by Colombo. They felt that unless the region improved its economic performance, the Central government would continue to deny it its rightful share of budgetary provisions and development funding. This logic was extended to the imperative of Indian help in building up the economy.

Civil society circles like the Jaffna Managers Forum acknowledged the major infrastructure projects done with Indian financial and technical assistance, such as, the reconstruction of the Northern Railway re-connecting Jaffna and Colombo and the construction of 46,000 houses in the former war zone, both of which were initiated and completed during the Rajapaksa's regime. Admittedly, a slew of infrastructural projects were initiated in 2017 during the Indian Prime Minister Modi's visit. But the fruits from them, such as, the rehabilitation of the Kankesanthurai (KKS) Harbour in northern Sri Lanka and the modernisation of a Lankan airport, would take some time to be tested. This new-found demand for Indian investment in the north-east was yet to be accorded a political demand, but a beginning was made in the wake of the drafting of a new constitution.

The Tamil leadership linked the full implementation of the 13th Amendment to the formation of a new constitution, arguing that only through a political solution to the ethnic question (which was guaranteed under the 1987 India-Sri Lanka Accord) could the north-east be developed, upon which the region's contribution to the GDP would improve and its value to the nation would be highlighted. In their view, all this could be achieved only with India's active participation in the process. So, however much New Delhi wished to shift its focus from the Tamil region to the Sinhalese region, Sri Lankan Tamils were not yet ready to forego what they believed to be their hereditary asset.[5]

RSS-BJP reorienting relations

However, there seems to be a new churning in bilateral relations with the fast emergence of the ruling Bharatiya Janata Party (BJP) and its ideological mentor the Rashtriya Swayamsevak Sangh (RSS) as an important factor with still unclear ramifications. Several academics I had talked to on the subject appear to be quite uncomfortable with the development. They argue that Sri Lanka's long, devastating experience with majoritarian chauvinism and its societal repercussions force them to be wary of any political entity that is identified with a comparable ideology.

This apprehension is caused by the rapid closeness developed between the BJP and the RSS on the one hand and Sri Lanka's Bodu Bala Sena (BBS or Buddhist Power Force) on the other hand in the last few years. The first signs of this otherwise unlikely relationship first surfaced in 2013 at the height of anti-Muslim attacks in Sri Lanka when the BJP's national general secretary and the then national spokesperson of RSS, Ram Madhav wrote in an RSS publication *Samvada* that 'The issues raked up by the BBS are worthy of active and sympathetic consideration'.[6] This was the first known record of the RSS expressing its plan to get into an ideological alliance with the racist Buddhist organisation in Sri Lanka.

The BBS chief ultra-rightist Buddhist monk Gnansara Thero apparently confirmed this development by disclosing in 2014 that discussions with the RSS were 'at the highest level' to create a 'Buddhist-Hindu peace zone' in the region to combat a 'growing threat of radical Islam', and 'to protect and defend the threatened Buddhists and counter Muslim extremists'. These contacts and consultations are obviously a continuing process, as has been confirmed by the BBS on several occasions since then. Vishwa Hindu Parishad, a more openly hard-core Hindutva outfit and member of the ubiquitous Sangh Parivar, invited Northern Province Chief Minister C.V. Wigneswaran to the World Hindu Congress in November 2014, in New Delhi where the Chief Minister's remark caused a flutter back in his country. He said that the difficulties faced by the Hindus in Sri Lanka had not ended after the war, opting not to mention the other two communities, Muslim and Christian, who were equal sufferers. His apparently motivated statement surprised and shocked Sri Lankans, but the trend towards grandstanding Hinduism at the expense of other faiths was clearly worrying.

Right from 2014, anti-Muslim and anti-Christian attacks by ultra-radical Buddhists have become a regular annual feature. What is truly worrying is the apparently inadequate governmental response to what may be described as a routine malady. Even though the government declared an emergency after two days of rioting in March 2018, facilitating deployment of the army to control the situation, reliable reports spoke about the security forces standing as mute spectators while Buddhists went about setting fire to Muslim business establishments in Kandy district. Newspaper reports spoke about soldiers telling each other that 'They are beating our people, bring your weapons and rush here'.[7] Another report said that the police and politicians backed by Rajapaksa joined anti-Muslim riots that rocked the Kandy district, as confirmed by witnesses, officials and CCTV footage reviewed by Reuters news agency. The role of the police and some local Buddhist politicians suggested that the government lost control of sections of the security forces deployed in the region and that the violence was more than a spontaneous outburst fuelled by fringe Buddhists extremists and hate speeches spread on social media.

Rajapaksa, however, denied that he had ordered party leaders who were found involved in the riots, to act as they did. The police said that the allegations of involvement of policemen and politicians were being investigated. Victims and witnesses, whose accounts were partly backed by CCTV footage, described members of an elite paramilitary police unit, the Special Task Force, assaulting Muslim clerics and leaders. 'They came to attack,' said A.R. Ramees, a clerk at a mosque.[8]

However, referring to the reported alliance between Sri Lanka's BBS and Myanmar's revivalist 969 group led by monk Ashin Wirathu, Breitbart News Network, (an American news website advocating ultra-rightist and reactionary views) wryly commented that the 'violence by Buddhists against Muslims in Sri Lanka has not yet reached the level of mass slaughter, mass torture, and mass rapes being committed by Buddhists led by Wirathu against Muslim Rohingyas. Perhaps the two Buddhist monks, Gnanasara and Wirathu, are in some kind of bloody contest with each other to see who can be responsible for the most atrocities'.[9]

The National Christian Evangelical Alliance of Kandy reported that since the national unity government came into power in January 2015, as many as 190 incidents of religious violence against churches, clergy and Christians had been recorded.[10]

From the above, it would appear that the joining together of the BBS and 969 group has sent a disturbing enough signal. If, on the top of this, the coming together of the RSS-BJP-VHP and the BBS adds its bit to the atmosphere of religious intolerance spreading across South Asia, it is but natural that sensitive Sri Lankans themselves—who are among the worst sufferers of bigotry—would be deeply disturbed. The spurt in Buddhist atrocities against Muslims and Christians in Sri Lanka since the end of the war seems to confirm the theory that as the Tamils have been ground under the heel and are not likely to hit back and demand respect in foreseeable future, the Buddhists' majoritarian chauvinism just needed a new victim, and that it has found them in the other two minority communities residing in the country, the Muslims and the Christians.

These acts of violence are seen to be as a direct fallout of the triumphalism and majoritarianism that took hold of some sections of the Sinhala Buddhist majority community after the military defeat of the LTTE, encouraging the Mahinda Rajapaksa regime as it went about tightening its political grip on the country. Since then, a raft of groups openly professing hatred for Muslims as well as Christians, has come up, some of them using social media to spread their venom. Apart from the Bodu Bala Sena, two other similarly fanatical groups, Sinhala Ravaya and Mahason Balakaya, are also busy in the business of ushering in yet another period of religious and racial strife.[11]

Viewed against this development, the prominence enjoyed by Ram Madhav, who seems to be the Indian government's point man for Sri Lanka, in the bilateral relations seems to bother Sri Lankan scholars. They feel that even if this RSS-BJP functionary may not be directly concerned with New Delhi's Sri Lanka policy, his party's institutional relationship and warmth toward a rabid ultra-rightist Buddhist group cannot bode well for either country. His perceived bonhomie with Wickremasinghe appears to be worrisome for them, too.

Senior Indian officials, however, discount any major influence that Ram Madhav may have on policy, asserting that the MEA is sufficiently capable of dealing with a close neighbour like Sri Lanka and need not depend on any political entity for guidance and policy formulation.

Irrespective of pooh-poohing, however, it is well-established that it is the Prime Minister's Office (PMO) and not the MEA that determines India's major foreign policy matters and that this may well ensure that inputs for policy formulations are not always governmental and may be based on inputs from other sources. This is a trend that was first initiated by former National Democratic Alliance (NDA) Prime Minister, BJP's Atal Bihari Vajpayee, during whose regime his National Security Advisor and Principal Advisor Brajesh Mishra (himself a former diplomat) came to largely determine India's foreign policy, effectively reducing the foreign affairs ministry to the status of a post office. The two Indian National Congress-led United People's Alliance governments by Dr Manmohan Singh during 2004-14 restored the MEA to its former status. The tables were again turned on the MEA when the Narendra Modi-led NDA government took office in May 2014.

While officials decline to comment, it is also well-established that career diplomats are being increasingly sidelined in determining foreign policy matters. This trend has been gaining traction as the PMO has taken the centre-stage and the MEA has become a mere communicator with other governments. Consequently, the MEA has been shedding the use of expertise which is otherwise traditionally available with Indian and foreign scholars and former diplomats. This assertion is supported by several Indian and Sri Lankan scholars who were earlier regularly consulted by the MEA on subjects pertaining to their expertise.

The Modi touch

In the particular instance of Sri Lanka, however, the role played by Indian Prime Minister Narendra Modi has evoked considerable appreciation. His visit in March 2015 ruffled Sri Lanka's domestic politics. During his first visit to Colombo he talked with the new government, praising its reversal of policies, his last-stage visit to Jaffna where he advised Tamils (he had already met the TNA leaders in Colombo) to be patient with the coalition in power and give it more time to sort out the Tamil-specific issues, invited severe criticism from the Tamils. The latter insisted that he should have been quite emphatic with the Sinhalese leadership and pressured it to meet the Tamils' demands without further delay. The trip to Jaffna was derided as a 'cosmetic' visit.[12] While the Tamils said they had welcomed his visit, they had been completely disappointed with his utterances which failed to show any light to them. There was a demonstration of Tamil men and women in front of the Indian Consulate at Nalloor, Jaffna. One of the organisers said, 'The Indian Prime Minister should take a victim-centric approach. That is why we are gathered in front of the Indian Mission at Nalloor.' The Sri Lankan state should be told by him in clear terms that Colombo should release those detained in the secret detention camps without delay and to clarify the status of those who were handed over at the end of the war in the Vanni region, the status of those who had surrendered, those who were filtered away from the people in the barbed-wire camps and those abducted by the white van squads run by the Sri Lankan military in the past and still believed to be held in secret detention camps. Three years later, the grievances remain right where they were; neither the political prisoners have been released nor the surrendered and filtered people have been accounted for. On the top of this recently came the news that at least a group of 280 Tamils, including 29 children, who had surrendered to the army in the last few days of the war, remain untraced till date.

Modi's next visit took place during the Vesak celebrations in May 2017, a rather deliberate choice of timing since Indian diplomacy took a turn to exploit the religious factor. This fitted well with the RSS-BJP establishment's world view as well, exploiting the so-called 'soft power' of Indian heritage. And, buoyed by Modi's oratorical skill, the trip was a resounding success. A Sri Lankan Minister spoke eloquently when he said, 'Modi's visit was a grand success. The chemistry between our President, Prime Minister and Modi was excellent...The interesting thing is that Modi made a clear statement that projects should be fast tracked.'

President Sirisena was as effusive as his Minister, 'It is wonderful to meet this great human being @narendramodi in Colombo again. Thank you for gracing #InternationlVesakDay.' Modi himself, was, however, singularly prosaic, 'Delighted to meet President @MaithripalaS in Colombo.4:41 PM-May 11.2017.'

The moot point was that Buddhist-Sinhalese fundamentalism could only feed on such specific religion-oriented visits by foreign dignitaries and their anti-minority fixation would only get further legitimisation. Logically, neither Modi nor his government could have any deliberate intention to help create such an impact, but in Sri Lanka's existing environment of intolerance and hatred, treading with extreme caution is always advisable.

This attempt to counter-balance the Chinese clout with its soft power clearly falls short of diplomatic requirements, for the truth is that while it appeals to the religious sentiments of the majority community it does not necessarily answer the target of the country's expectations. The most charitable way to describe this stance is by comparing it with a poor man's response to the insufferable display of wealth and might by a rich man. India can never hope to beat China either in terms of loans or of trade. There was a time when India's neighbours were yet to taste the Chinese bounty and used to be happy recipients of Indian assistance. But once China appeared on the world stage and turned its attention to Asia, and especially since Xi Jinping came to dominate its politics and economy, India has been simply overwhelmed by the scale of economic relationship that China has developed with Asian countries. Besides, the pace of economic and strategic domination of South and South-East Asia accelerated with the launch of the One Belt One Road (OBOR) Initiative or Belt and Road Initiative (BRI) for increasing connectivity via road, ports, railway and infrastructure between China, Asia, Indo-Pacific nations and Europe.

It is also time to question and take a re-look at the effectiveness of soft power as a foreign policy tool. Has the facilitation of travel from Nepal to Ayodhya changed in any way the hardened and disillusioned Nepali mindset about India? Especially when at every moment Nepal loves to remind India of its folly of blocking overland supply of fuels and other essential commodities which affected the common citizen terribly? Has the Nepali foreign ministry forgotten the Indian warning whenever Kathmandu sought out Chinese assistance? It is time for New Delhi to accept the fact that the neighbours tolerate India only because they cannot get away from it. There is a strong feeling in these countries that the free India merely inherited the British Raj's mindset towards its neighbours. As an analyst puts it, 'Small states like Sri Lanka will need to keep their diplomatic options open as to wide a range of influence as possible, without committing themselves to any single course of action. What is required is not a systematic linkage but a partial one. Regional groupings are, by and large, the least disadvantageous, if not the most desirable, for small states.' All of India's neighbours in South Asia will continue to face the common problem of a relationship in which every possible calculation is weighted in favour of India.[13] Even though the statement is obviously an over-simplification of a whole range of diplomatic relationship in a region and seemingly prejudiced, but its significance lies in the fact that most of India's neighbours would tend to agree with it. India has not been able to address this vital problem. This view also does not take into account the new complications of a situation—as presently obtaining in India-Sri Lanka relations—in which the regional power has to try to solve intra-regional problems as part of responding to the challenge of an outsider's aggressive foray into the region.

India's realpolitik

How is India's deliberate shift in policy from a normative and value-based one to one of realpolitik working? In the last five years of the BJP rule, India has increasingly projected itself as a hard-bargaining, tough-talking and pragmatic country giving no quarters to anybody and being bent on securing its own interests above everything else. There is only one test to ascertain the efficacy of such a policy, to find out if it is yielding results. In the instant case, we can have a look at how the economic cooperation between India and Sri Lanka is progressing. As the reader will soon see, India is being asked again and again to prove its bona fides as a benefactor and not as a usurper in the garb of a philanthropist.

Neighbourhood, the hardest nut

New Delhi is clearly under an exceptional pressure to re-establish its status in its neighbourhood, which has been badly destabilised by China. Each and every South Asian country except Bhutan has crossed over to the Chinese side by more than half the distance. Most sensibly, they have all chosen not to antagonise either contender and opted for optimising the benefits for themselves by balancing their act. By no means, they can be faulted for an intelligent choice they have made.

In my interactions with South Asian diplomats at various times and places, I have always glimpsed a constant strain, namely, that Indian leadership is primarily responsible for the failure of the South Asian Association of Regional Cooperation (SAARC). As the regional leader, the SAARC should have taken off automatically under India's stewardship. And that it has not done so because the regional body has become a prisoner of India-Pakistan rivalry. After seventy years of this enmity, the region is thoroughly tired and wishes to forge ahead on its own. And this is precisely what the neighbours are doing, especially since China's emergence as the second most powerful nation on earth.

While the soft power diplomacy (which China has been practising on a global scale) has its merits, economic diplomacy is far more effective in today's intensely competitive and globalised world. China has succeeded in establishing itself as India's chief competitor mainly because of its economic power. It is in this context that the buzz in Sri Lanka during Modi's 2017 visit can be better understood.

The MoU for Co-operation in Economic Projects, which was signed between the two countries during Wickremasinghe's New Delhi visit in April 2017 is a document full of attractive possibilities of ideal cooperation in several vital sectors of economy between the two neighbours. The projects envisaged in the MoU include a 500 MW Liquid Natural Gas (LNG)-fired power plant, an LNG terminal or floating storage Regasification Unit in Colombo and along with other associated projects, such as, Compressed Natural Gas (CNG) outlets, a 50 MW solar power plant in Sampur near Trincomalee, for all of which Sri Lanka issued

Letters of Intent by May 2017; joint development of the Upper Tank Farm containing 84 tanks in an area of 800 acres by Lanka IOC and Ceylon Petroleum Corporation for which the two corporations would set up a joint venture by the end of July 2017 and make business development plans ready by September 2017; a port, petroleum refinery and other industries in Trincomalee for which a joint working group was set up by the two governments by the end of June 2017; and road and railway projects in Trincomalee, Mannar and Jaffna.

The MoU makes it clear that if implemented properly and in a timely manner, the Indian-assisted projects would enable the ushering in of a major economic and industrial change in Sri Lanka. Therefore, its importance cannot be over-emphasised. The Indian government said that the MoU was important in the context of growing Chinese footprints in Sri Lanka. The two countries were at that point finalising an MoU for joint development of the Trincomalee port. 'Held comprehensive talks with PM Ranil Wickremasinghe on way to strengthen India-Sri Lanka ties for the benefit of our citizens,' Modi tweeted after the meeting. 'The discussion of the Indian leadership with the visiting dignitary (Wickremasinghe) provided both sides an opportunity to review the progress in the implementation of the decisions taken during various high-level exchanges in the past two years or so, including the visit of the Prime Minister Modi to Sri Lanka in March 2015 and the visit of the President and the PM of Sri Lanka to India in February 2015,' the External Affairs Ministry said. The Indian side reiterated India's commitment to promoting prosperity in the neighbourhood and affirmed the continued support to the leadership for a stable, peaceful and prosperous Sri Lanka. The flurry of agreements that had materialised between the two countries covered a wide range of economic sectors, such as, orbit frequency coordination of satellite for the SAARC region, development of small developmental projects, medical equipment, emergency ambulance services, peaceful uses of nuclear energy, cultural cooperation (enabling Sri Lanka to participate in the Nalanda University), and agriculture. Indian cooperation is also extended to defence, notably to the Sri Lankan navy.

Murkiness of politics

The extent of pitfalls for India in cultivating its neighbours can be realised by the fact that the April 2017 MoU was met with an immediate and severe attack. The opposition to its implementation was so severe that the Sri Lankan Prime Minister was obliged to speak in Parliament in its defence, pointing out that Lanka IOC had been paying $100,000 per year for a lease signed in that year for the tank farm. 'None said no to the monies,' he said.

The deliberate misinformation campaign had succeeded in creating the general impression in the country that the MoU in no way bound Sri Lanka to anything to do with India. In a token of coercive diplomacy, the Indian Prime Minister, who was in Sri Lanka in about three weeks after the MoU was signed, conveyed 'quietly but firmly' that India was serious about implementing each of the projects and expected Sri Lanka to reciprocate. It came as no surprise that Mahinda Rajapaksa led the assault, seeking to belittle the significance of Modi's visit. 'The information I have is that all deals have already been signed. So the Indian Prime Minister's arrival or non-arrival would be immaterial,' he said. Interestingly, in a complete volte-face from this anti-India public posture, he called on Modi in Colombo and discussed economic relations between the two countries, which he later described as 'very cordial and friendly' talks. Completely skipping any political subject, he spoke only of forging close economic relations with India. More interestingly, while he had led the protests against such relations, he listed the 'deficiencies' in the present government's economic policy and regretted the stalling of the projects he had initiated. He declared his strong desire to strengthen economic cooperation with India as well and argued that investor confidence in Sri Lanka was lacking and should be addressed. He also expressed his happiness at Modi's presence in the International Vesak Day celebrations. Reports suggest that despite all this verbal dishonesty, Modi was not taken in and emphasised that Indian economic cooperation was meant for Sri Lanka's welfare and not the other way round. He also assured that India would not try to launch any project harmful to Sri Lanka.[14] It was as if he was responding to each of the silent thoughts of Rajapaksa, sought to be hidden away from him. The impression the meeting left (which was held at Rajapaksa's request) was that both the leaders were trying to set up a new friendly relationship with each other on the assumption that while Modi would continue to be in power, Rajapaksa, too, would be staging a comeback soon and, therefore, a cordial relationship between them would help both the countries. However, Rajapaksa's meeting with Modi left a trail of surprise, disappointment and grumble in his own camp, since he had kept it a secret from his closest allies and followers. One report claimed that even his request for a meeting—when Modi had had a tight schedule leaving little room for further engagement—came to be acceded to only because President Sirisena had agreed to it after being informed by the Indian envoy Taranjit Singh Sandhu. Along with his party, the whole country was caught by surprise because the meeting had followed a prolonged acerbic and openly anti-India agitation led by Rajapaksa. Picking up the Indian project for the Trincomalee port as a devilish conspiracy to engineer a division of the country to satisfy Indian aggrandisement, Rajapaksa had kept mum when one of his close followers called for a black flag demonstration against Modi, which was read as a sign of his approval. Rajapaksa sought to dilute this by saying later that the person was misquoted in the media. To learn that the same man had sought an interview with the 'arch-enemy' and had kept it a secret, appeared to have shocked and confused his party.

The MoU that 'nobody was talking about' (as a news analysis said at the time)[15] and signed in New Delhi on 26 April 2017, about three weeks after Modi's visit, sought to provide a fillip to bilateral economic relations, with both the countries expressing commitment to expeditious implementation. Clearly, its importance derives from the growing Chinese economic footprint in Sri Lanka. But behind all the sweet talk lurked several irritants which came out in the open in the course of time.

Apart from the 2017 MoU and the Trincomalee port project, the most contentious issue is the Economic and Technical Cooperation Agreement (ETCA), which has been hanging fire for sometime in the face of a stiff opposition organised by the Rajapaksa-led Joint Opposition and other frontal associations like the Professionals' National Front (PNF). The ETCA seeks to include 'services' in the economic sectors in which the bilateral economic cooperation is to be expanded under the MoU and other agreements signed so far. However, the ETCA has not progressed due to the stiff opposition from the Sri Lankan public.

Interestingly, though the initial opposition was to a presumed and unconfirmed Indian design to bring about the dominance of Indian labour and technical expertise for constructing the massive infrastructural projects under the ETCA, it has since shifted to the very projects themselves and taken on an overt political overtone. The PNF said in a letter addressed to the Indian Prime Minister on the eve of his 2017 visit that India should first solve the problem of the unfavourable balance of trade between the two countries before 'forcing' another unequal agreement on Sri Lanka. Arguing that the Indo-Sri Lanka Free Trade Agreement (ISFTA) signed in 2000 had allowed the Indian state governments to impose non-tariff barriers on Sri Lankan imports which led to them getting out-priced, as a result of which the deficit with India stood at over a massive $3.5 billion in 2016, the new ETCA would only aggravate the situation for Sri Lanka. 'As professionals we cannot agree on your government's influencing the Sri Lankan government to enter into a new free trade agreement (meaning the ETCA) to include services in addition to trade, without taking any tangible step to solve the existing serious issues with the prevailing ISFTA,' it said. The agreement on the Trincomalee oil tanks was sought to be held back due to a case filed in the Supreme Court. The PNF also objected to the construction project linking Trincomalee and Talaimannar and termed it, along with the Talaimannar-Medawachchiya railway line, as potentially encouraging a division between the north and the south considering that 'separatist threats' were still present in the country. Coupled with the railway line and the highway, the Indian government's ambition to connect the Trincomalee harbour through the projected construction of a so-called 'Hanuman Bridge' to Dhanuskody (India) presented a 'great threat' to the independence and sovereignty of Sri Lanka.

While there is scarcely a discussion in India on the hare-brained concept of building a road-rail link between the two countries, seeking to revive and institutionalise a much-told episode from the epic *Ramayana,* it appears that Sri Lanka continues to be much exercised over it. Wickremasinghe's categorical denial in Parliament about such a project having been discussed, was of no avail. Instead, the media reported the Indian government had finalised the project, the engineering design and related planning completed, a $5-billion-loan from the Asian Development Bank approved, and even preliminary discussions with the Sri Lankan government initiated. The reports also re-read the 'true' import of Modi's address to the Sri Lankan Parliament during his May 2017 visit talking of coming to Sri Lanka 'with the hope of building this bridge' (at the time, thought to be a metaphorical reference to building friendship) but now revealed in its actual purpose (of gobbling up the island-nation).[16] The origins of this hoo-ha in Sri Lanka about the project lay in the overtly ebullient Indian road and transport minister Nitin Gadkari's announcement in June 2017 following the signing of the Bangladesh, Bhutan, India and Nepal (BBIN) Motor Vehicles Agreement in Thimphu, that 'The government is also looking at connecting India and Sri Lanka. The road connectivity built across (the) Palk Strait could possibly be a combination of a sea-bridge and an underwater tunnel.' The plan was to construct a 23-km sea bridge linking Dhanuskodi (India) with Talaimannar (Sri Lanka) on the grounds that it would increase the trans-SAARC road and transport network.

Interestingly, it was the British who had originally conceived such a link between the two neighbouring countries, both then part of the British empire; they had even done the costing by 1894 naming it the Indo-Ceylon Bridge; and then abandoned the whole project in favour of a ferry service which was naturally found to be much cheaper. The doubtful credit for reviving the idea belongs to Ranil Wickremasinghe who, as the then Prime Minister, mooted a land bridge as it would 'offer both (the) sides huge economic benefits, with industry springing up on both (the) sides of the project.'

Be that as it may, how effective has the road project linking Bhutan, Bangladesh, India and Nepal been so far? Proposed first at Kathmandu during the SAARC summit in 2014 by Modi, it was only in January 2018 that India was able finally to persuade Bangladesh and Nepal—just two out of a larger number of member-countries—to be signatories to the Bhutan-Bangladesh-India-Nepal Motor Vehicles Agreement (BBIN-MVA). Bhutan, the owner-country of the very first letter of the 'awkward' (as a media analysis called it) acronym, had till then resisted the project firmly, citing its environmental concerns. A signatory country would be obliged by the agreement to permit passage to vehicles of the other signatories in order to ensure a smooth transport flow of commodities thus facilitating growth of sub-regional trade, the basic concept behind the project. Modi's concept itself owed its inspiration to Pakistan's walkout at the Kathmandu summit in protest against India's push for the SAARC Motor Vehicles Agreement. At the time the Indian Prime Minister said that regional integration in South Asia would go ahead 'through (the) SAARC or outside it, among all of us or some of us.' Ultimately, it is only three, out of the eight (this is rather academic since the eighth member, Afghanistan, can never hope to be part of the agreement as it shares a land border in South Asia only with Pakistan) member-nations, which are participating in the BBIN-MVA. Even though for diverse reasons, and with Pakistan never agreeable to cooperate with India, the principal South Asian country managed to carry along only two others, and this cannot be complimentary to its foreign policy. India's desire to include Sri Lanka merits sympathetic consideration, but the probability of Mahinda Rajapaksa regaining power in a little over a year the door there might be closed again.

Returning to the Modi visit in May 2017, an immediate fallout could well be Sri Lanka's straight refusal to allow a Chinese submarine to dock at Colombo. 'They asked for permission for May 14 and 15 to dock the submarine. We refused,' a senior defence official said. To be on the safe side, the government also decided that such requests would be turned down in future, too.[17] Three years ago, Colombo did not pay much attention to Indian concerns and allowed two Chinese submarines to dock at the Colombo harbour. This act of open defiance angered New Delhi so much that it promptly called for an explanation from Colombo.

China in a swift diplomatic move sought to calm down India's raw nerves by pointing out that it was the common practice for all navies in the world to dock at nearby ports for logistical support. Two years earlier, Beijing also issued a lengthy statement assuaging India's nervousness by saying that 'The People's Liberation Army has never established a military base overseas. The PLA Navy ships, while conducting long-distance voyages, often go to close ports of littoral countries for logistic supply. This is a common practice of the world's navies. According to the needs of escort missions and other long-distance voyages we would also consider having logistic supply or short rests at appropriate ports of other countries. Such logistic supply activities do not have any connection with establishing military bases overseas.' In May 2017, however, Colombo did not make any such mistake and nipped another recurrence of a similar diplomatic row in the bud by outright refusal of the Chinese request. Quite interestingly, three separate events almost coincided.

Apart from its obvious success, Modi's second visit was also marked by the ghost of a dispute, ghost in the sense that while the two governments denied the existence of any 'deals' and an 'MoU' secretly signed, sections of Sri Lankans continued to agitate over it. Understandably, the cries over the supposed secret understandings reached by the two governments were raised by the political opponents of the present Sri Lankan government; in other words, the Rajapaksa-led SLPP and the Joint Opposition. The reference to an MoU is not lost in mystery. It was to the MoU signed by the Sri Lankan Prime Minister during his first official visit to New Delhi in 2015, a pact that evoked a tremendous wave of protests back home, led naturally by the Rajapaksa-led Opposition parties.

It is a fair measure of the arduous job that Indian diplomacy is constantly called upon to perform while dealing with the neighbourhood that even after several explanations from the highest quarters about the benefits of the ETCA for Sri Lanka that the issue was still hanging fire in mid-2018 with little indication of an acceptance in the offing.

The toughest nut?

The prolonged dispute over deep-sea fishing by Indian fishermen in Sri Lankan territorial waters continues to elude an amicable settlement. Several attempts have been made in the last decade or so, but Sri Lanka continues to be highly aggrieved over what it perceives to be India's inability or otherwise to introduce a change in the fishing pattern of Tamil Nadu-based fishermen so that they do not intrude into its exclusive maritime region.

The inability of the two countries to resolve this festering issue of poaching by Indians in Sri Lankan waters offers an ideal opportunity to study the various intricacies which play a major role in the inter-relationship. Once again the big state of a sub-continental proportion with its vast coastline and the small state, an island, with its much smaller coastline are essentially dissimilar players in this relationship. India operates in maritime affairs on a much higher plane, enabled by its vast coastline, the 12th largest exclusive economic zone in the world, its *pioneer investor* status earning it (thirty years ago) a 150,000 sq. km. mine site in the central Indian Ocean for sea-bed mining of poly-metallic nodules.[18] It was also the first country in the world to have earned the pioneer investor status to explore the central Indian Ocean. However, based on a resource evaluation, India has now retained an area of 75,000 sq. km. with an estimated resource of about 100 million tons of strategic metals, such as, copper, nickel, cobalt, manganese and iron. A First Generation Mine site with an area of 18,000 sq. km. has been identified, and the technology for extraction of metals from the mined poly-metallic nodules has also been developed. In short, India is on the threshold of acquiring vast resources from exploring and exploiting an indeterminate wealth of poly-metallic nodules from the sea-bed of the central Indian Ocean.[19]

India has a total coastline of 7,515 km. of which a mere 344.88 km. is shared with Sri Lanka but managing this small stretch of ocean to mutual benefit has so far defeated all bilateral mediation efforts. As many as four maritime agreements exist between the two neighbours. They are worded in mutually agreed words and graphics and the precise extent of each party's exclusive territory with exact locations where their sovereignty and ownership overlap each other. Yet, there are violations of the rights of one country's citizens by those of the other, and the dispute continues. The agreements are 1) The Boundary in historic waters of the Palk Strait between the two countries and related matters (signed on 26-28 June 1974, and put into effect on 8 July 1974); 2) The Maritime Boundary in the Gulf of Mannar and the Bay of Bengal and related matters (signed on 22 March 1976, and put into effect on 10 May 1976); 3) The Determination of the tri-junction point between India, Sri Lanka and the Maldives in the Gulf of Mannar (signed on 23-24 and 31 July 1976, and put into effect on 5 February 1977); and 4) The Extension of the maritime boundary in the Gulf of Mannar (signed on 22 November 1976 and put into effect on 5 February 1977).

The importance of what is popularly called the fishermen's issue lies in the fact that it involves the question of livelihood of a few hundreds of thousands of Indian and Sri Lankan fishermen. This is why the issue has always demanded an amicable, mutual settlement. While both the countries have failed to strike a deal acceptable and beneficial to all the stakeholders, the flare-ups including deaths of Indian fishermen due to shootings by the Sri Lankan navy seem to have become a thing of the past. However, large-scale and stray arrests of Indian fishermen poaching in Sri Lankan waters by the Sri Lankan navy continue to occur. Their release from Sri Lankan prisons also follows in due course after the Indian government takes up individual cases with its Sri Lankan counterparts.

This is obviously not an ideal situation and cannot be allowed to continue indefinitely, since at times the issues gather enough traction to complicate bilateral relations. Both India and Sri Lanka are well aware of this and are genuinely committed to settling the dispute.

What then prevents a solution? An examination of the past efforts would suggest that while prior to the outbreak of the ethnic war in Sri Lanka in July 1983, Indian and Sri Lankan fishermen went about their jobs reasonably peacefully, but the situation began to change after 1983. Fishing boats began to be used to smuggle out both Tamil Tigers and civilians across the bay to India and smuggle in arms and ammunition on return trips. The Sri Lankan navy first used to intercept and arrest or shoot the militants. When the LTTE developed a naval wing with powerful and armed boats, the government put a ban on fishing by Sri Lankan fishermen in the Palk Strait.

Prior to this development, Indians were regularly crossing the International Maritime Boundary Line (IMBL) to poach in Sri Lankan waters as the area was extremely rich in marine wealth. The turn of events subsequent to the outbreak of the civil war stopped their visits. Thus, the livelihoods of fishermen on both the sides of the Palk Strait were suddenly turned upside down.

Intrepid Indians were, however, always ready to risk their lives and continued to poach in Sri Lankan waters. Once the Sri Lankan navy took me and several other foreign correspondents on a patrolling trip to the end of the Sri Lankan territorial waters, and, sure enough, several Indian boats were intercepted. The Navy Chief of the time good-humouredly asked the Indians why they were in Sri Lankan waters. Only too aware of their crime, they apologised and begged to be allowed to return to India. The Sri Lankan navy, of course, could not just release them even though a group of foreign correspondents comprising two more Indians were present. We saw the reality and reported accordingly.

Katchatheevu, the bone of contention

The fisheries dispute, however, consists of several other issues as well, among which the question of the sovereignty of the Kachchtheevu island reigns supreme. The maritime boundary agreements of 1974 and 1976—which delimited international boundaries in the Palk Bay and the Gulf of Mannar and the Bay of Bengal respectively—were concluded by the two governments in the name of good neighbourly relations. But they did not reflect realities on the ground because the people concerned, namely, fishermen were not consulted on either side. The principle of national sovereignty underpinned both the agreements. A close personal relationship the two Prime Ministers, Indira Gandhi and Sirimavo Bandaranaike, facilitated the successful conclusion of the talks. However, from the perspective of Tamil Nadu, the ceding of the island of

Katchatheevu in the Palk Bay to Sri Lanka was an unpardonable mistake on the part of Gandhi.[20]

With the island previously falling under the *zamindari* system of land tenure established by the British Indian government, New Delhi and Tamil Nadu continued to debate the question of sovereignty. At the time of ceding, New Delhi did not consider Katchatheevu to be part of India but rather 'a disputed territory.'

To New Delhi, the boundary agreement's worth lay more in cementing bilateral relations and Katchatheevu or fishermen's livelihood did not appear to have weighed much. The strong opposition that surfaced in Tamil Nadu was, therefore, quite natural, and even though all the political parties got together to start a movement, the government continued to ignore its probable repercussions. According to one point of view, what New Delhi did at the time out of ignorance and callousness could have sparked off a systematic disintegration of the country, since many parts of India—even though united under the British rule—were originally and also during the foreign domination—were governed under the zamindari, ryotwari and mahalwan systems of land tenure.[21]

The government tried to soothe the rough feathers of Tamil Nadu by explaining that though the sovereignty of Katchatheevu had been ceded to Sri Lanka, Tamil Nadu fishermen would continue to enjoy their traditional fishing rights in and around the island without hindrance, would continue to dry their fishing nets on the island and attend the St. Anthony's annual festival as before, and all these without obtaining Sri Lankan visas. However, Tamil Nadu did not accept the government's clarification and stuck to its standpoint that their traditional fishing rights had been impeded. The state continued to agitate over the 1976 Agreement and in an effort to exploit the public sentiment, in 2008 the then Chief Minister J. Jayalalithaa filed a writ petition challenging the two agreements with Sri Lanka. Three years later, the state legislative assembly adopted a unanimous resolution based on Jayalalithaa's petition. The case continued to hang fire in the Supreme Court. Meanwhile, Colombo also kept up putting pressure on New Delhi to resolve the dispute once and for all. In the fitness of things, the present

Sri Lankan government routinely took up the matter whenever interactions took place and as usual when Modi visited Colombo in 2017.

In all these years many concerned Indian politicians, scholars, lawyers and diplomats have pondered over the peculiarity of the dispute and the inability of the two governments to resolve it despite an abundance of mutual good will. Ultimately, it is reduced to the question of jeopardising the assured livelihood of Indians versus returning a traditional zone of earning livelihood to Sri Lankans in their own territory. A very hard nut to crack, to say the least.

Two eminently sensible and workable solutions have long been in the pipeline, but New Delhi has been equally steadfast in refusing to consider them. One is to follow what may be called the *Teen Bigha model,* which solved a long-ending territorial dispute between India and Bangladesh. The India-Bangladesh Boundary Agreement of 1974 handed over the ownership of Teen Bigha to India which resulted in denying Bangladeshi farmers their traditional right to farm the land there. A subsequent agreement led to the rendering of a *lease in perpetuity* to Bangladesh, thus retaining the Indian ownership but allowing Bangladesh to cultivate the land in perpetuity. Why can India then not apply the same formula in the case of the Katchatheevu island which would satisfy both the contenders? But New Delhi continues to remain silent on the question.

The other option offered is Sri Lanka-specific. Can Sri Lanka permit *licensed* Indian fishermen to fish in Sri Lankan waters up to five nautical miles from the IMBL; this proposal drew its inspiration from a provision in the 1976 agreement allowing licensed Sri Lankan fishermen to fish in the Wadge Bank, a fertile fishing ground located near Kanyakumari for a period of three years. In return, Sri Lankan fishermen could be permitted to fish in the Indian Exclusive Economic Zone (EEZ) under the same terms and conditions applicable to Indian fishermen. There has been a consistent support to this course of action by the successive governments in Tamil Nadu, but New Delhi has remained deaf and dumb.[22] In 2003, the Sri Lankan government agreed for the first time to consider licensed fishing, but neither New Delhi nor Chennai could produce sufficiently reasonable proposals in this respect and, therefore, a rare chance to make progress got lost.

Years have rolled past, but a solution to the dispute remains elusive. Meanwhile, irreparable damage is being inflicted daily on the marine life and sea-bed. Indian mechanised trawlers which scrape the bed to extricate as much catch as possible, are the main culprits. Trawlers have in fact been rechristened 'hoovers of shelf bottom' and 'bulldozers' by the International Collective in Support of Fish workers. After Indians started using trawlers, the Indian side of the bay quickly became devoid of fish. While there was poaching from all fishing harbours, it was fishermen from Rameswaram (Tamil Nadu) who reaped the maximum benefits. Rameswaram at the time had about 1,000 mechanised trawlers and a few hundred country boats, many of them mechanised. Allowing Indians to fish in Sri Lankan waters for a restricted period of three days proved to be disastrous as trawlers and boats rushed like an invading flotilla and even shot over to the north-eastern coast of the island. This kind of aggressive behaviour so unnerved Sri Lankans that they refused to enter the waters at the same time. Such intensive fishing also brought in instant results; Indian exports of marine fish shot up by an incredible 5,400 per cent between 1961 and 2012. This forced Sri Lankan fishermen to protest, arguing that if this practice was allowed to continue, fish stocks would be depleted on the Sri Lankan side as well, just as it had on the Indian side.

At long last, it was in July 2017 that Sri Lanka finally banned bottom-trawling by mechanised trawlers in its waters, subjecting violators to two years of imprisonment and a fine of approximately $20,000. Passed unanimously, an amendment to the existing Fisheries and Aquatic Resources Act was warmly greeted by the fishing community. The Tamil National Alliance welcomed the ban as a 'huge victory' for the Sri Lankan fishing community that had been battling the issue for about a decade. In April 2015, M.A. Sumanthiran had moved a private member's bill seeking a ban on bottom trawling, which for obvious reasons sparked protests from a section of indigenous fishermen who had started using mechanised trawlers to maximise profits. After the war ended, north Sri

Lankan fishermen began to look to rebuilding their destroyed lives by going out again to the sea. But the fierce Indian competition shattered their dreams, and they were compelled to agitate against Indian fishing. Tempers flew on both the sides; fishermen from the two countries held several rounds of discussions but failed to reach a settlement. The Sri Lankan navy continued to take strict punitive measures like long-time seizure of trawlers and arrests of Indians. The first few years after the end of the war saw a dramatic rise in the number of arrests (over 2,500 arrests between 2010 and 2017) which showed a decline from 2016. 'A complete ban on bottom trawling is an important and very positive step,' said N.V. Subramanian, secretary, Association for Northern Province Fisher People's Unity. 'It will not only deter Indian fishermen but also prevent local trawlers from engaging in the practice.'[23]

It is time to take note of some positive changes that have taken place in recent times concerning the dispute. Incidents of poaching by Indians in Sri Lankan waters have decreased substantially. Northern Sri Lankans have been back in fishing in their waters in increasing numbers. Both the countries continue to be seriously engaged in finding a permanent solution to the prolonged clash of interests and actions. On 23 May 2017, New Delhi announced a three-year scheme, evolved jointly with the Tamil Nadu government, to equip Tamil Nadu fishermen with 2,000 Tuna Long Liners-cum-Gill Netters so that they could switch over to deep-sea fishing instead of poaching in Sri Lankan waters. The families transitioning to deep-sea fishing would also be paid a monthly stipend of INR 5,000 during the transition period. The state government explained that Indians were no longer interested in poaching as their boats were being seized and catches destroyed followed by their long periods of detention in Sri Lanka. It was obvious that Sri Lanka's punitive measures had at last begun to be effective in dissuading the rampant encroachment in its waters which was bringing immense misery to Sri Lankan fishermen. This turn of events appears to indicate that the long-pending dispute may not last much longer. If a permanent solution is finally found, a major irritant in bilateral relations would be removed.

NOTES

1 Prof. Jayadeva Uyangoda, interviewed at his residence in a Colombo suburb on 14 November 2017.

2 Meera Srinivasan, 'Call for change in India's perspective on Sri Lanka,' *The Hindu,* 10 March 2017.

3 Pragmatic Mubarak, 'India overhauls policy towards Sri Lanka,' *Geopolitics,* New Delhi, Vol.VIII, Issue XII, May 2018.

4 NewsIn Asia, 'India gives livelihood assistance to 70,000 farmer and fishermen's families in Hambantota district in south Sri Lanka,' 9 April 2018, https://newsin.asia/india-gives-livelihood-assistance-to-70000-farmer-and-fishermens-families-in-hambatota-district-in-south-sri-lanka/

5 T. Ramakrishnan, 'Economic push needed,' *The Hindu,* 28 May 2018, https://www.thehindu.com/opinion/op-ed/economic-push-needed/article24007712.ece

6 Meera Srinivasan, 'Building solidarity beyond borders,' *The Hindu,* 10 July 2017.

7 Meera Srinivasan, 'Muslim shops, buildings targetted again in Kandy,' *The Hindu,* 8 March 2018.

8 Tom Allard and Shihar Aneez, 'Police, Rajapaksa-backed politicians accused of joining Sri Lanka's anti-Muslim violence,' *Reuters,* 24 March 2018.

9 John J. Xenakis, 'World View: Sri Lanka Targets Radical Nationalist Buddhists in Bodu Bala Sena (BBS),' *Breitbart,* 12 June, 2017, https://www.breitbart.com/national-security/2017/06/12/12-jun-17-world-view-sri-lanka-targets-radical-nationalist-buddhists-in-bodu-bala-sena-bbs/

10 World Watch Monitor, 'Sri Lanka: over 20 attacks on Christians this year,' 13 June 2017 https://www.worldwatchmonitor.org/2017/06/sri-lanka-20-attacks-christians-year/

11 Nirupama Subramanian, 'In Sri Lanka's anti-Muslim violence, an echo of postwar Sinhala triumphalism,' *The Indian Express,* 7 March 2018.

12 TamilNet, 'Jaffna voices grief at Indian PM's cosmetic visit', 14 March 2015.

13 K.M. de Silva, 'Sri Lanka: The security problems of a small state,' *Defence and Peace Economics,* published online: 19 October 2007.

14 NewsIn Asia, 'Modi and Rajapaksa skip politics, talk about economic cooperation in a very friendly meeting,' 12 May 2017.

15 Nirupama Subramanian, 'Modi in Sri Lanka: The MoU nobody is talking about during his visit,' *The Indian Express,* 11 May 2017.

16 Don Manu, 'India's new 5-billion-dollar one-way Hanuman Bridge to Lanka,' *The Sunday Times,* 27 September 2015.

17 The Quint, 'Modi Visits Sri Lanka to Celebrate "Shared Heritage" of Buddhism,' 12 May 2017.

18 Madhumanti Sengupta, 'Geopolitics of India's Maritime Boundaries,' *Geopolitics Journal*, New Delhi, Vol. VI, Issue VIII, January 2016.

19 Prakash Kamat, 'Union Ministry to launch "Deep Ocean Mission",' *The Hindu*, 31 May 2017, and Ministry of Earth Science, Government of India, 'India's Exclusive Rights to Explore Polymetallic Nodules from Central Indian Ocean Seabed Basin…', 21 August 2017.

20 V. Suryanarayan, 'The India-Sri Lanka Fisheries Dispute: Creating a Win-Win in the Palk Bay,' *Carnegie India*, 9 September 2016, https://carnegieindia.org/2016/09/09/india-sri-lanka-fisheries-dispute-creating-win-win-in-palk-bay-pub-64538

21 Ibid.

22 V. Suryanarayan, *Conflict Over Fisheries in the Palk Bay Region*, (New Delhi: Lancer Publishers and Distributors, New Delhi, 2005), pp.138-140.

23 Meera Srinivasan, 'Sri Lanka bans bottom-trawling,' *The Hindu*, July 7, 2017.

Epilogue

I too still have my dreams and desires,
but my only visitor is disappointment.
—Luxika Nagendiran, *Isolation* (Write to Reconcile II)

IF one single word is needed to describe the present national mood in Sri Lanka, 'disappointment' would fit the bill perfectly. I believe that this book has dealt with the Sri Lankan situation in sufficient details and has been able to explain in the process why this particular mood prevailed in this idyllic island in the middle of 2018.

In another manner of describing the situation, one could say that the entrenched demons of Sri Lanka have once again succeeded in wresting the initiative from the people and condemned them to a distasteful replay of the historical fallacies of a diverse society which refuses to acknowledge that it is diverse.

While corruption is a universal malady irrespective of society and political system and can, therefore, infect any country, Sri Lanka has been living with some specific maladies. These are religious and racial incompatibilities exacerbated by religious fundamentalism, casteism, and social and economic problems in communication and interaction. These imperfections have given rise to majoritarianism.

Sri Lankans themselves appear to be fully conscious of the enormous challenges their divisive society has thrown up. A workshop organised by the Ministry of Education in 2007 (during the Rajapaksa regime) to identify the obstacles to building up a cohesive society identified a whole bunch of issues:

> 1) Intercultural disharmony; 2) Lack of, or problems in communication and interaction, among different cultural groups; 3) Not looking at problems with an open mind; 4) Lack of respect for human rights of others or children's rights; 5) behaviour Violence; 6) Unwillingness to share resources or helping others, and selfishness; 7) Mistrust among communities due to ethno-centric ideas; 8) Not respecting and following rules and regulations; 9) Religious knowledge not transferred to practice in everyday life; 10) Lack of teamwork, lack of common values among children; 11) Lack of gender equity and socio-economic equity; 12) Lack of environment awareness and health awareness; 13) Lack of public awareness of peace values.[1]

The conclusion reached at the workshop sounds quite appropriate for today even after a period of eleven years. It said that the 'desired' citizen who is a product of education, for the sake of social cohesion should be able to live in a multicultural society, tolerate other cultures, trust others, treat others as human beings, be democratic in decision-making, communicate well in each other's language, etc. All policy makers in plural societies believe that education is a key instrument in the promotion of social cohesion through the transmission of appropriate knowledge and shaping of attitudes of individuals towards accepting diversity and change. But how does one relate this conclusion to Sri Lanka which has a literacy rate of 98.1 per cent? Not of any recent origin but of a long legacy, inherited right from the colonial days. Sri Lanka has always had an enviable position among South Asian nations with its high standards of living and high levels of education. The answer probably lies in acknowledging the negative impact that education can generate if so misdirected, as was seen in the fascist Germany and militarist Japan.

Corruption in Sri Lanka is closely related to politics. Its rampant proliferation under its rule was one of the main charges against the Mahinda Rajapaksa government and brought about its downfall and victory of the national unity government. Three years later, it is corruption again which has pushed the national unity government to the brink, if not disintegration, then definitely of disability.

It is but natural that in this scenario—which was not on the agenda when the people chose the Sirisena-Wickremasinghe coalition over the Rajapaksa clan—the most deprived community, ethnic Tamils, continue to remain disadvantaged, dispirited and disillusioned. Will they rise again in rebellion? Not by the longest stretch of imagination. If one asks why, the answer is that the Tamil backbone has been crushed and that they are fully conscious of the futility of seeking independence. That lesson has been well delivered and learned. But a far more enduring fact is that the community is disappointed and, hence, resentful. That is not a healthy sign for any diverse society.

They had banked heavily on the capacity of the Sirisena-Wickremasinghe government to deliver on their promises concerning reconstruction, reconciliation and rehabilitation of their shattered lives. This book carries plenty of facts and figures within itself to explain why the maximum losers, the ethnic Tamils, are also the most helpless community to strike out on their own and rebuild their lives within the country.

This is really hurtful because the period since May 2009, when the war had ended, was the most promising period for ethnic Tamils as indeed for the entire country and the international stakeholders. After a long period of time, Sri Lanka was enjoying goodwill all around. Everybody and every country wished it well.

Three years later, much of the bonhomie evaporated. The government has dealt with various issues in fits and starts, in a curious mix of competence, honesty and bad faith, incompetence and plain dishonesty.

However, a vital point to remember is that the government has not enjoyed a free hand in tackling national problems. It did not take long for Rajapaksa to stage a comeback with a heady platter of malevolence, revenge and an obsession with resuming and continuing with his unfinished agenda of turning Sri Lanka into a full-fledged autocracy. It is difficult to accept him at face value that he makes no difference between the Sinhalese and the minorities in his policy pronouncements and treatment. While the minorities have adequately expressed their lack of trust in him, his consistent failure to honour his own commitments during his tenure concerning the minorities (such as, bringing in the so-called 13th Amendment and the devolution package) discourages one from taking his words seriously.

It is significant that in their media interviews quoted above, neither Mahinda nor his brother Gotabaya Rajapaksa have admitted to any wrongdoing on their part or any moral deficiencies in the execution of the policies they had followed while in government. Also significant is the fact that they were successful in creating an atmosphere of rising public support for themselves in the local government polls. But it was also a fact that they had failed to recapture the major portion of the Sinhalese electoral constituency. Their party, the SLPP, could not match Rajapaksa's performance in 2015 when his reputation had reached a nadir but even then he could garner 55 per cent of the total Sinhalese vote. The party's share of the majority community's vote in February 2018 was not readily available to make a qualitative assessment but the general impression left in the wake of the local body polls was that his party, Sri Lanka Podujana Peramuna, would do well in the next presidential election.

Not everything lost yet

However, as has been noted above, the popular impression of a massive Opposition victory in February 2018 does not hold water if examined deeper. This local government election saw the first implementation of the first-past-the-post system in addition to the traditional proportional representation system on a 60:40 formula. As usually happens in the first system, the number of seats won by a party does not reflect the precise extent of popular support. If judged by this perspective, the SLPP which won a vast majority of seats in the local polls had actually obtained only 44.6 per cent of the total votes cast. The other parties had, therefore, in reality obtained a larger percentage of votes. When pitted against his performance in the last presidential poll in 2015, his vote share in 2018 had actually declined. Besides, the SLPP would be obliged to run local governments in coalition with other parties as it did not have the majority electoral support. The decline in the Sinhalese vote share could partly have been explained by a larger than before number of Sinhalese voters turning away from exercising their franchise in a kind of protest against the politics of the country. (This practice has lately become so rampant in India, the world's largest democracy in terms of the number of registered voters, that the Election Commission had to introduce a new button to be pressed by voters, called NOTA [None Of The Above] indicating that they do not support any of the candidates).

Therefore, robbed of an actual majority support, Rajapaksa's party in effect allowed the ruling coalition some leeway to rebuild their support base and fight back to prevent the former autocrat from advancing further.

Looked at from this perspective, the flood of rather harshly critical appraisals of the performance of the Sirisena-Wickremasinghe government that swept the Sri Lankan narrative throughout 2017 and 2018, does not perhaps reflect the ground realities in the island republic.

In addition, there are some positive achievements by the government too. Compared to 2014, Sri Lanka is a remarkably free society today and the credit should go entirely to the government. It succeeded in demolishing many of the barricades that the previous government had built up to retain its iron grip on the people.

The most notable aspect that caught my eye during the November 2017 visit was the easy portability of different communities across the country. It was no mean achievement that hundreds of Sinhalese students, boys and girls, were now studying in the Jaffna and other universities in the north and the east. During my stay, a group of forty Tamil women-activists travelled from Jaffna to Colombo to demonstrate before government offices in support of their political, economic and social demands. Haunted by a high degree of unemployment, Tamil youths were travelling to the south in search of jobs. Sinhalese traders had opened up shops in Jaffna and were being patronised by the Tamils. Muslims, too, had returned in large numbers to the north, something they had done earlier in the Eastern Province after it was liberated from the LTTE.

The most important success of the government was in cutting down on the virtual police state that Rajapaksa had built up and imposed on the country. The military and the police were strictly told to stick to law and not to resort to extra-legal measures, which were widely in vogue during the previous regime. All these have been described in detail in the book.

The above narration also takes note of the unfortunate fact that despite the impressive improvement in democratic norms by the state, remnants of the police state continue to blacken the records of the present government. That is one of the major failures of the government, for only when Sri Lanka attains true democracy, the government of the day can take due credit and not before.

The most significant factor today, in the context of Sri Lankan politics, is the ability of the present ruling coalition to effectively counter Rajapaksa. As per a frank assessment of the situation: 'There are many Sri Lankans who do not regard Rajapaksa as a monster but rather as a hero, particularly among the island's Buddhists, ethnically Sinhala majority. He was the person who led them to victory in the long civil war with the Tamil minority. They want a strong man like him at the helm. In fact, says Alan Keenan of the International Crisis Group, a think tank, the former President never really went away. His grassroots support remained nurtured by the well-financed family political machine. 'He has a strong core constituency, a clear narrative and a good set of issues,' says Keenan, 'whereas the government has to pull together a range of minority constituencies—Tamils, Muslims, Sinhala liberals—and find something to deliver to each one.' He says 'Sri Lanka is set on a bumpy course. With Rajapaksa gleefully stoking Sinhala chauvinism, the country could slip backwards into the kind of polarisation that led to its long civil war.'[2]

Are we crying 'wolf' out of panic and too early? For instance, there is a feeling that since the true selves of Rajapaksa and his brothers stand exposed to the people, even pure ethnic and clan fidelity may not be a sufficient glue to undermine the bloody memories of their regime. If this happens, some of those who had switched over to the Rajapaksa side might have second thoughts at the time of the next election and may either decide to vote against their party or to abstain from voting. Such an eventuality would be of substantial help to the ruling coalition.

But this would at best be of peripheral help. The minorities and liberal Sinhalese would necessarily vote against the SLPP out of compulsion, but a huge Sinhalese turnout in favour of the Rajapaksas would not be thwarted by such a gathering of forces. The January 2015 presidential election was won by the combined opposition led by an inconsequential candidate only because the anti-Rajapaksa forces were joined by as much as 45 per cent of the Sinhalese electorate. As it stands now, the majority or almost the entire Sinhalese electorate is with the Rajapaksas.

The safest way for the ruling coalition would have been to woo the Buddhist-Sinhalese chauvinist section of the population by adopting an unashamed pro-Sinhalese attitude in governance. Logically this would be an impossible act of volte-face. But the coalition is an entirely different kettle of fish from the Rajapaksas. It came into power on the plank of uniting the divided people and it has little option but to follow it to its logical conclusion. It is not that the coalition members are all liberals devoid of religious and racial prejudices but political compulsions work both ways; they can persuade the politicians to remain faithful to their parties that are currently part of the ruling coalition or defect to the SLPP to share the spoils of a possible election victory. Their loyalty would be determined by the way the fortunes of the contending sides shape up in the coming months.

A reflection of this reality was already available during 2018. Take, for example the very issue of a new constitution. The necessary work is completed; Parliament has approved the framework which promises to usher in substantive devolution of power to the provinces. But a new constitution is not on the horizon. The Buddhist clergy have declared a war over it and that is one way of putting a seal on its fate. The Rajapaksa-led Opposition is loath to let such a golden opportunity to compromise the government go waste. Part of the campaign to whip up Buddhist-Sinhalese chauvinism, Rajapaksa's trump card, is to rant and rile against the new constitution, which is seen as an appeasement of the minority communities.

Sri Lanka's malady is that irrespective of wherever one starts from, the discourse eventually comes around to the issue of ethnic divide. One cannot simply get away from it.

Political reform is another major plank on which the Opposition coalition won the two elections in 2015. The most important item in this is the abolition of the executive presidency system, rightly identified as the main source of authoritarianism of the state ever since it was introduced. Soon after the inauguration of the new presidency, the government introduced a bill to amend the relevant act of Parliament, and curtailed the presidential tenure from six to five years. That is where the matter rests till today. As noted in detail above, it soon became clear that President Sirisena had begun to feel differently on the subject and by the end of 2017 he went ahead with a petition to the Supreme Court to allow him to continue in office for an additional year. His prayer was rejected but it definitely left a bad taste in the mouth. Step by step, the 'good governance' government began to lose its credibility. Coupled with the Central Bank bond scam which involved several ministers and senior government officials, apart from the Prime Minister, all these developments swiftly destroyed the credibility of the government. The last nail in its coffin was driven by the public bickering among the government leaders and the clear split in the government between the Sirisena camp and the Wickremasinghe camp (or the SLFP and UNP camps). By February-March 2018, the government had lost its face.

Dire implications

Certain possible end-results of the present Sri Lankan situation are already discernible. Judging by the overall shoddy performance in office, the government would find it very difficult to implement the pending promises, all of which have a direct bearing on the inter-community relations. Take, for instance, the undertaking to punish those military officers and men who are alleged to have violated human rights on a mass scale during the last phase of the civil war. As a matter of fact, the President and the government have been quite categorical in rejecting the two main demands of the international community, both manifested in UN resolutions, namely, that only a hybrid trial court system would be accepted; and the allegation of a genocide against the Tamils resulting in the death of about 40,000 civilians including women and children and LTTE cadre who had surrendered in April-May 2009, must be investigated by a hybrid court and the guilty identified and punished. Both the government and the army are in stiff denial, and have pitched for a nationalistic platform of protecting the Sri Lankan sovereignty.

However, the implications of this stand for ethnic reconciliation in Sri Lanka are equally palpable. The government and the ruling parties, all Sinhalese, barring a few junior minority ministers, dare not touch the question lest whatever hold they still have on the majority community should evaporate. At the same time, this act or lack of action by the ruling elite would rob the Tamils of their last hope of getting justice from their motherland. Easily the most traumatised section of Sri Lankans, would the Tamils be able to absorb this final betrayal by the state?

There are equally important international implications of an eventual failure of the Sirisena-Wickremasinghe dispensation. From the international standpoint, this government is on trial to prove its capacity to return the country to the status of a constitutional, liberal and democratic republic where the people choose their government and the government in turn honours its commitments to them. Its present status of a constitutional, liberal and democratic republic is more academic than realistic.

It is unnecessary at this stage to stress the aphorism that Rajapaksa's return to power would upset this arrangement and push the country back to where it was in 2014. If this happens, it is not only Sri Lanka but the world as a whole that would be the losers.

There would be an immediate impact on India, which has already shaken off its exclusive responsibility for Sri Lankan Tamils and now professes to work for the Sinhalese and other communities as well. But where would an all-out Sinhalese chauvinism, thriving in re-run of Rajapaksa's Sri Lanka, place India? Can New Delhi, in such a scenario, tell the Tamils not to seek its support to ward off renewed Sinhalese assaults? Would India not be drawn back again into the vortex of Sri Lanka's racial politics? Besides, what would happen to the Sri Lanka-India equation, already heavily tilted in favour of China, if Rajapaksa returns to power? Already, by the end of 2017, China had invested $15 billion worth of infrastructure projects in Sri Lanka. Sri Lanka had also stopped dithering and had prostrated itself at China's altar. India's space in between China and Sri Lanka had been squeezed further. Its troubles would only multiply in the coming days as Sri Lanka hurtles through time towards a re-enactment of both ethnic chauvinism and religious fundamentalism both, as we have seen, are already present and active.

The future of Sri Lanka can perhaps be better read if one listens to Cheng Xueyuan, the Chinese ambassador in Sri Lanka, speaking in Colombo in May 2018, 'When standing and trembling on the war ruins, Sri Lanka called for urgent support from the international community to rebuild this beautiful country, but surprisingly (it) found that most countries chose to remain silent and watch the situation going on with folded arms. At this critical moment, it was China once again that stood up with open arms to Sri Lanka and participated comprehensively and deeply in the post-war reconstruction of the country.' While I travelled in the north on India-financed and built railway tracks and passed through rebuilt railway stations, the Chinese ambassador said that the infrastructure of Sri Lanka like roads, railways and ports had 'all' been improved with China's assistance in the last decade. In due course, he acknowledged Sri Lanka's role in joining hands with the Belt and Road Initiative.[3]

The China factor

In fact, China seems to be all over the island. The Colombo Galle Face Green has changed for the worse with the gigantic Colombo Port City project reclaiming a large part of the harbour. Chinese tourists are still relatively low in numbers when compared to the overwhelming Indian tourist presence but, compared to the world-wide presence of Chinese tourists, the case in Sri Lanka is definitely on the slim side. Indian tourists continue to dominate the tourism scene in Sri Lanka accounting for 7.8

per cent of the total arrivals in 2017, with China coming second with lesser arrivals than before but already dislodging the U.K. from the second position. As the Sri Lankan tourism board carries on an intensive campaign in China, the number of Chinese tourists is expected to grow faster and further.[4] On another plane, while Sri Lankans are fighting hard to prevent large-scale deployment of Indian professionals in their country under the stalled ETCA, as many as 6,000 Chinese technical personnel were working in various projects at the time the ambassador was listing his country's munificence towards the South Asian nation. As in my time, so also now, Indian restaurants are a minor source of food and entertainment but Chinese restaurants continue to be as dominant as before.

However, the most dramatic presence of China is in the Jaffna peninsula, of all places. More interestingly, the country has made deep inroads into the northern media, transporting large numbers of media persons for familiarisation to China. The Chinese state media have established a close relationship with the resurrected *Uthayan,* a one-time mouthpiece of the LTTE (for which the newspaper and its employees had to pay very dearly at the hands of the security forces). Several Tamil newspapers and TV channels are also said to be in regular and close touch with the Chinese media.

As Sri Lankan media reports and interactions with foreign correspondents stationed in the island suggest, this is obviously part of a larger Chinese design of installing the Chinese media as a formidable presence in the island. There is a lot of curiosity in diplomatic circles about this particular development, especially because no plausible explanation for it is available.

According to one Sri Lankan media report, closely following the spurt in Chinese investment, there has been a regular 'invasion' of Chinese media in Sri Lanka. Most Chinese media if not all, which have established bases in Colombo or have correspondents in Colombo, are either linked to the Chinese government or follow the unwritten rule that they work in the best interests of China. The Xinhua news agency was the first major Chinese news service to set up a bureau in Sri Lanka with two Chinese nationals and four Sri Lankans in Colombo. Xinhua has expanded in the last couple of years all over the country. Among the other Chinese media are China Radio International, Asia Pacific Daily and China Times. While the agencies are being headed by Chinese nationals, the leg work is being done by Sri Lankan correspondents (some of them are stringers from local news organisations) all of whom have been instructed to ensure that their reports and writings serve to enhance Chinese interests in the country. One of the major tasks of the Chinese media functioning in the island is to orchestrate praise of Chinese-aided infrastructure projects, acting as publicity agents. This indicates a well-maintained coordination between Chinese companies and Chinese media working together to advance their country's foreign investment, policy and strengthening of ideological reach. This is also indicated by the well-calculated manner in which some Chinese media persons have cultivated 'close links' with leading Sri Lankan personalities in politics and academia, the motive for which is not difficult to surmise.[5]

A veteran foreign correspondent based in Colombo informed me that the Chinese media, Xinhua in particular, covers every little bit of news in Sri Lanka which are at times not covered by the local media. 'This cannot be explained easily,' he mused. 'But the impression is that the Chinese media's job is to transmit every kind of news from Sri Lanka so that they can be picked up at the right quarters and exploited to advance Chinese interests.' Perhaps the media in such a scenario acts more like an intelligence agency than as purveyor of news. Considering the relatively less importance of the island in international affairs, this seems to be an unusual show of interest by the world's second most powerful country in a small island-nation. As a result, not just India but the western governments as well, are quite worried and keeping a watch on the developments on the media front.

Try as it does to avoid getting caught up in a fresh irritant, the China factor continues to colour India-Sri Lanka relations. Once it was claimed that Sri Lanka's sudden harsh refusal to Chinese submarines to dock in Sri Lankan waters in 2017 was at India's prompting, a Chinese scholar, apparently speaking his government's mind, shot back, 'Sri Lanka's promise (not to do so again) is unnecessary because the port is meant for civilian use and shows that India has interfered in Sri Lanka's internal affairs. But if India has a problem with the programme and oppresses its neighbour, it only shows it is interfering in other countries' domestic affairs. China has no intention to offend India and the programme is good for Sri Lanka's economic development.' Chu Yin, an Associate Professor at the University of International Relations, told the Global Times. Lin Minwang, a Professor at the Institute of international Studies, Fudan University, added, 'Sri Lanka initially wanted India to develop the Hambantota port, but it finally turned to China for help since India faces financial difficulties.' This port continues to evoke strong reactions from both the sides as it sits on a strategically sensitive location on the Indian Ocean.

The latest controversy erupted around February-March 2018 after India got the news that the Chinese were planning to set up, in collaboration with the Ruhuna University, High-Frequency Short Wave (HFSW) radar station at Dondra in south Sri Lanka with a range of 180 km towards the Indian Ocean and coverage of 120° 'to keep an eye on Indian shipping.'

Sri Lanka's foreign secretary Prasad Kariyawasam, an old India hand, assured New Delhi that 'There is no platform in Sri Lanka that might threaten any country in the region, including India. No platform, whether on land or sea, will be used to threaten peace and tranquillity in the region. All platforms will operate within that framework and we will ensure that.' (Interview to *Times Now*, an Indian TV news channel).

However, a Sri Lankan naval and strategic expert, Adm Jayanath Colombage, felt it 'highly unlikely' that the radar would be of high frequency because such an installation would not stay hidden from public view. He felt that the planned radar could just be an ordinary weather tracking installation used in oceanographic research.

Following its intelligence reports, Indian officials visited the newly established Sino-Lankan Oceanographic Institution at Ruhunu University and were briefed on the proposed radar project. As far as the university was concerned, it was informed by the Chinese collaborators (the South

China Sea Institute of Oceanography and the Chinese Academy of Sciences) that the radar station would be used for oceanographic studies, and that ship-tracking abilities 'could happen later.' However, India's suspicions about the actual or eventual purpose of the project could not be allayed as it believed that even oceanographic surveys could be used to collect hydrological and bathymetric data 'valuable for submarine deployments and operations under sea.' India was also concerned over China's reported keenness to bid for the Maritime Rescue Coordination Centre in Sri Lanka with funding and technical support. New Delhi was apparently looking at this development as a further shrinking of its strategic space in the immediate neighbourhood and a further confirmation of China's so-called encirclement strategy. It would obviously not be happy to allow China any space in this project as it was about to embark on financing it. Interestingly, even though India had been preparing to invest in the project, China had started butting in, giving rise to a suspicion in New Delhi that the Sri Lankan navy was being kept 'out of the loop' in this project. However, it did not mean that some political interests could not be working behind the scene in order to facilitate China's backdoor entry, bypassing India.

Sri Lankans friendly to India looked at this interplay of international players in the Sri Lankan theatre in the following manner. By virtue of its naval and technological strength, India should be the natural security provider for the south Indian Ocean Region but its capacities were being held back by its inability to match China's funding capabilities. Even a supposedly anti-Indian President Rajapaksa usually began to look around for funding projects at India's door and ended up at China's. There was another section of Sri Lankans who felt that 'certain powers' could be interested in driving a wedge between India and China in order to keep them permanently divided so that a fearsome India-China combine might not upset the international power equilibrium in which the West had maintained its traditional commanding position.

Sri Lanka was passing through a period of uncertainty and grave consequences in the middle of 2018. While the political Opposition sensed a victory in the making, the rulers were re-arranging their armour and earmarking targets. The timeline for a final showdown was shrinking by the hour. The 'socialist-nationalist' President Sirisena had been turning the wheel with a determined hand towards the east and away from the west and the immediate northern neighbour. He had shrunk Prime Minister Wickremasinghe's hold over the economic policies which had been pro-capitalist and begun to introduce pro-poor and pro-labour policies in order to win over the Sinhalese rural and urban poor, who constituted the bulk of Sinhalese voters. He had also taken over foreign policy which would gradually have a bearing on Sri Lanka's relations with various global players. Observers felt that his aim was to veer close to China and Russia away from the West, Japan and India. A year ago in May 2017, Wickremasinghe reshuffled his ministers in order to tighten his grip on the economic and foreign policies, introducing a more effective pro-Western stance. In about a year later, Sirisena signalled a further and deeper change by appointing a known Russophile Dr. Saman Weerasinghe, as his foreign policy adviser (who was also Rajapaksa's foreign policy adviser). He deftly reversed the unpopular economic policies and programmes being pursued by his government and introduced a pronounced pro-China nuance. Taking the cue, Wickremasinghe spoke in March 2018 about Chinese assistance enabling his government to bring benefits to greater numbers of 'grassroots people'.

In the last two years of its rule, the *Yahapalanaya* government is expected to institutionalise populism, socialism and nationalism, hoping to counter the challenge from Rajapaksa with a judicious mix of policies that should prove to be strong enough to neutralise the autocrat's popular appeal. It would be unfortunate and undesirable if Sri Lankan society is pulverised further in the process. The demons are already roused, the festering wounds hurt and the wounded psyche cries for healing. The world waits and watches.

NOTES

1 S. Sandarasegaram, 'Education & Reconciliation; The Sri Lanka Case,' *Colombo Telegraph*, 26 May 2016, https://www.colombotelegraph.com/index.php/education-the-sri-lanka-case/

2 The Economist, 'In Sri Lanka, local elections have rattled the government,' 17 February 2018.

3 NewsIn Asia, 'By the end of 2017, China has invested $15 bln worth of infrastructure projects in SL, says envoy,' 23 May 2018, https://newsin.asia/by-the-end-of-2017-china-has-invested-15-bln-worth-of-infrastructure-projects-in-sl-says-envoy/

4 N.R Ravindra Deyshappriya, 'Chinese tourist numbers in Sri Lanka: a case for improving growth,' *South Asia @ LSE*, 27 February 2018.

5 Harshana, 'Eyes wide open on Chinese media invasion in Sri Lanka,' *LankaNewspapers.com*, 12 March 2018, https://www.lankanewspapers.com/2018/03/12/eyes-wide-open-chinese-media-invasion-sri-lanka/

Index

Index

Index